FROGS

Awesome Amphibians

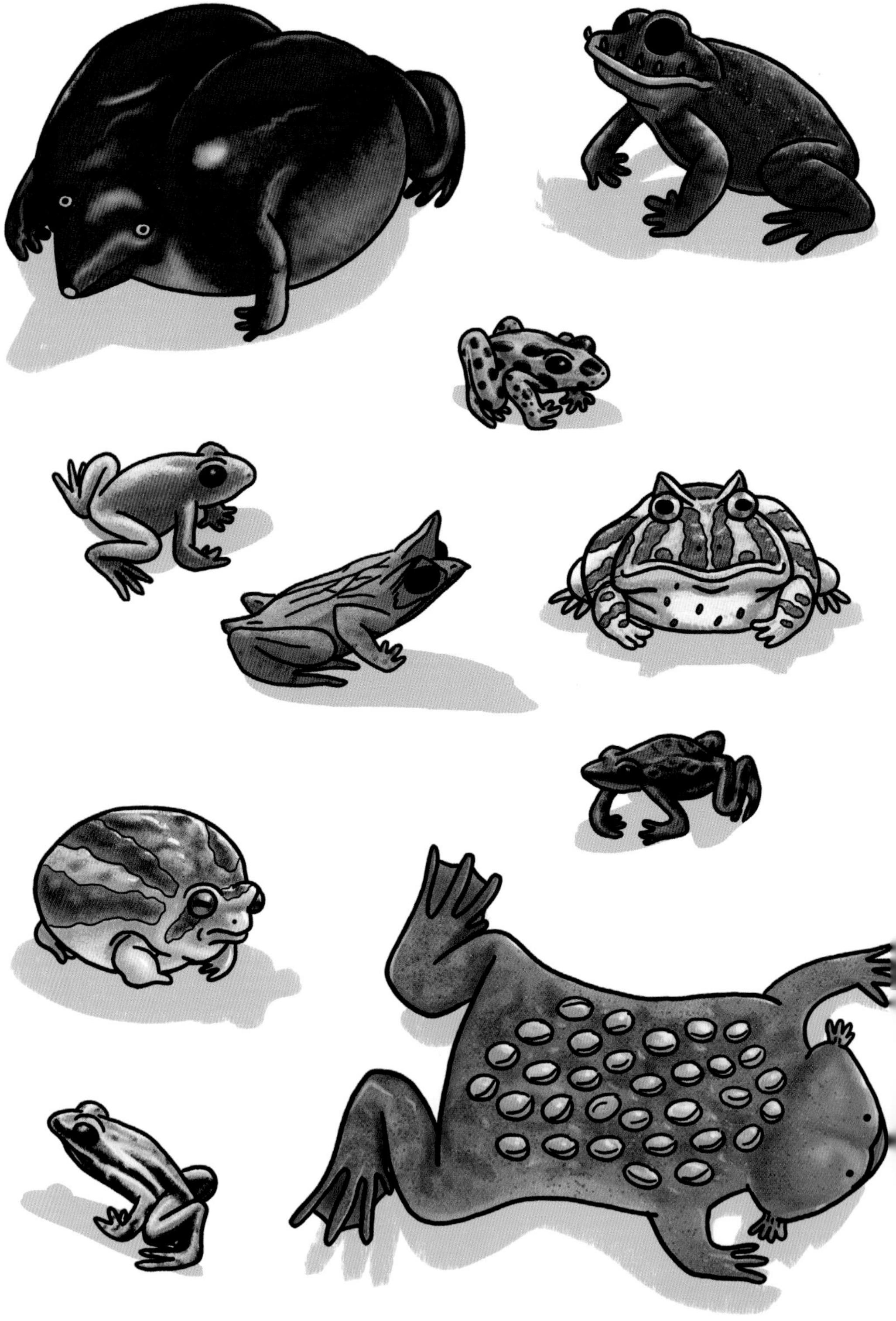

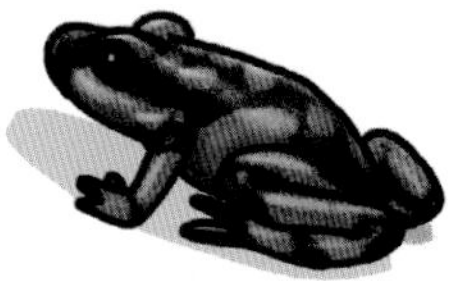
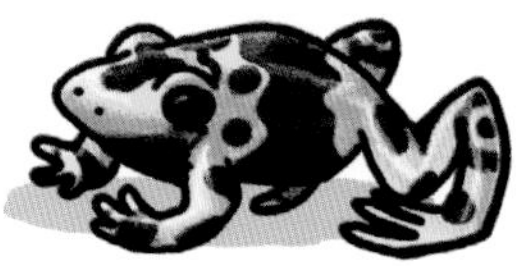
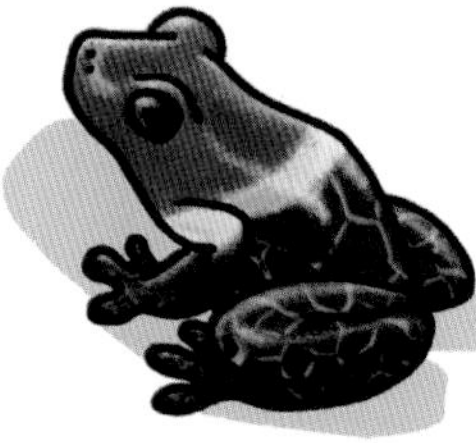

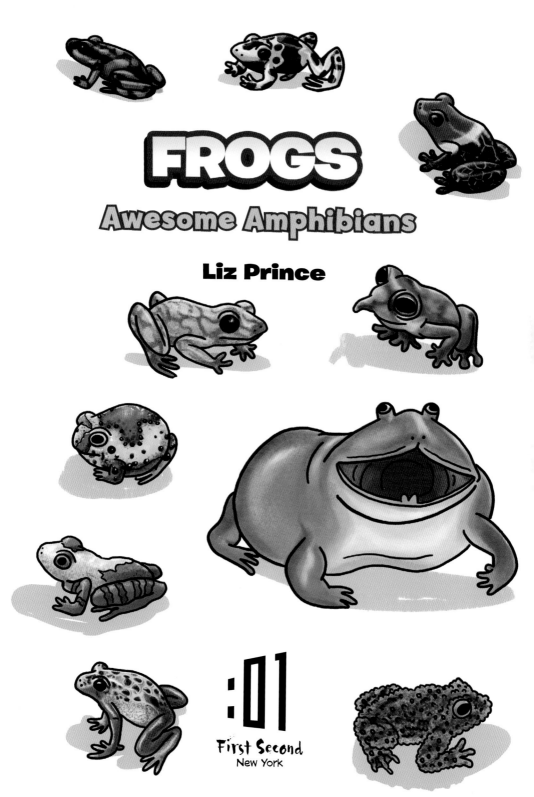

FROGS

Awesome Amphibians

Liz Prince

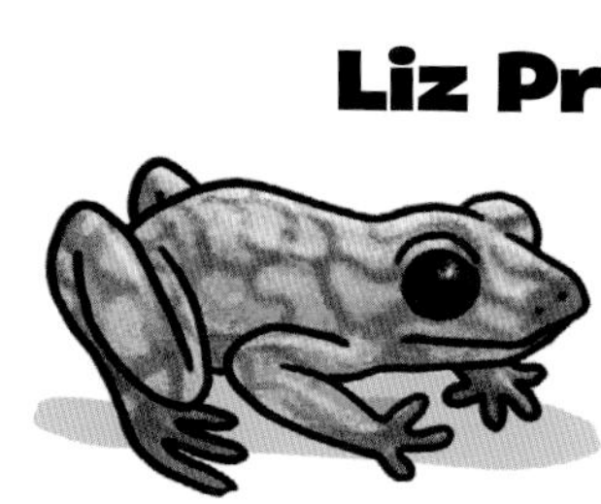
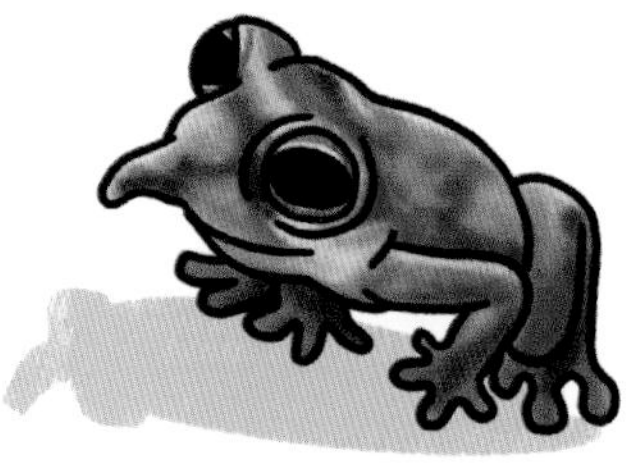
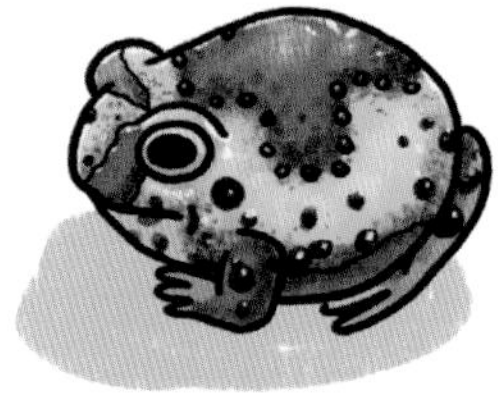
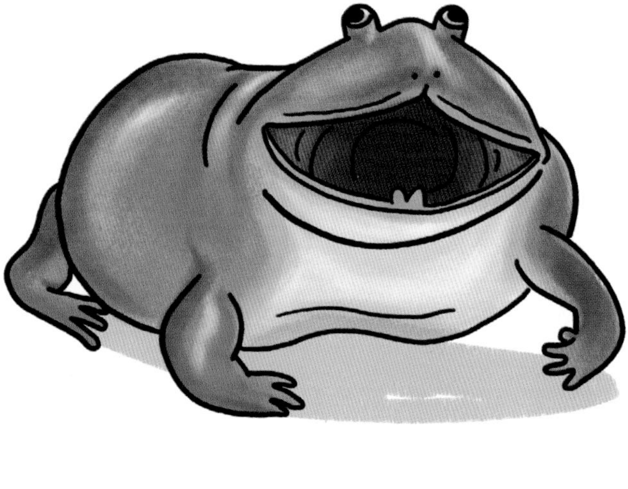
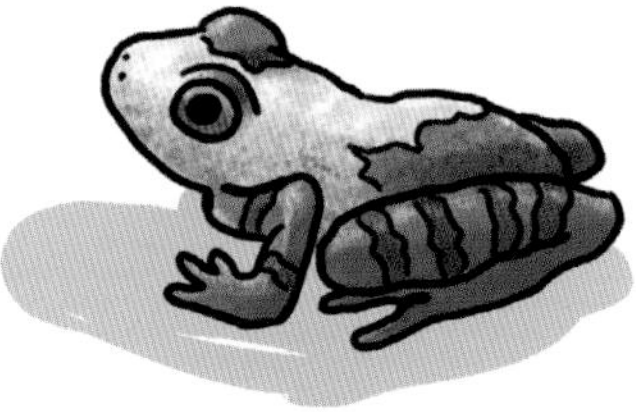
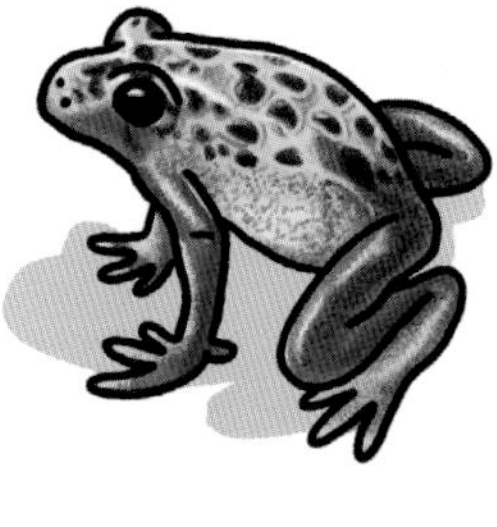

First Second
New York

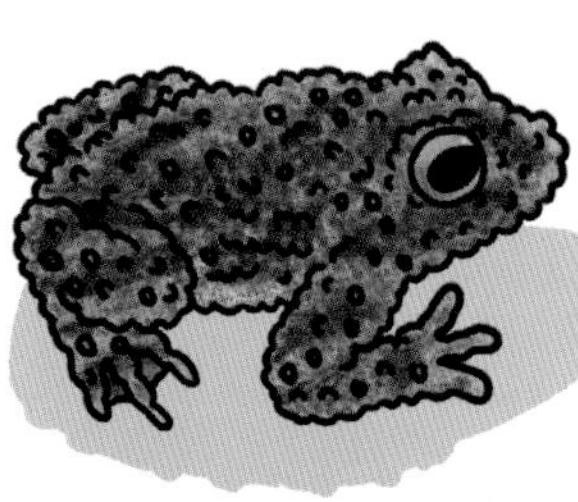

:01

First Second

Published by First Second
First Second is an imprint of Roaring Brook Press,
a division of Holtzbrinck Publishing Holdings Limited Partnership
120 Broadway, New York, NY 10271
firstsecondbooks.com
mackids.com

Library of Congress Control Number: 2022920405

Our books may be purchased in bulk for promotional, educational, or business use. Please contact your local bookseller or the Macmillan
Corporate and Premium Sales Department at (800) 221-7945 ext. 5442 or by email at MacmillanSpecialMarkets@macmillan.com.

First edition, 2023
Edited by Dave Roman and Tim Stout
Cover design and interior book design by Sunny Lee and Casper Manning
Color and lettering by Jim Kettner
Production editing by Avia Perez
Frog consultants: Dr. A. Z. Andis Arietta and Lauren A. O'Connell, PhD

Penciled and inked in Procreate, colored in ClipStudio, and lettered with the Comicrazy font from Comicraft.

Printed in China by Toppan Leefung Printing Ltd., Dongguan City, Guangdong Province

ISBN 978-1-250-26886-0 (paperback)
10 9 8 7 6 5 4 3 2 1

ISBN 978-1-250-26885-3 (hardcover)
10 9 8 7 6 5 4 3 2 1

Don't miss your next favorite book from First Second!
For the latest updates go to firstsecondnewsletter.com and sign up for our enewsletter.

BY ART WE LIVE

Bronk, bronk, bronk . . ." the bullfrog sings. Every summer night when I was growing up, I would hear the bullfrogs call from the pond near our house. To help me fall asleep, I would count their calls like sheep. During the day, I could see little tadpoles wriggling around the shore, sometimes getting eaten by a fish or a turtle. When some of the tadpoles became little froglets, I would say to them, "Good job, little froglets. You made it!"

Amphibians are amazing animals. They have figured out how to live in many different environments by changing their behavior and the way their body functions. I'm a scientist, and my job is to study those differences. I mostly study amphibians that are poisonous. They are usually very colorful as a signal to predators that says, "Don't eat me or you will regret it!" One question I ask is how those poisons work on their predators because this tells me how the poisons can be used to heal diseases and relieve pain in humans. Another question is how the amphibians protect themselves from their own poisons. Different amphibians use different strategies to do that. Poisonous amphibians often have very different behaviors and can be very bold in their choices. For example, most frogs are nocturnal, but some poisonous amphibians, like the poison dart frogs I study, are awake during the day and have elaborate social lives that include moving their tadpoles around with piggyback rides. The tadpoles even let their parents know they are hungry by wiggling back and forth. Imagine letting your parent know you are hungry by dancing in the kitchen!

My job takes me all around the world, from the deserts of Australia to the cloud forests of Madagascar to the Amazon rainforest of South America, all to find frogs in different habitats. My experience listening to frogs when I was younger comes in handy because that is how I find them now! I listen to the environment and find different frogs by being still and patient and listening to their songs. However, you do not have to rely only on your ears. Lots of amphibians are awake during the day and the poisonous ones are easy to spot because they are usually bright and colorful and come in all colors of the rainbow. There is still so much that we do not know about amphibians, and we need scientists like you to study them. A scientist is someone who asks questions and then answers those questions with experiments. To become a scientist, you can learn about science in school and college. Many scientists have a doctorate degree, which means that a college will pay you a salary (like a real job!) to become an expert on your study topic.

When I go back home now as a grown-up, there are no bullfrogs calling at night. Our pond is smaller than it used to be because our summers are hotter and it does not rain as much. Wild nightlife around the world is quieter because there are fewer amphibians due to changes in climate, habitat loss, and amphibian diseases. Amphibians are very important members of healthy ecosystems, and the fact that their numbers are decreasing means our global habitat is in trouble, too. You can help by learning more about amphibian conservation in school and at zoos. One of the best things you can do is build natural ponds for your local amphibians and protect undeveloped land where amphibians live. If we work together, we can live in a world where the frogs sing at night in full chorus once again.

—Lauren A. O'Connell, PhD
Assistant Professor in the Department of Biology,
Stanford University

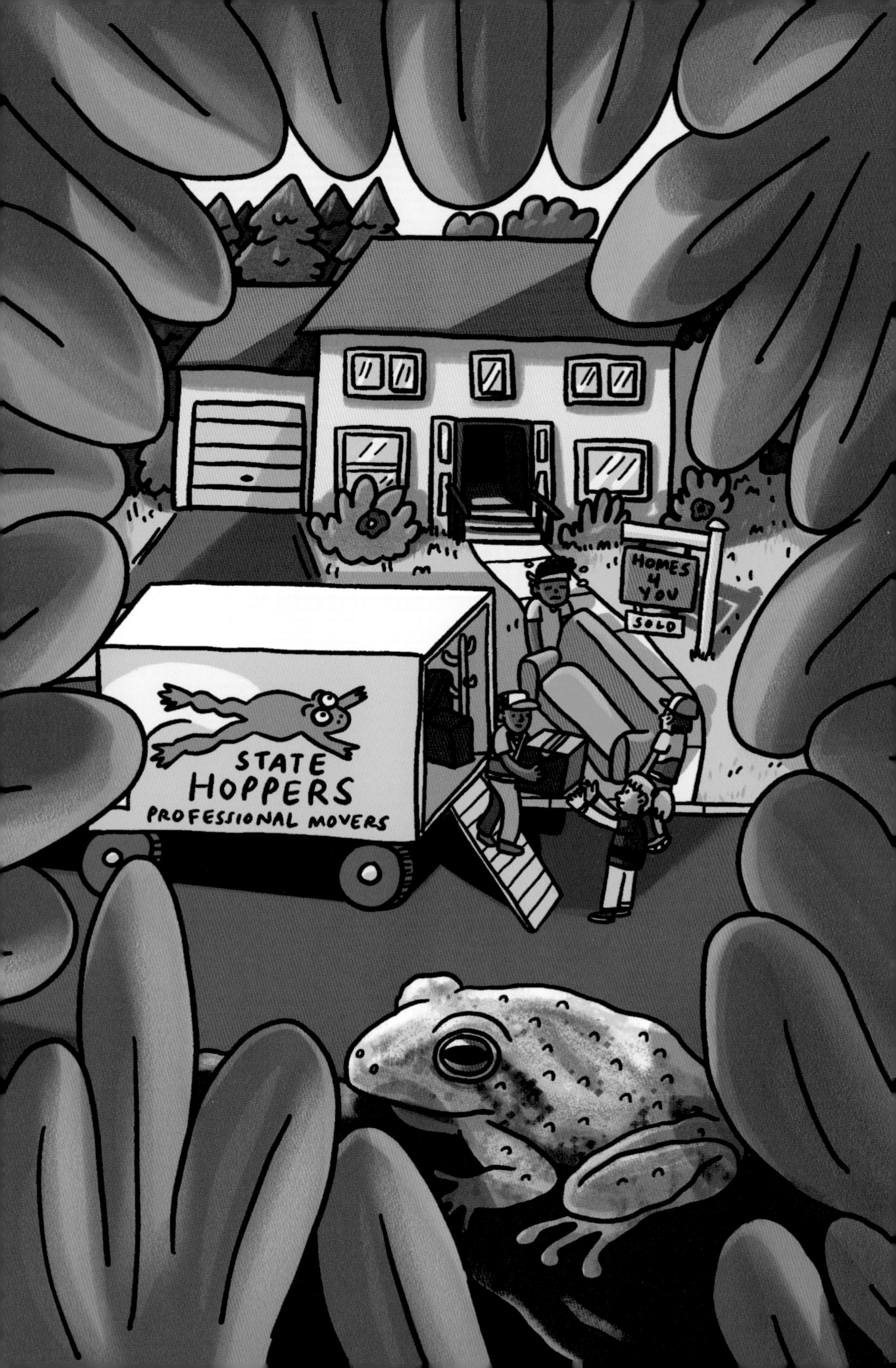
HOMES 4 YOU
SOLD
STATE HOPPERS
PROFESSIONAL MOVERS

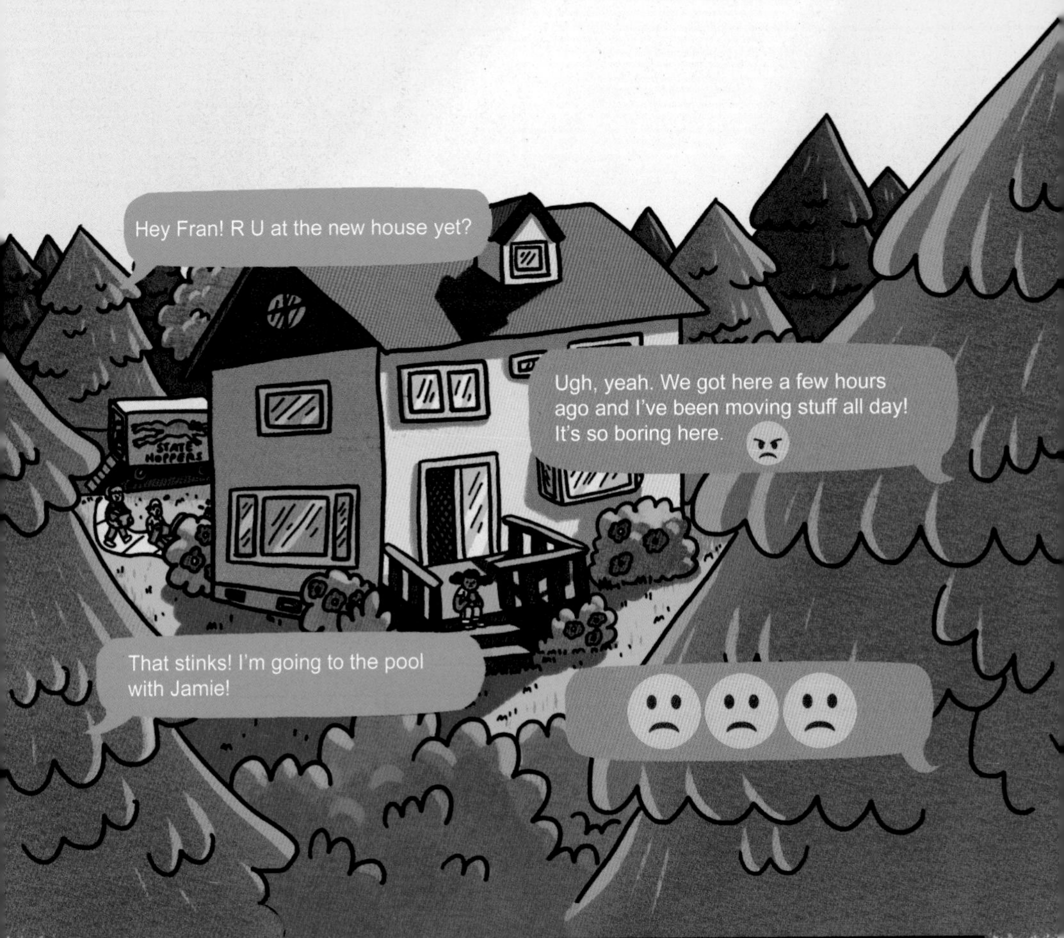
Hey Fran! R U at the new house yet?
STATE HOPPERS
Ugh, yeah. We got here a few hours ago and I've been moving stuff all day! It's so boring here.
That stinks! I'm going to the pool with Jamie!

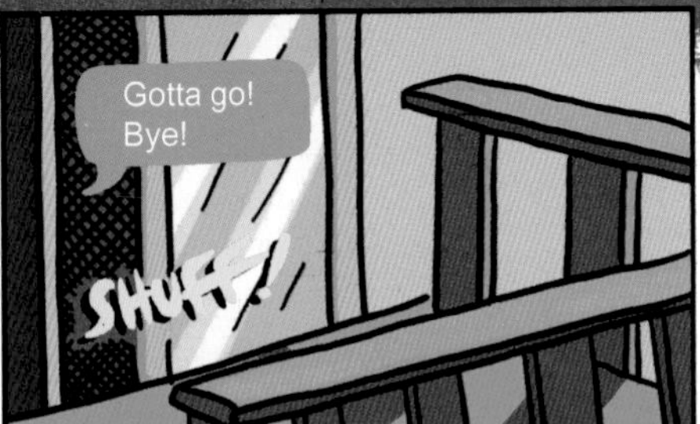
Gotta go! Bye!
SHUFF
sigh

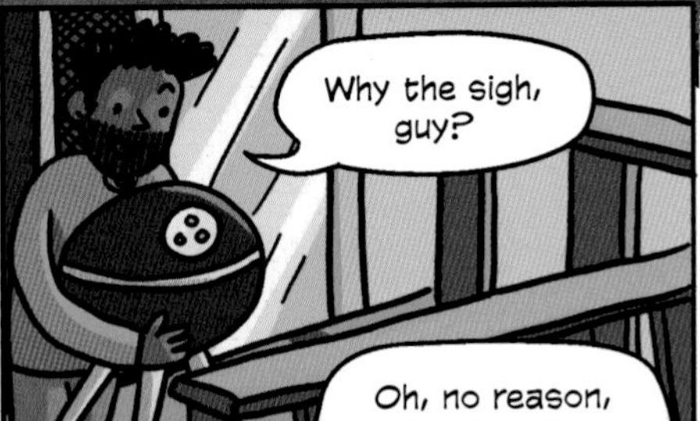
Why the sigh, guy?
Oh, no reason, just my dads picked us up and moved me out to the middle of nowhere.

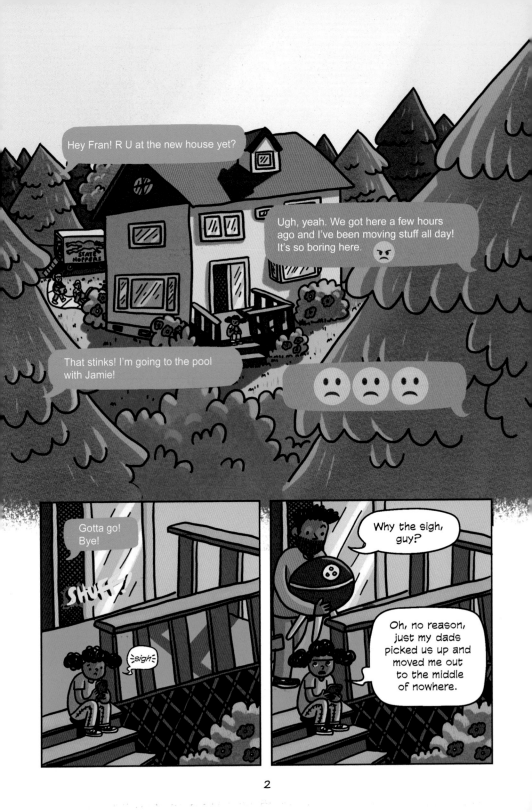

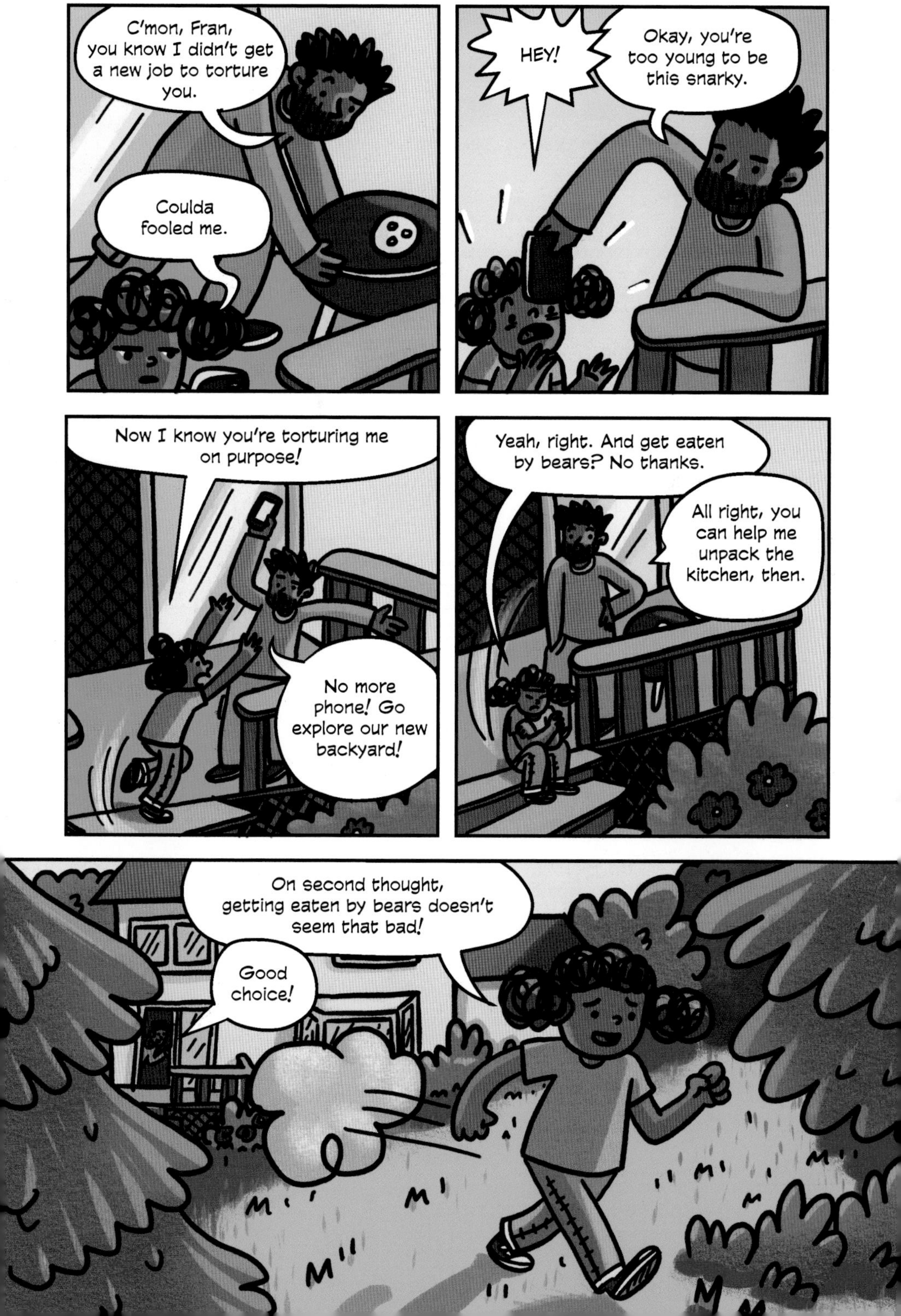
C'mon, Fran, you know I didn't get a new job to torture you.
Coulda fooled me.
HEY!
Okay, you're too young to be this snarky.
Now I know you're torturing me on purpose!
No more phone! Go explore our new backyard!
Yeah, right. And get eaten by bears? No thanks.
All right, you can help me unpack the kitchen, then.
On second thought, getting eaten by bears doesn't seem that bad!
Good choice!

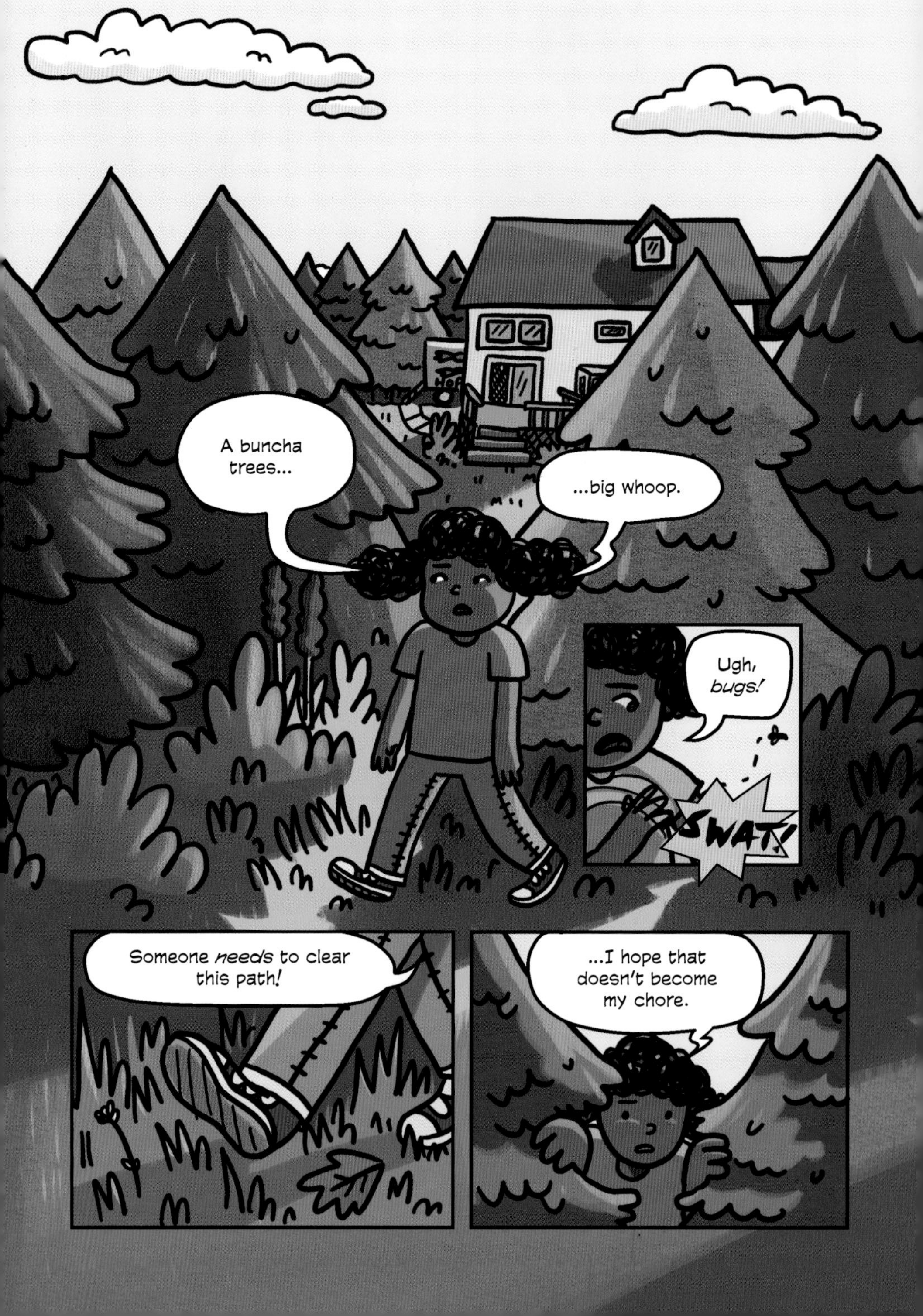
A buncha trees...
...big whoop.
Ugh, *bugs!*
SWAT!
Someone *needs* to clear this path!
...I hope that doesn't become my chore.

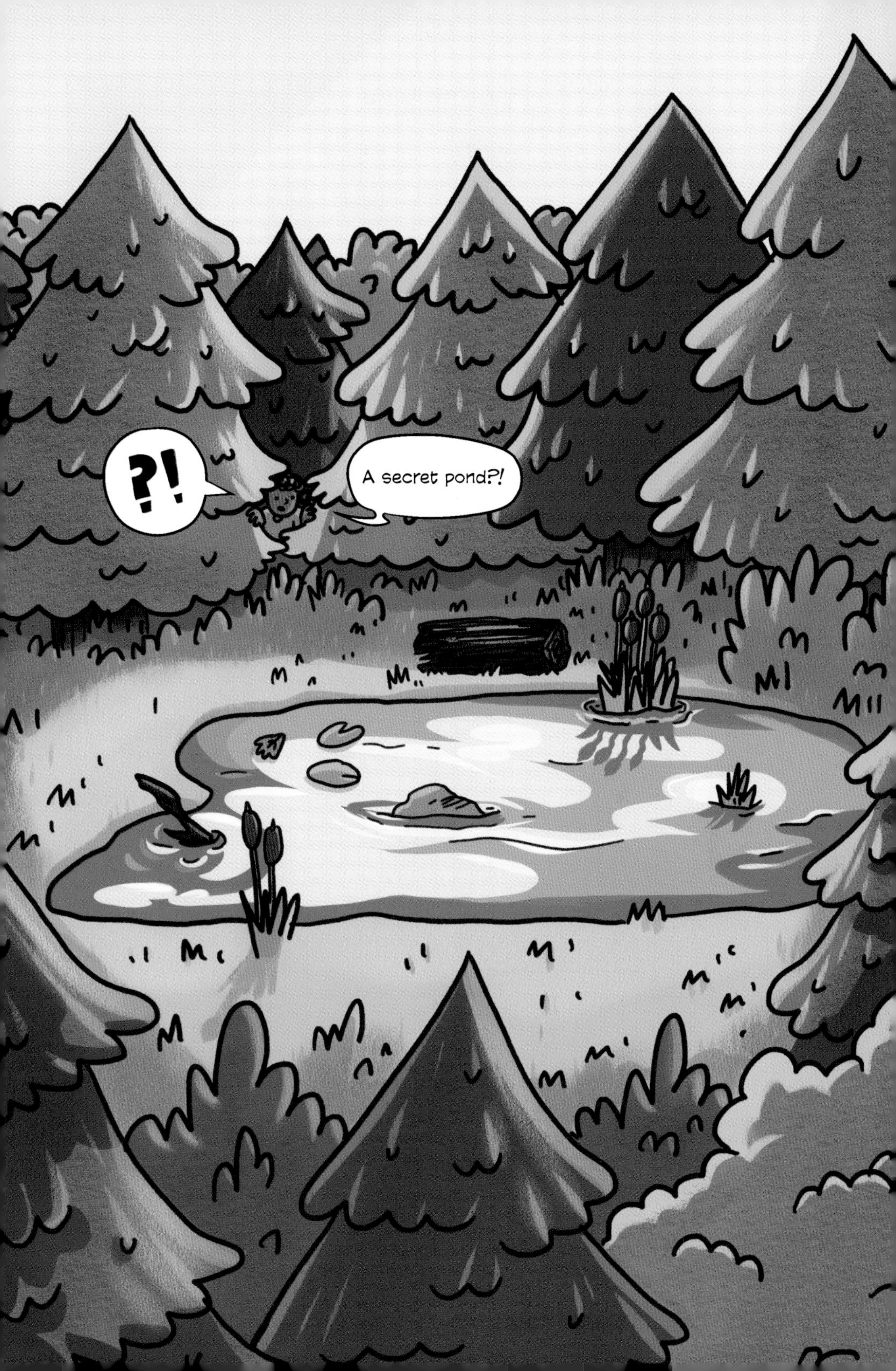
?!
A secret pond?!

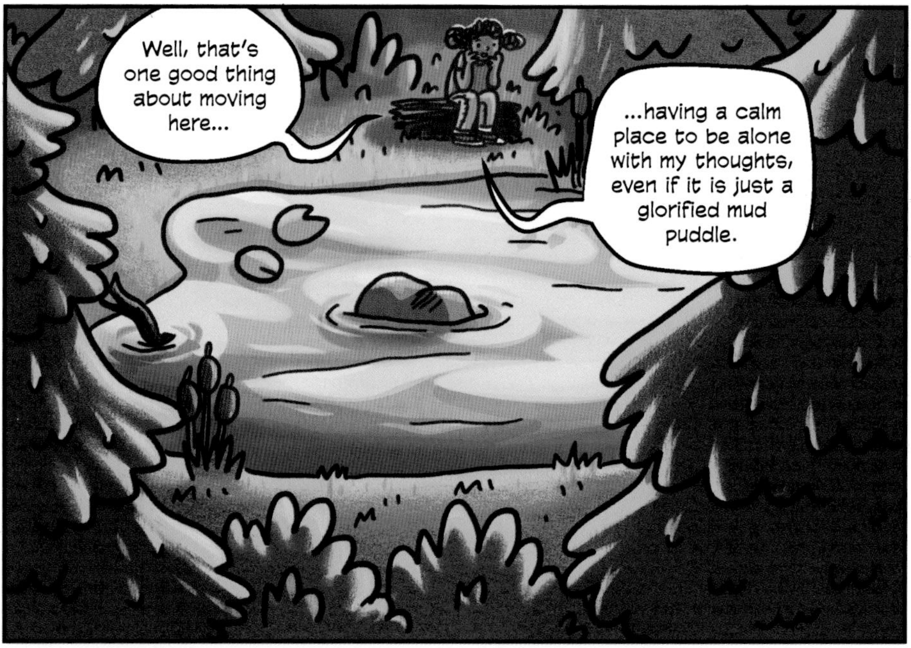
Well, that's one good thing about moving here...
...having a calm place to be alone with my thoughts, even if it is just a glorified mud puddle.

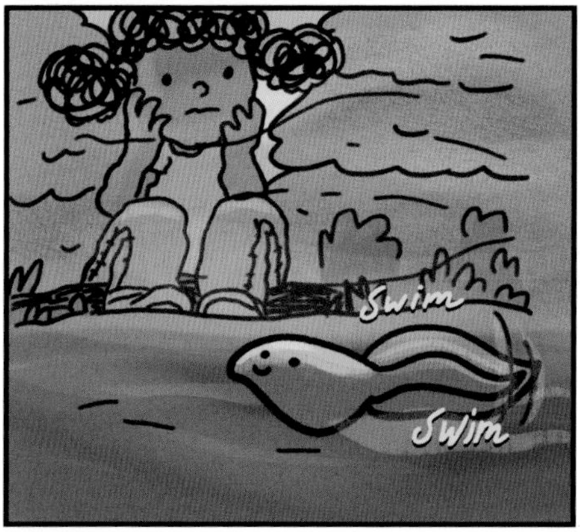
Swim
Swim

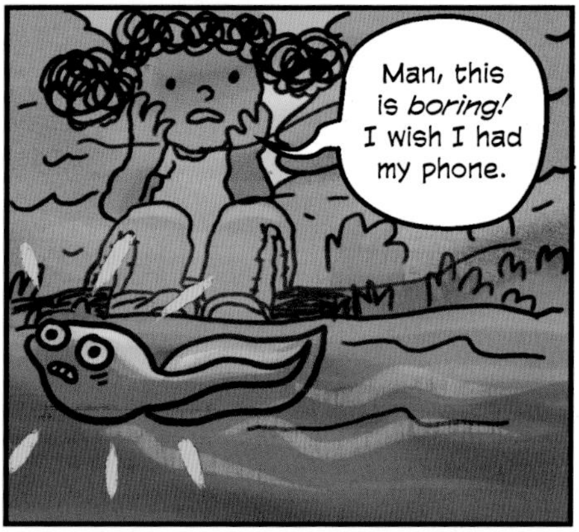
Man, this is *boring!* I wish I had my phone.

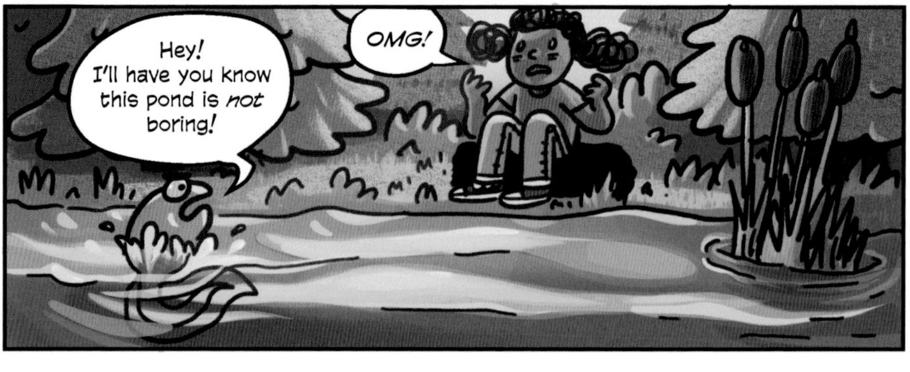
OMG!
Hey! I'll have you know this pond is *not* boring!

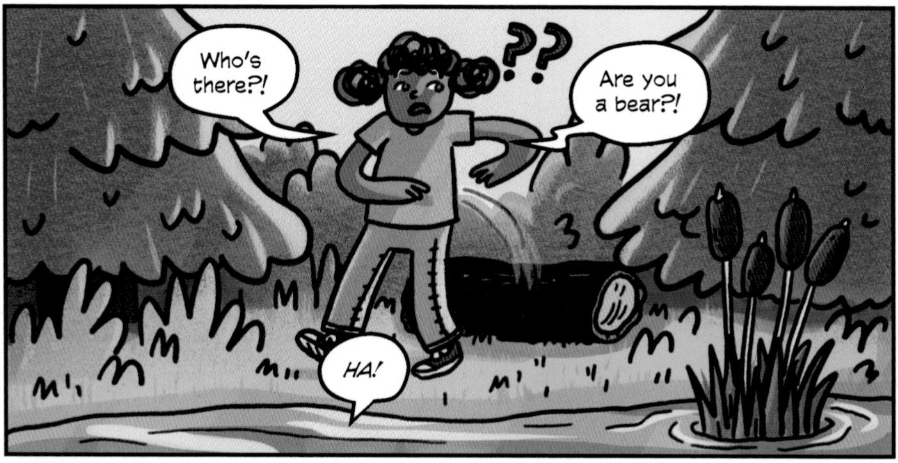
Who's there?!
??
Are you a bear?!
HA!

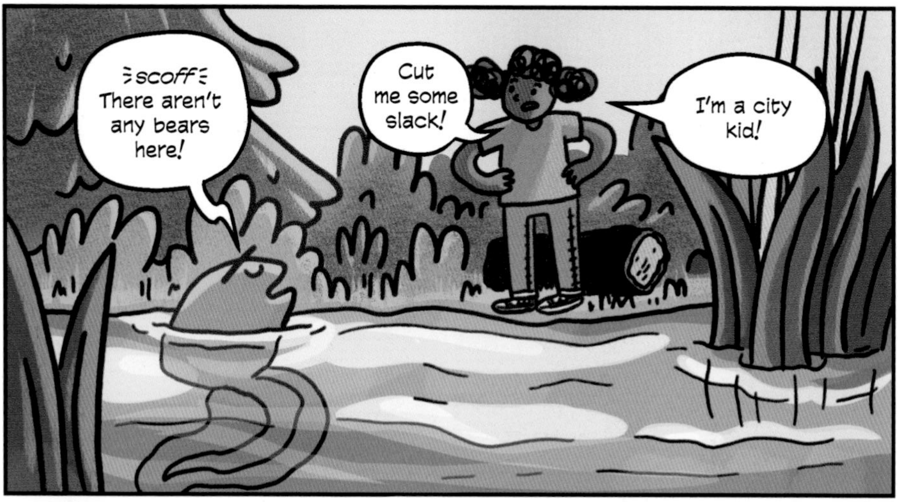
scoff
There aren't any bears here!
Cut me some slack!
I'm a city kid!

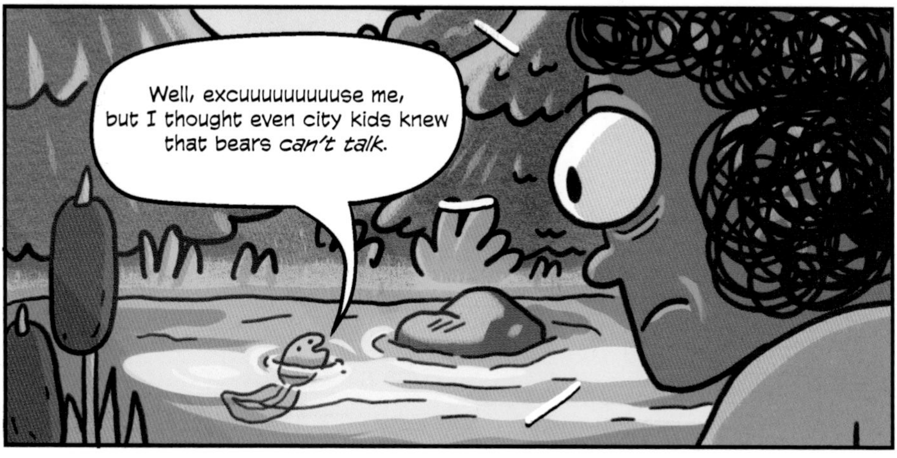
Well, excuuuuuuuuuse me, but I thought even city kids knew that bears *can't talk*.

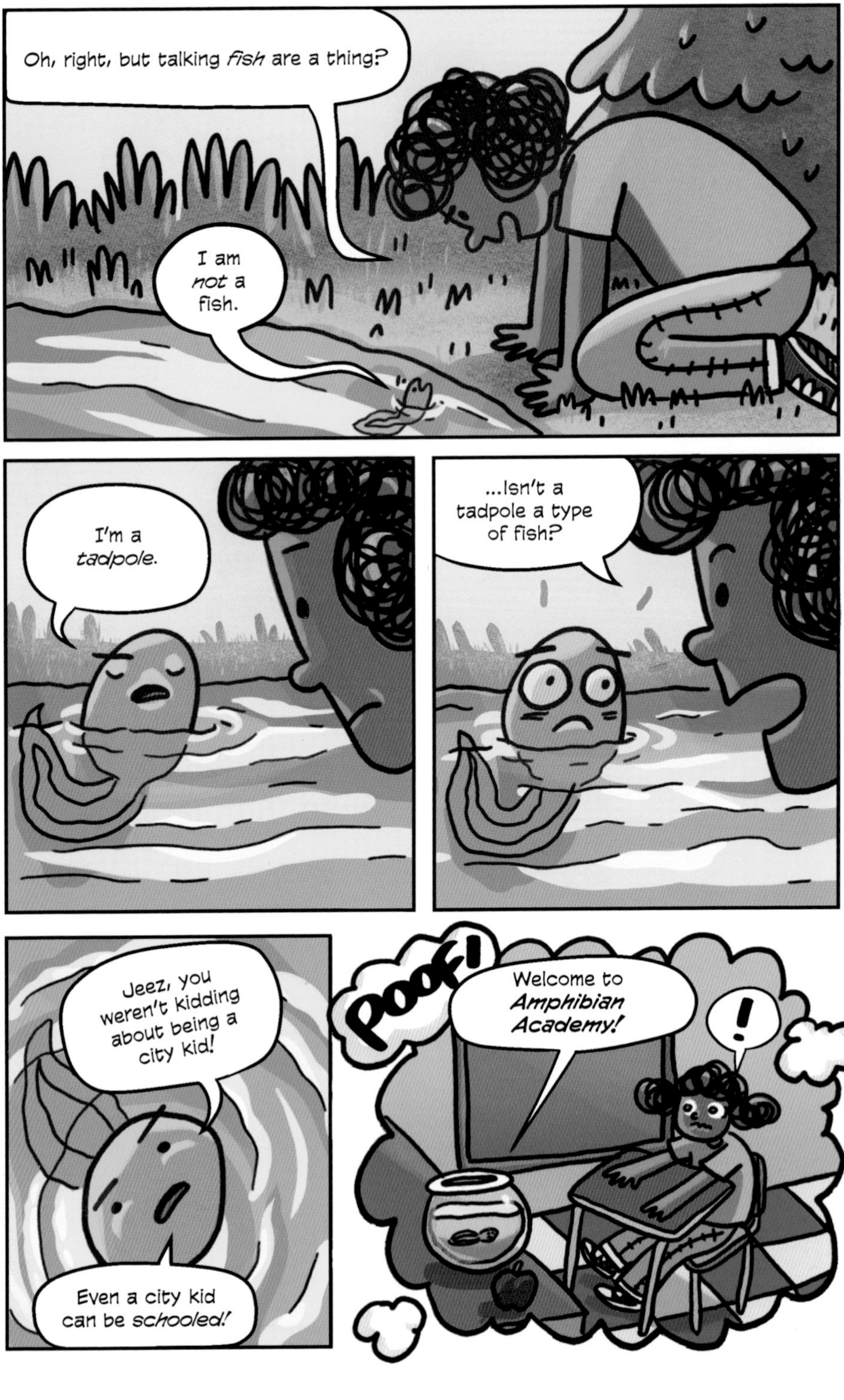
Oh, right, but talking *fish* are a thing?
I am *not* a fish.
I'm a *tadpole*.
...Isn't a tadpole a type of fish?
Jeez, you weren't kidding about being a city kid!
Even a city kid can be *schooled!*
POOF!
Welcome to *Amphibian Academy!*
!

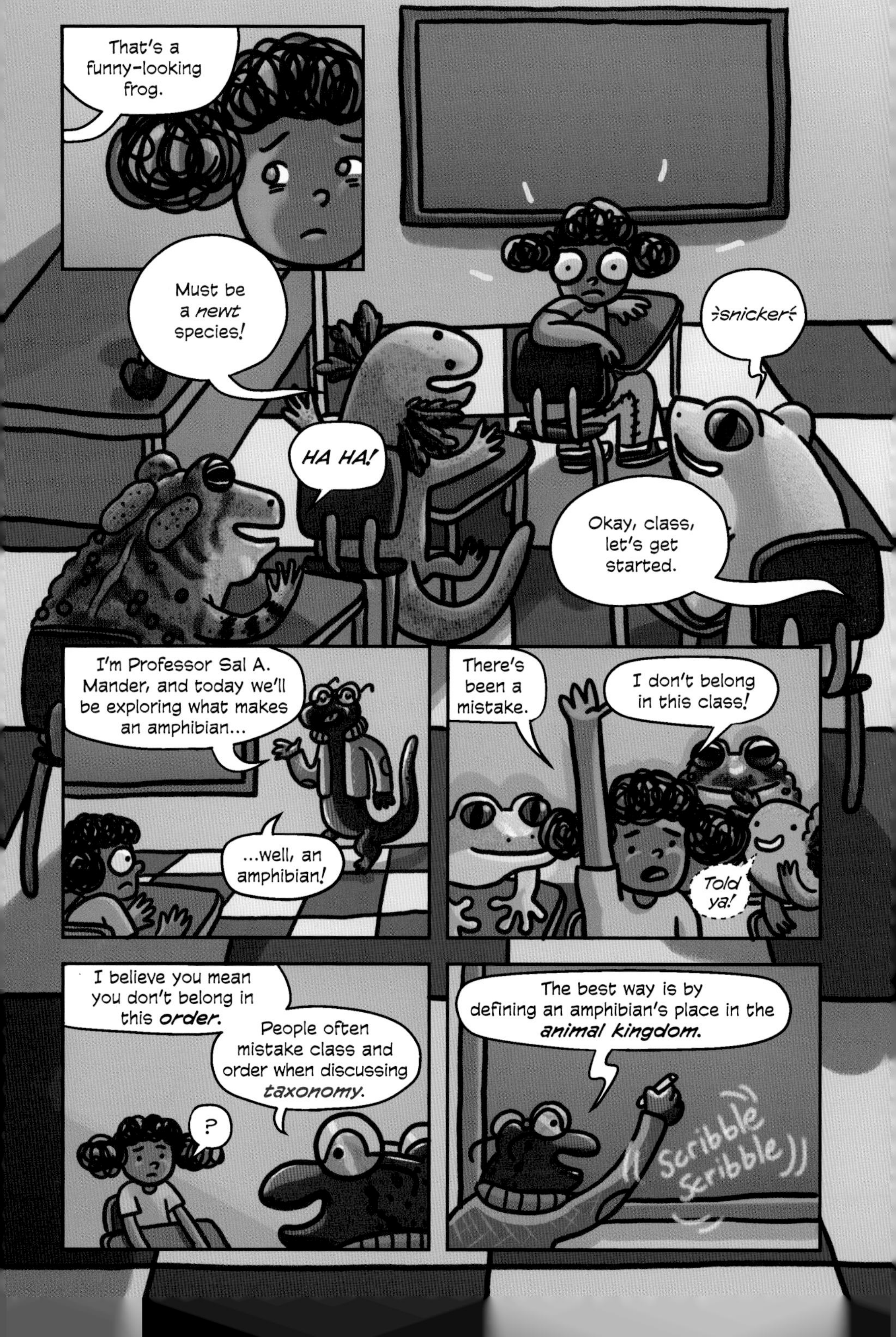
That's a funny-looking frog.
Must be a *newt* species!
HA HA!
snicker
Okay, class, let's get started.
I'm Professor Sal A. Mander, and today we'll be exploring what makes an amphibian...
...well, an amphibian!
There's been a mistake.
I don't belong in this class!
Told ya!
I believe you mean you don't belong in this *order*.
People often mistake class and order when discussing *taxonomy*.
?
The best way is by defining an amphibian's place in the ***animal kingdom***.
Scribble Scribble

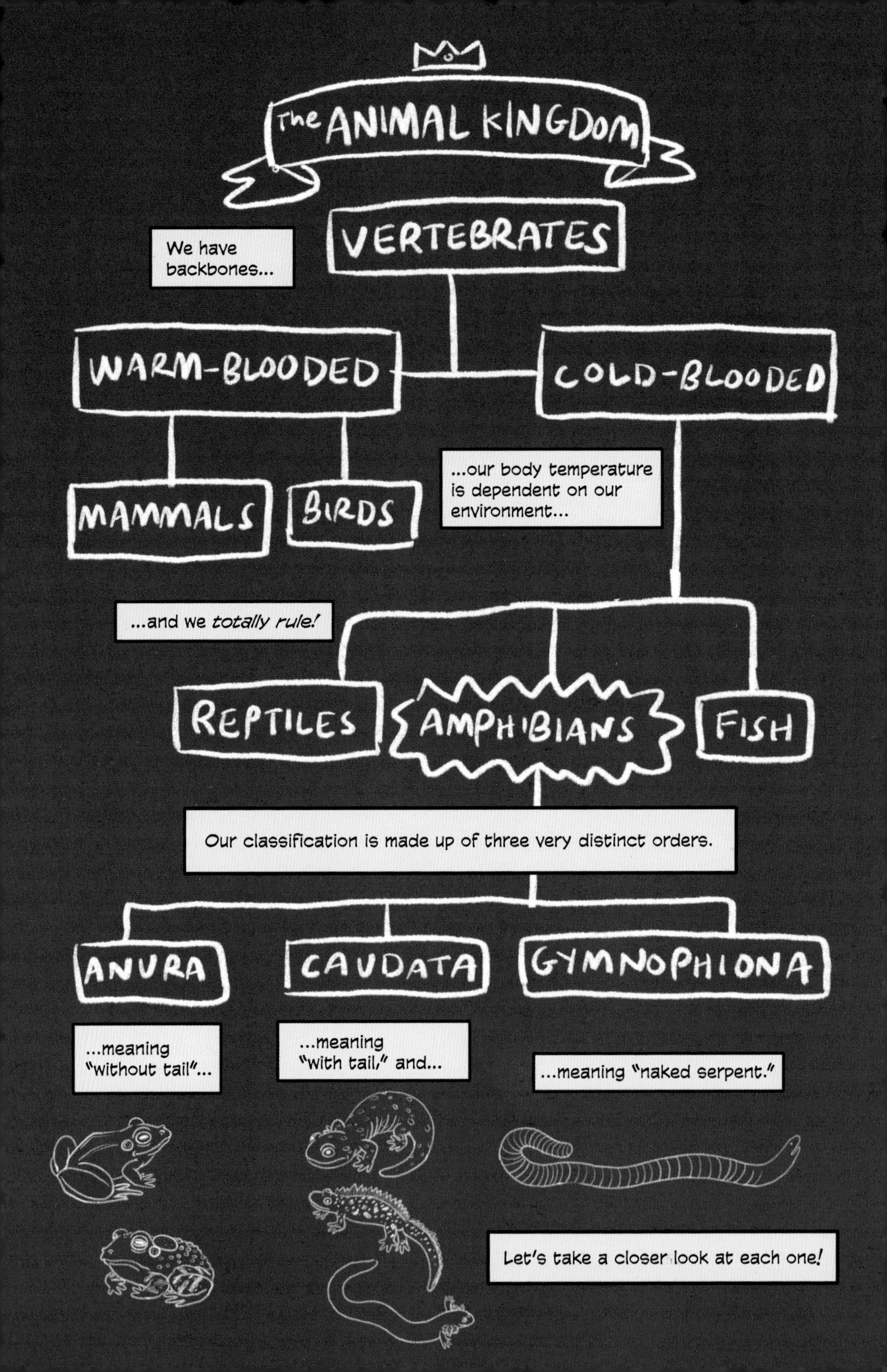
The ANIMAL KINGDOM
VERTEBRATES
We have backbones...
WARM-BLOODED
COLD-BLOODED
MAMMALS
BIRDS
...our body temperature is dependent on our environment...
...and we *totally rule!*
REPTILES
AMPHIBIANS
FISH
Our classification is made up of three very distinct orders.
ANURA
CAUDATA
GYMNOPHIONA
...meaning "without tail"...
...meaning "with tail," and...
...meaning "naked serpent."
Let's take a closer look at each one!

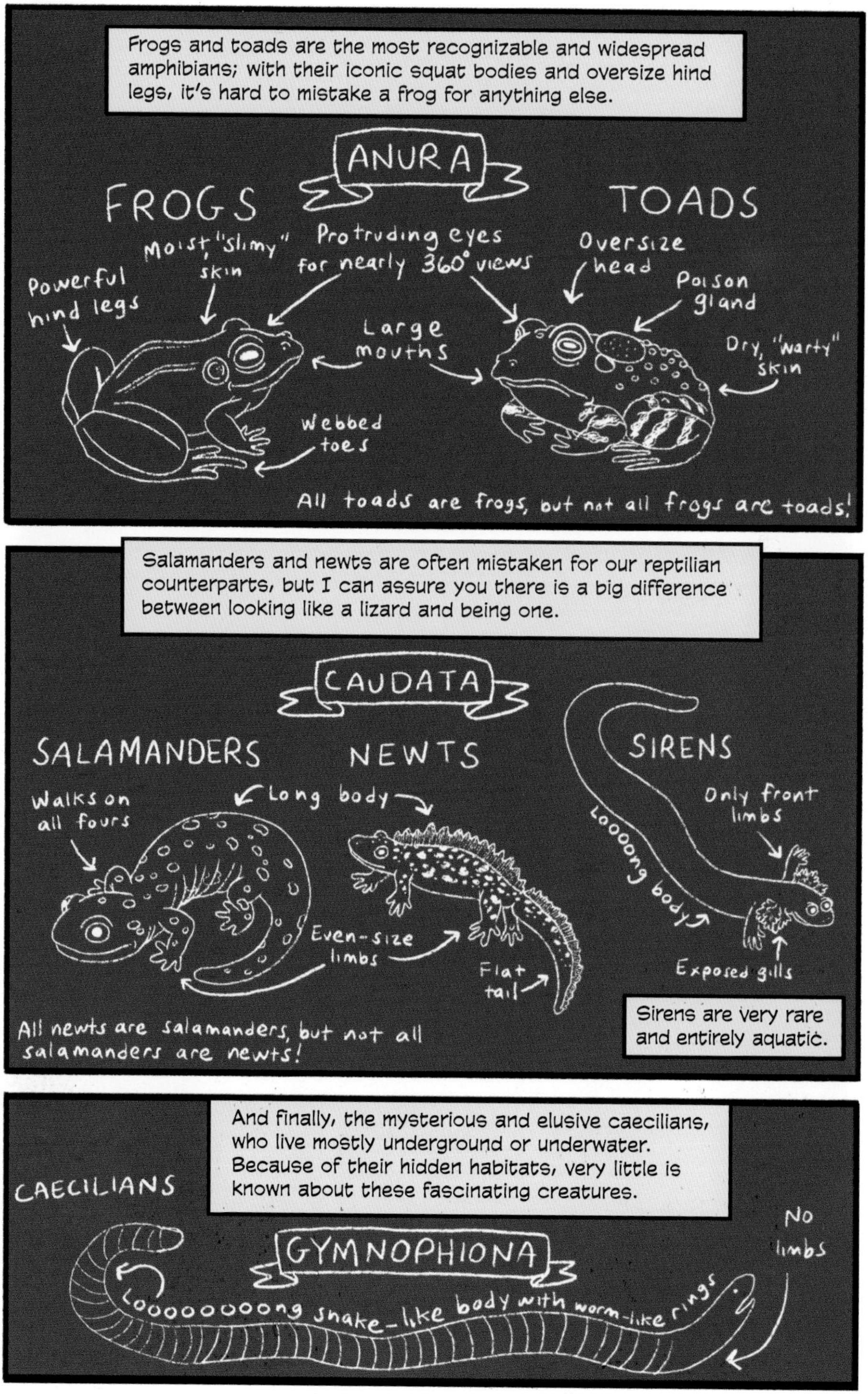
Frogs and toads are the most recognizable and widespread amphibians; with their iconic squat bodies and oversize hind legs, it's hard to mistake a frog for anything else.
ANURA
FROGS
TOADS
Moist, "slimy" skin
Protruding eyes for nearly 360° views
Oversize head
Powerful hind legs
Poison gland
Large mouths
Dry, "warty" skin
Webbed toes
All toads are frogs, but not all frogs are toads!
Salamanders and newts are often mistaken for our reptilian counterparts, but I can assure you there is a big difference between looking like a lizard and being one.
CAUDATA
SALAMANDERS
NEWTS
SIRENS
Walks on all fours
Long body
Only front limbs
Looooong body
Even-size limbs
Flat tail
Exposed gills
Sirens are very rare and entirely aquatic.
All newts are salamanders, but not all salamanders are newts!
And finally, the mysterious and elusive caecilians, who live mostly underground or underwater. Because of their hidden habitats, very little is known about these fascinating creatures.
CAECILIANS
GYMNOPHIONA
No limbs
Loooooooong snake-like body with worm-like rings

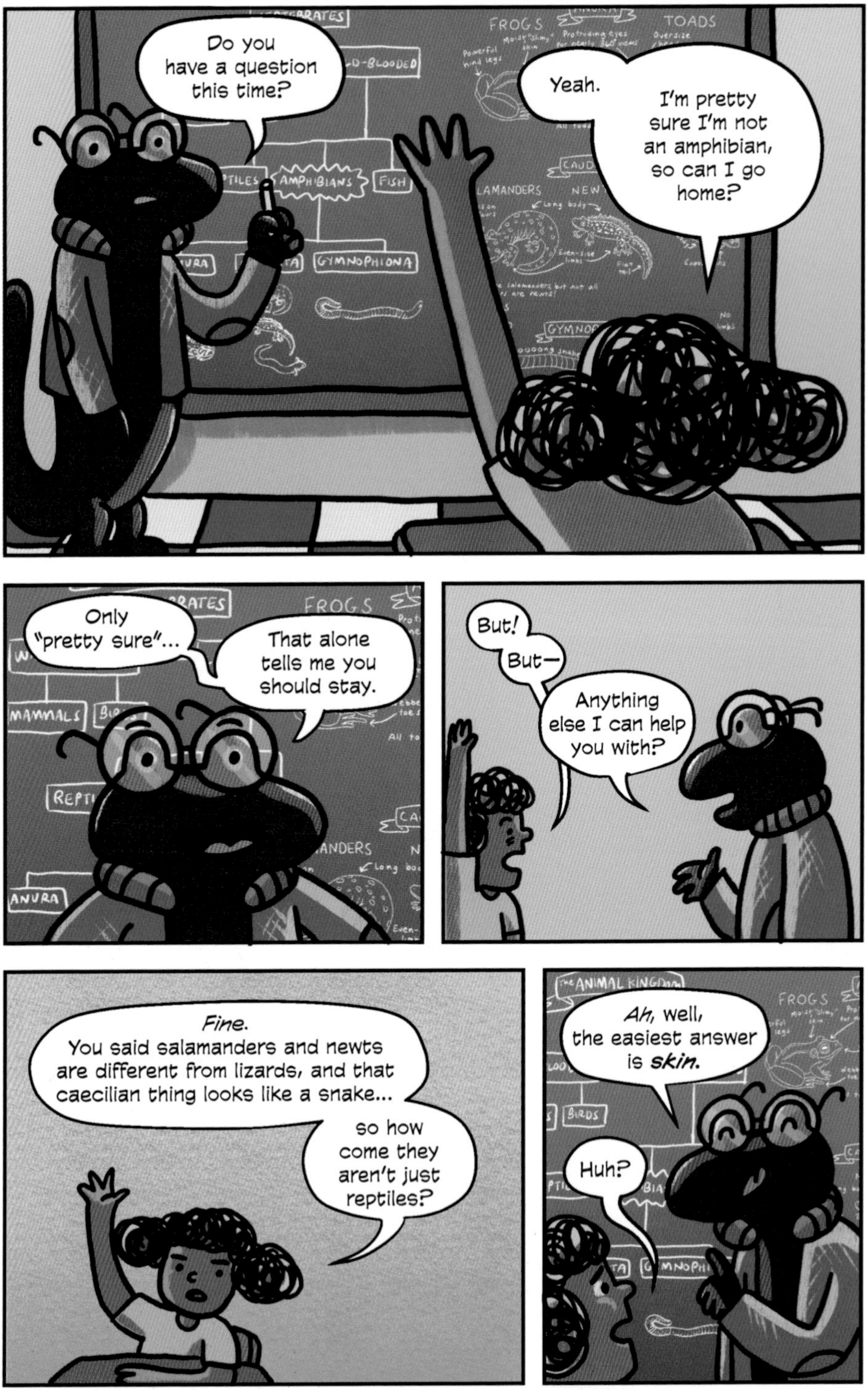
Do you have a question this time?
Yeah.
I'm pretty sure I'm not an amphibian, so can I go home?
Only "pretty sure"...
That alone tells me you should stay.
But!
But—
Anything else I can help you with?
Fine. You said salamanders and newts are different from lizards, and that caecilian thing looks like a snake...
so how come they aren't just reptiles?
Ah, well, the easiest answer is ***skin.***
Huh?

Remember that chart of the animal kingdom? Each classification has a pretty specific outer layer that not only aids in identification, but also provides a type of armor against the elements of their natural environments.

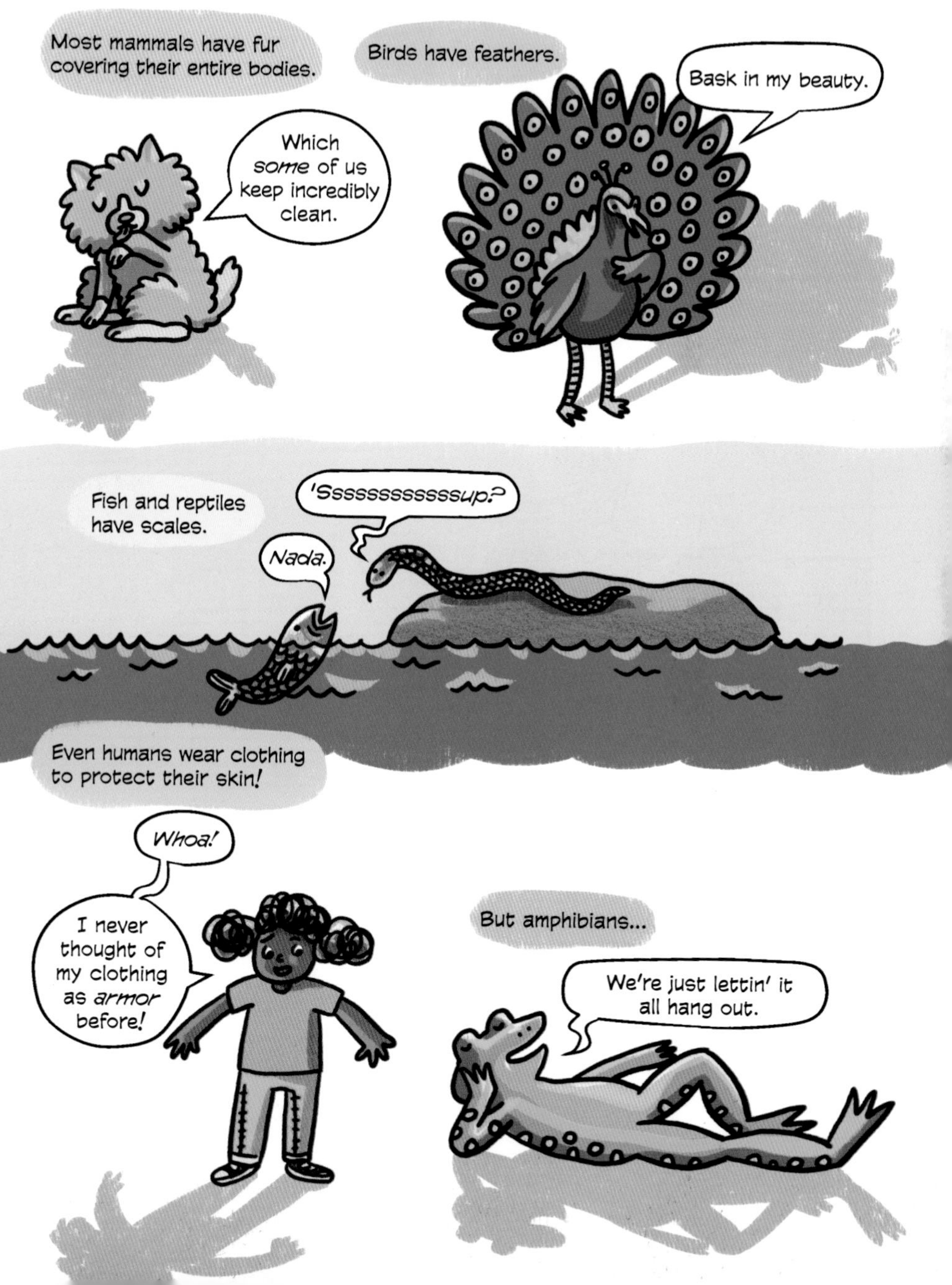
Most mammals have fur covering their entire bodies.
Which *some* of us keep incredibly clean.
Birds have feathers.
Bask in my beauty.
Fish and reptiles have scales.
'Sssssssssssup?
Nada.
Even humans wear clothing to protect their skin!
Whoa!
I never thought of my clothing as *armor* before!
But amphibians...
We're just lettin' it all hang out.

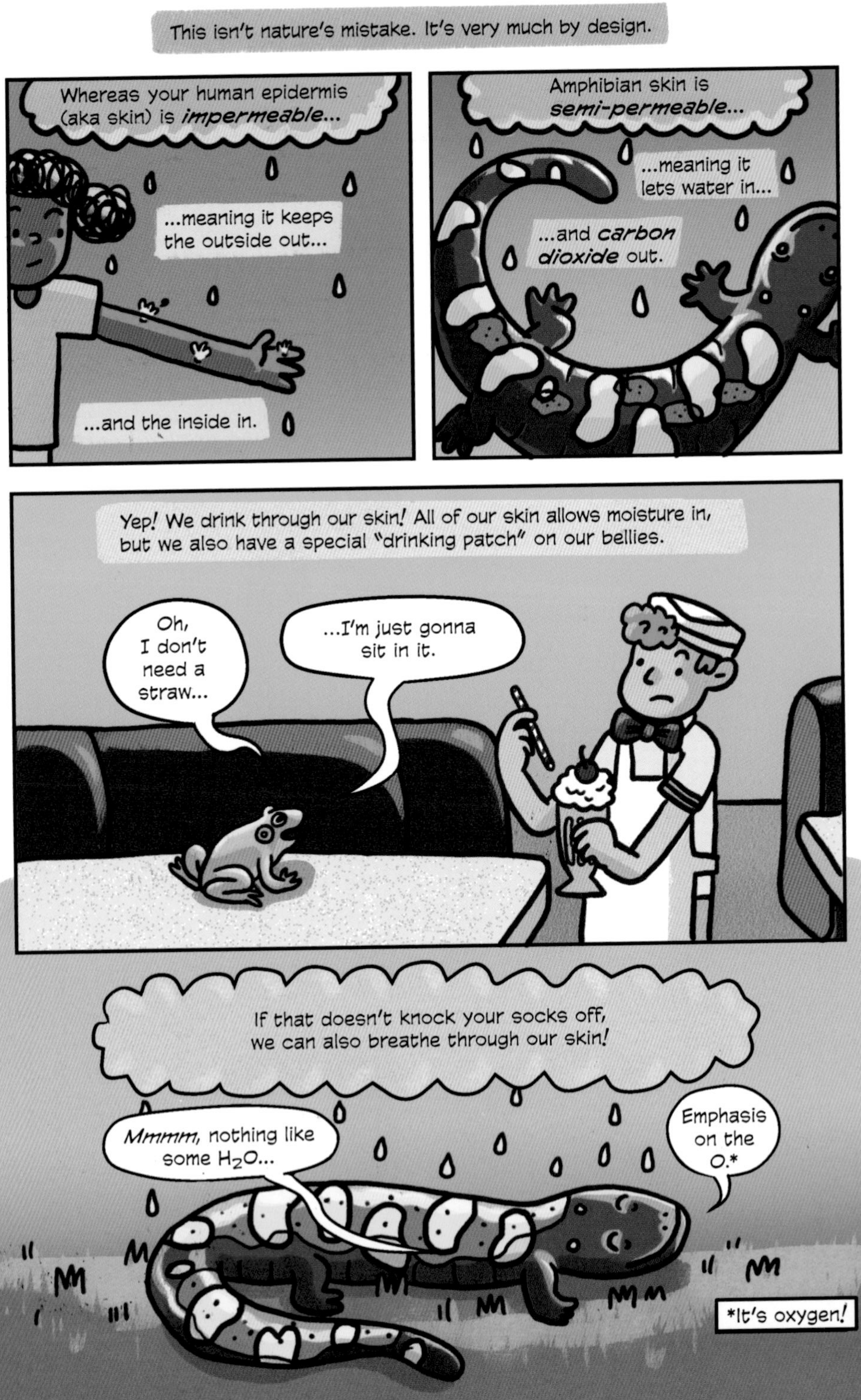
This isn't nature's mistake. It's very much by design.
Whereas your human epidermis (aka skin) is *impermeable*...
...meaning it keeps the outside out...
...and the inside in.
Amphibian skin is *semi-permeable*...
...meaning it lets water in...
...and *carbon dioxide* out.
Yep! We drink through our skin! All of our skin allows moisture in, but we also have a special "drinking patch" on our bellies.
Oh, I don't need a straw...
...I'm just gonna sit in it.
If that doesn't knock your socks off, we can also breathe through our skin!
Mmmm, nothing like some H_2O...
Emphasis on the O.*
*It's oxygen!

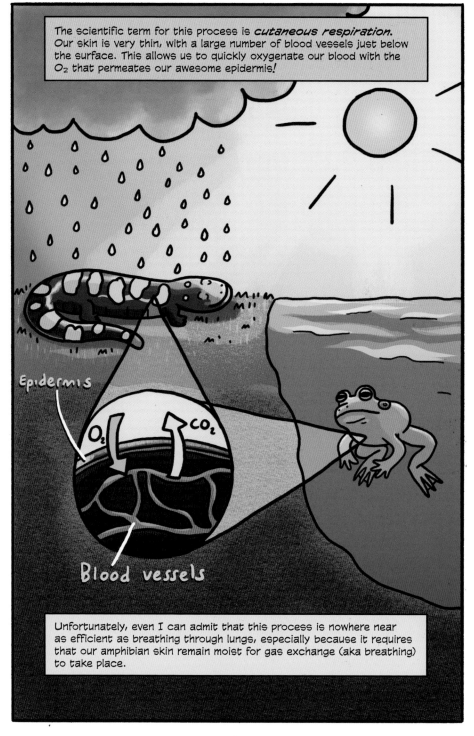

The scientific term for this process is *cutaneous respiration*. Our skin is very thin, with a large number of blood vessels just below the surface. This allows us to quickly oxygenate our blood with the O_2 that permeates our awesome epidermis!

Epidermis

O_2

CO_2

Blood vessels

Unfortunately, even I can admit that this process is nowhere near as efficient as breathing through lungs, especially because it requires that our amphibian skin remain moist for gas exchange (aka breathing) to take place.

On land, most amphibians breathe through both their lungs and their skin. When you see a frog's throat inflate and deflate, you are witnessing them breathing through their lungs, although the process is pretty different from the way humans use their lungs.

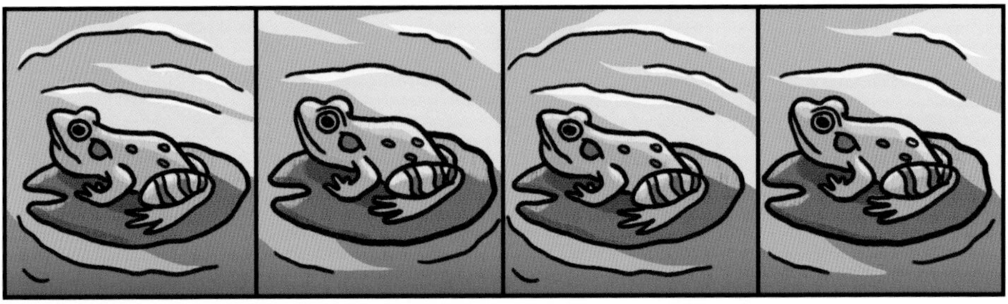

Amphibians do not have *diaphragms* (the muscle that pulls air into the lungs and pushes it out), so in order to use our lungs we have to fill our mouths with air, which is when our throats inflate. Then we push the floor of our mouths up, forcing the air down into our lungs, kinda like we are swallowing air—this is when the deflation occurs.

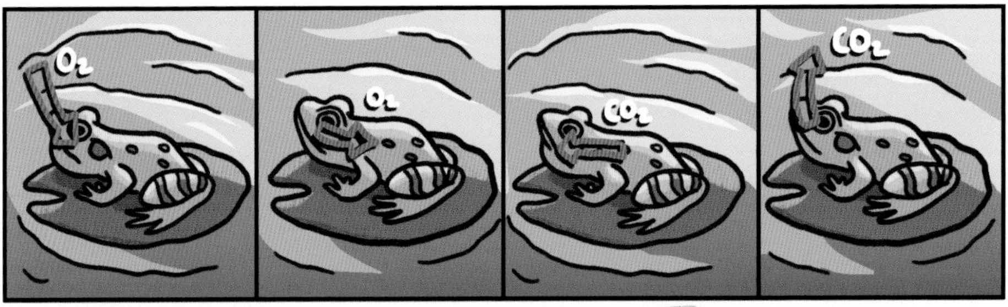
O_2
O_2
CO_2
CO_2

We then have to repeat the process in reverse to expel the CO_2 from our lungs. This time, the inflation is pulling air out of the lungs into the mouth, and the deflation is that air being pushed out through our noses.

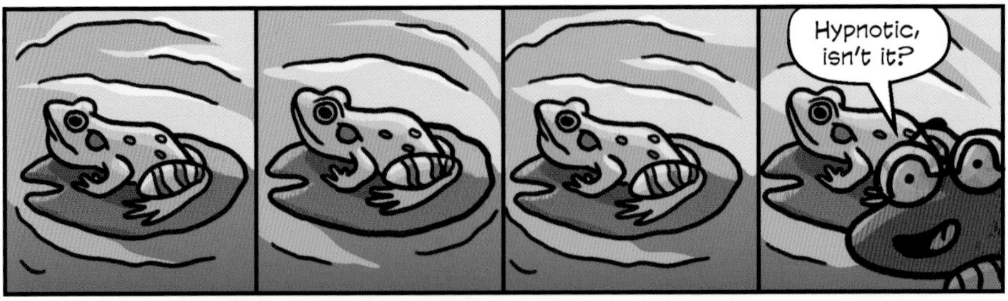
Hypnotic, isn't it?

All the while, cutaneous respiration is also occurring to aid in this pared-down breathing style.

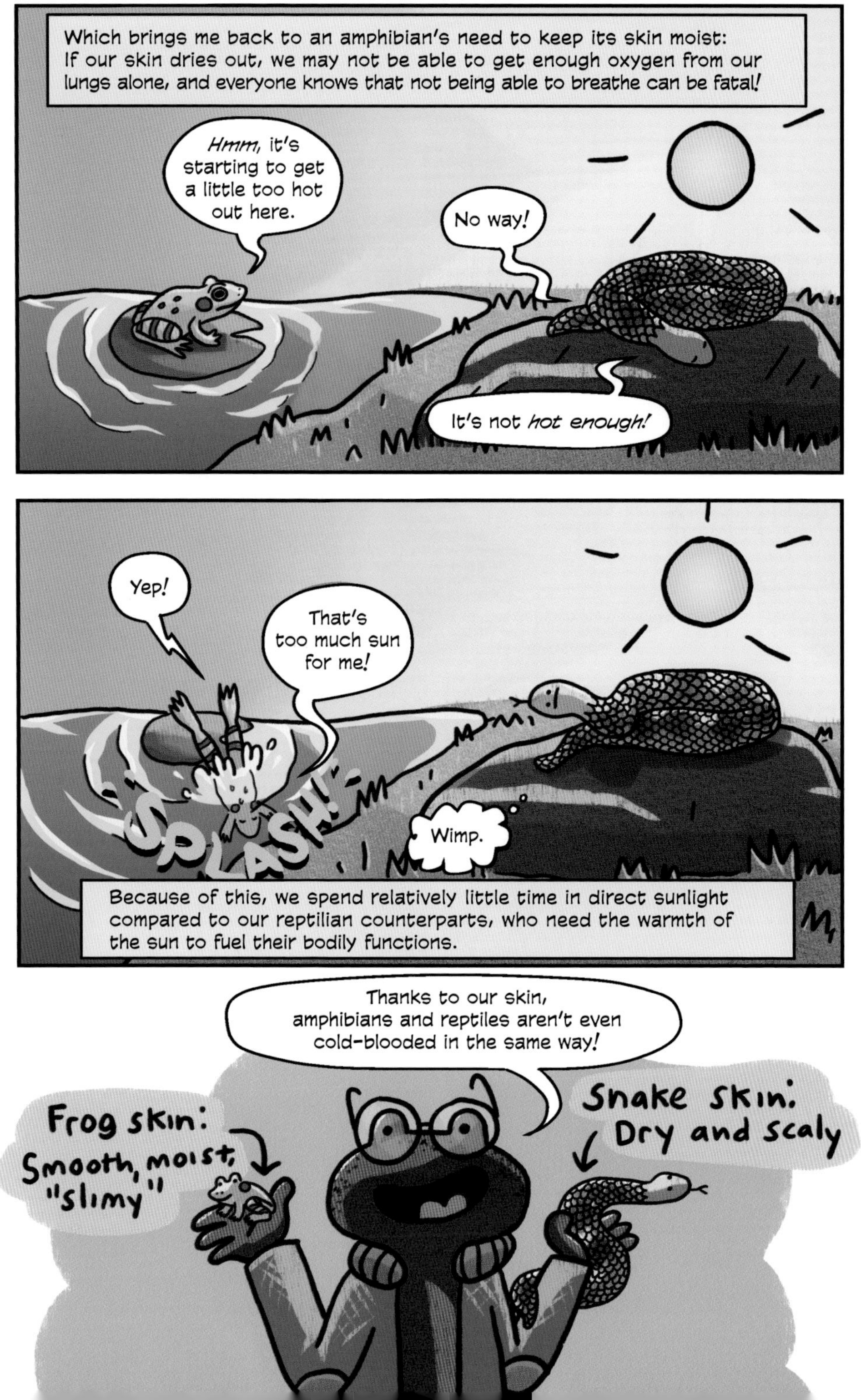
Which brings me back to an amphibian's need to keep its skin moist: If our skin dries out, we may not be able to get enough oxygen from our lungs alone, and everyone knows that not being able to breathe can be fatal!
Hmm, it's starting to get a little too hot out here.
No way!
It's not *hot enough!*
Yep!
That's too much sun for me!
SPLASH!
Wimp.
Because of this, we spend relatively little time in direct sunlight compared to our reptilian counterparts, who need the warmth of the sun to fuel their bodily functions.
Thanks to our skin, amphibians and reptiles aren't even cold-blooded in the same way!
Frog skin: Smooth, moist, "slimy"
Snake skin: Dry and scaly

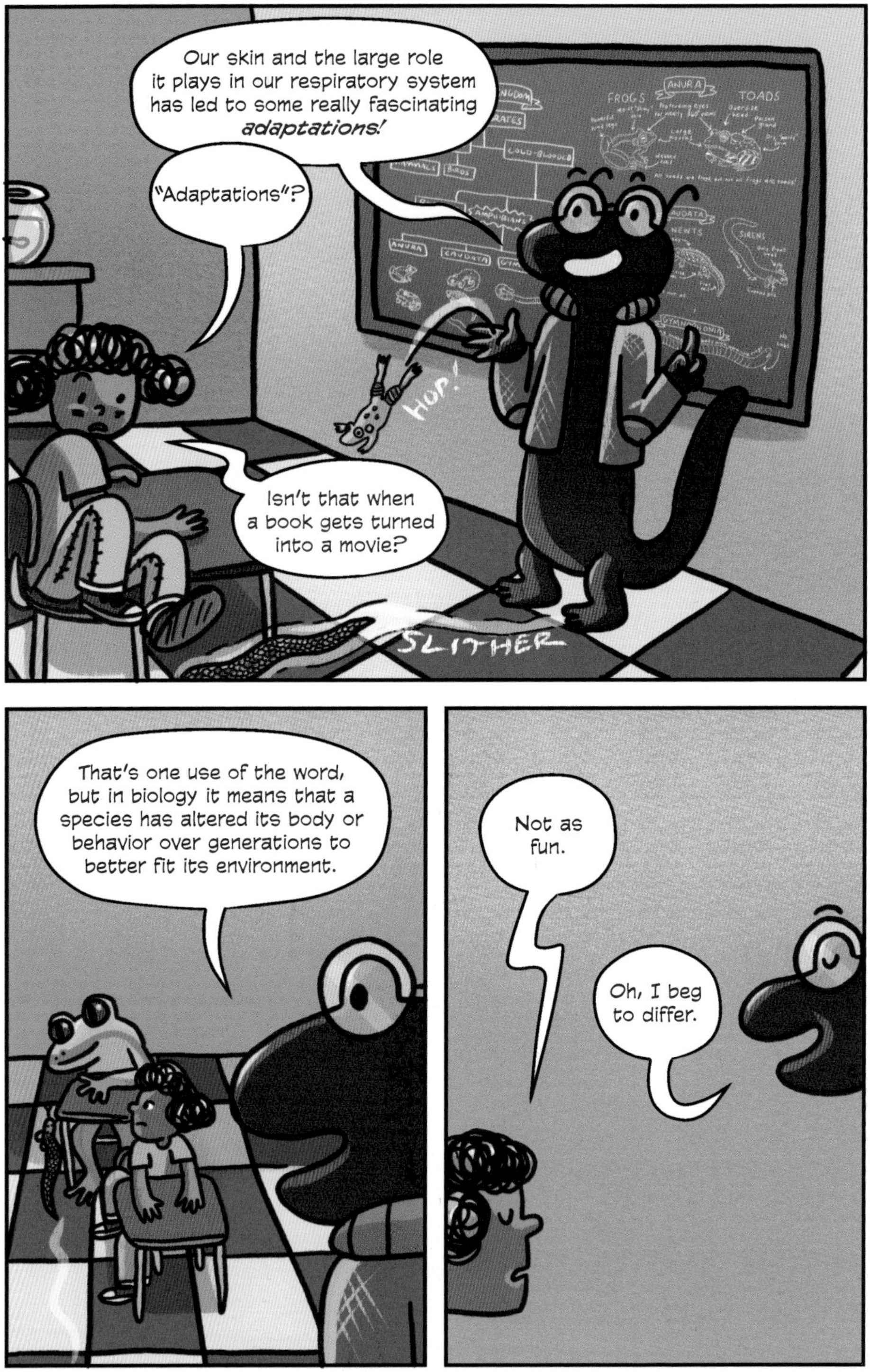
Our skin and the large role it plays in our respiratory system has led to some really fascinating *adaptations!*
"Adaptations"?
ANURA
FROGS
TOADS
NEWTS
SIRENS
HOP!
Isn't that when a book gets turned into a movie?
SLITHER
That's one use of the word, but in biology it means that a species has altered its body or behavior over generations to better fit its environment.
Not as fun.
Oh, I beg to differ.

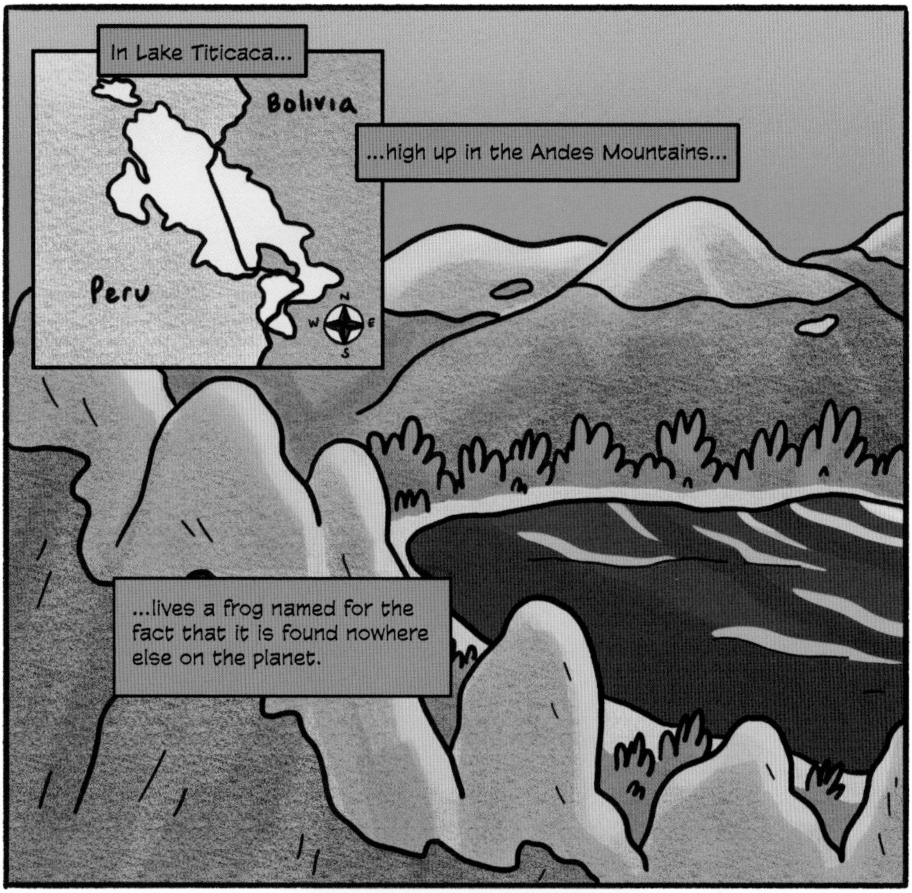
In Lake Titicaca...
Bolivia
Peru
N
W
E
S
...high up in the Andes Mountains...
...lives a frog named for the fact that it is found nowhere else on the planet.

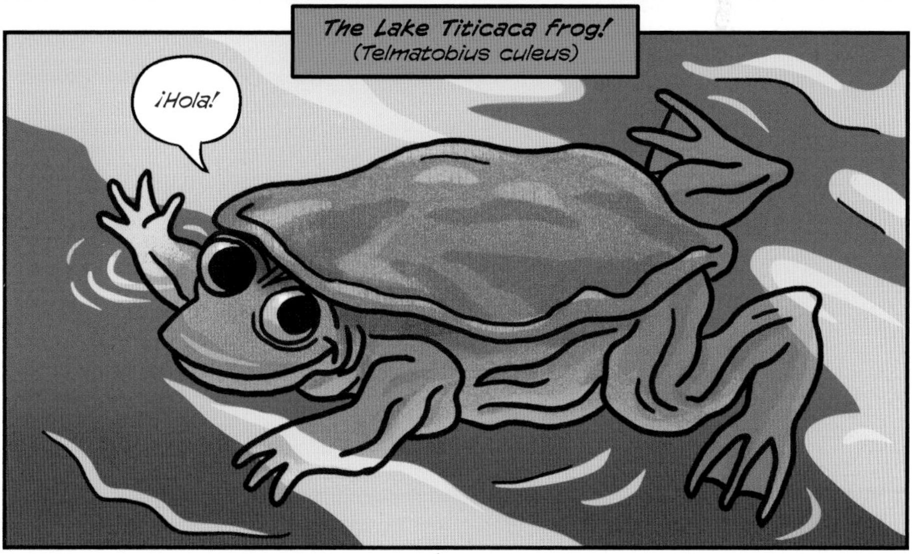
The Lake Titicaca frog!
(Telmatobius culeus)
¡Hola!

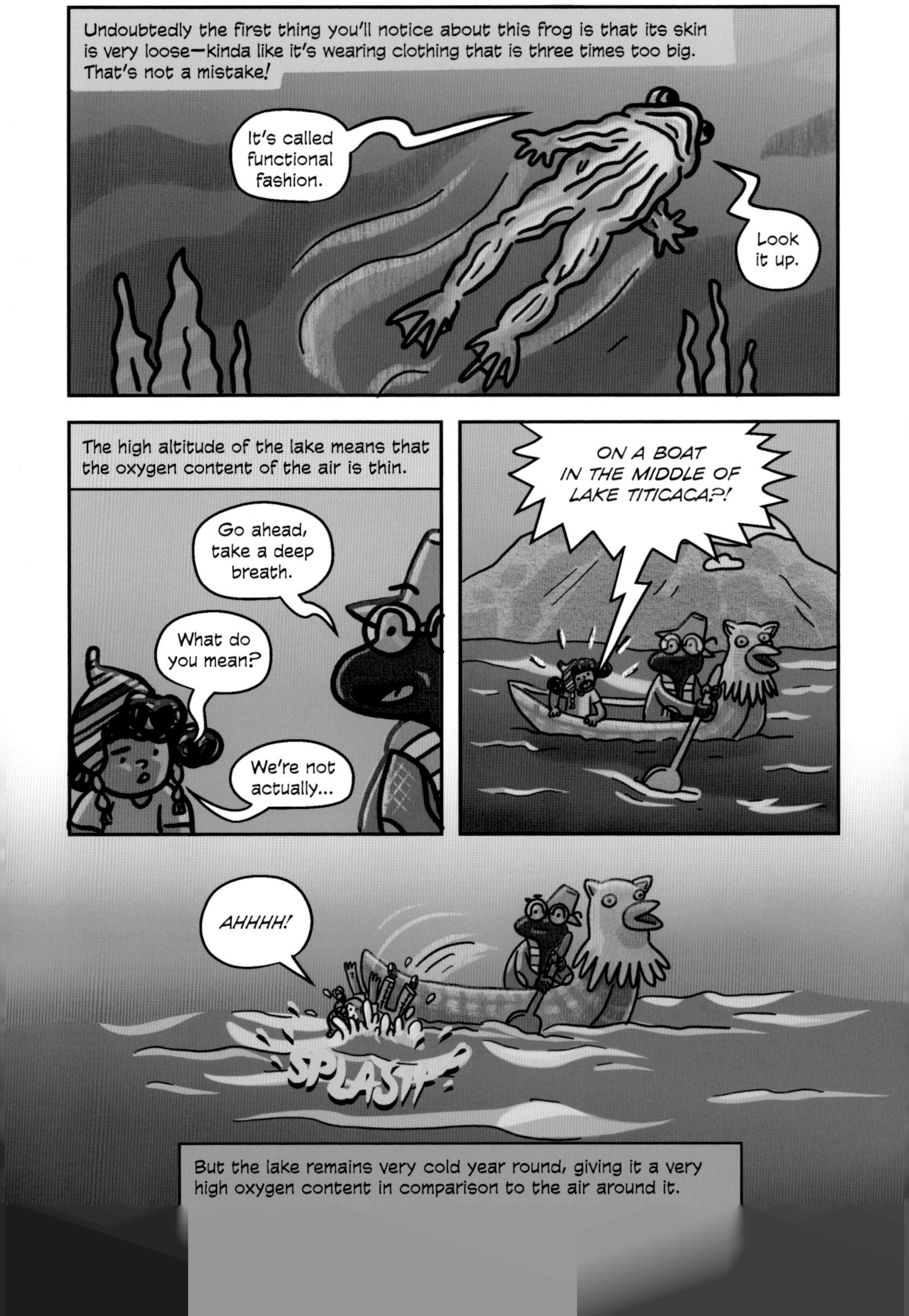
Undoubtedly the first thing you'll notice about this frog is that its skin is very loose—kinda like it's wearing clothing that is three times too big. That's not a mistake!
It's called functional fashion.
Look it up.
The high altitude of the lake means that the oxygen content of the air is thin.
Go ahead, take a deep breath.
What do you mean?
We're not actually...
ON A BOAT IN THE MIDDLE OF LAKE TITICACA?!
AHHHH!
SPLASH
But the lake remains very cold year round, giving it a very high oxygen content in comparison to the air around it.

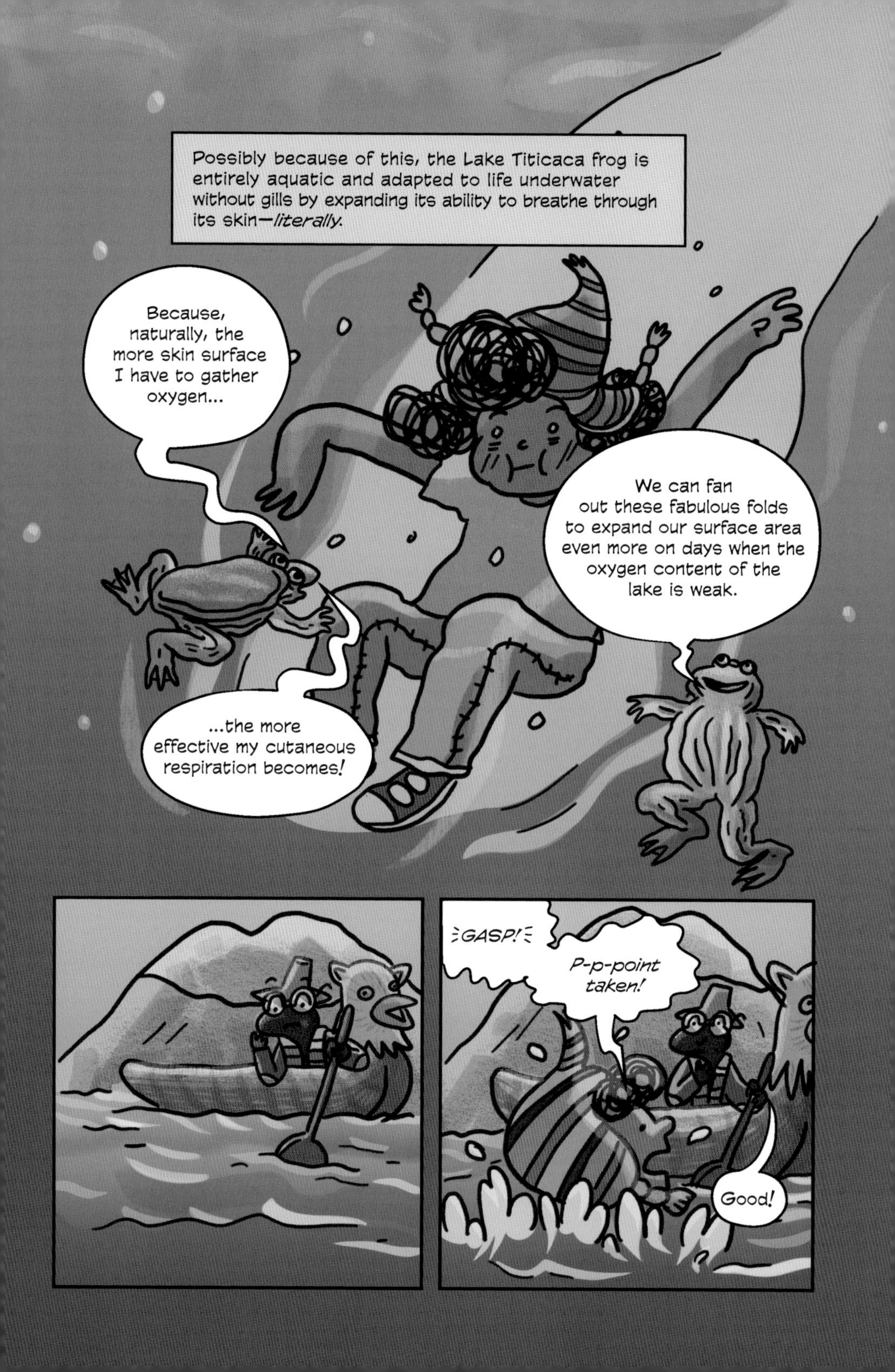
Possibly because of this, the Lake Titicaca frog is entirely aquatic and adapted to life underwater without gills by expanding its ability to breathe through its skin—*literally*.
Because, naturally, the more skin surface I have to gather oxygen...
...the more effective my cutaneous respiration becomes!
We can fan out these fabulous folds to expand our surface area even more on days when the oxygen content of the lake is weak.
GASP!
P-p-point taken!
Good!

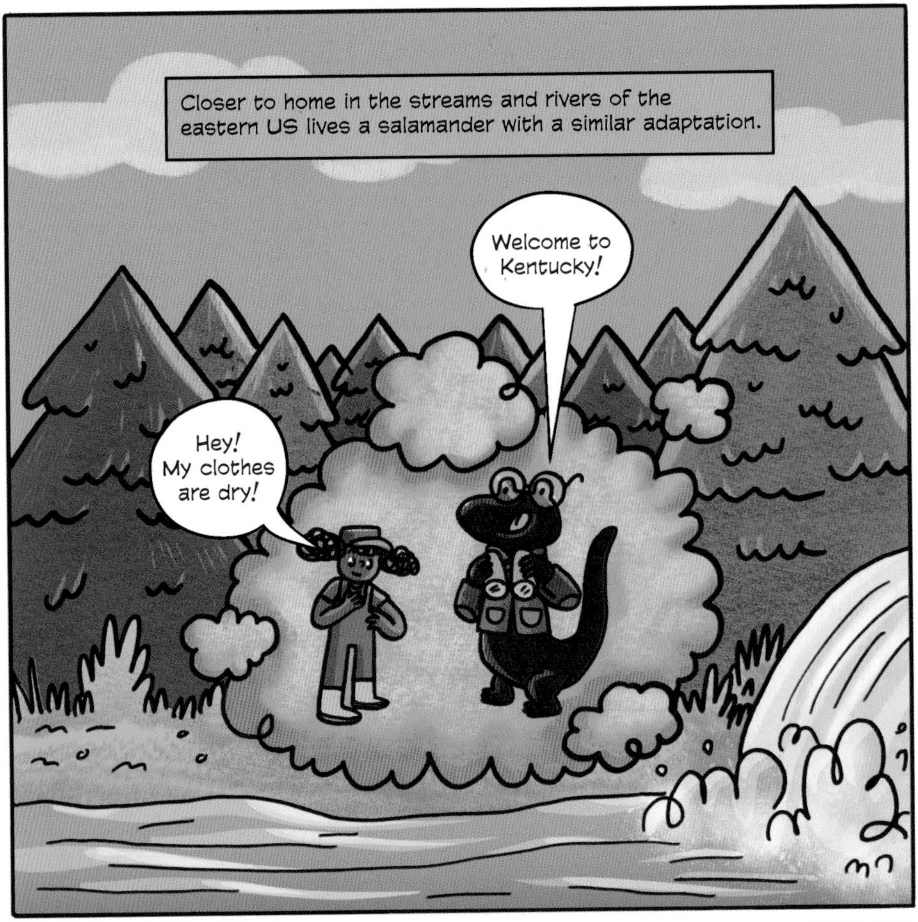
Closer to home in the streams and rivers of the eastern US lives a salamander with a similar adaptation.
Welcome to Kentucky!
Hey! My clothes are dry!

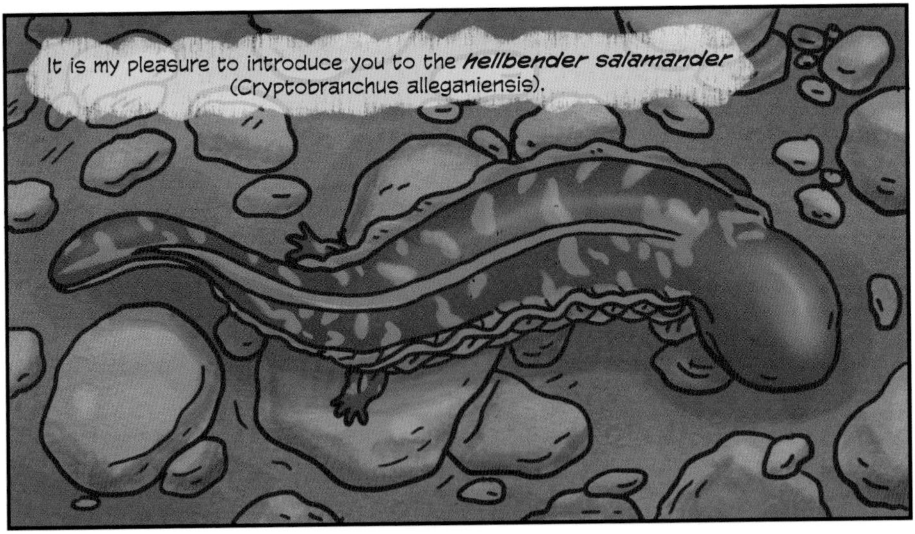
It is my pleasure to introduce you to the ***hellbender salamander*** (Cryptobranchus alleganiensis).

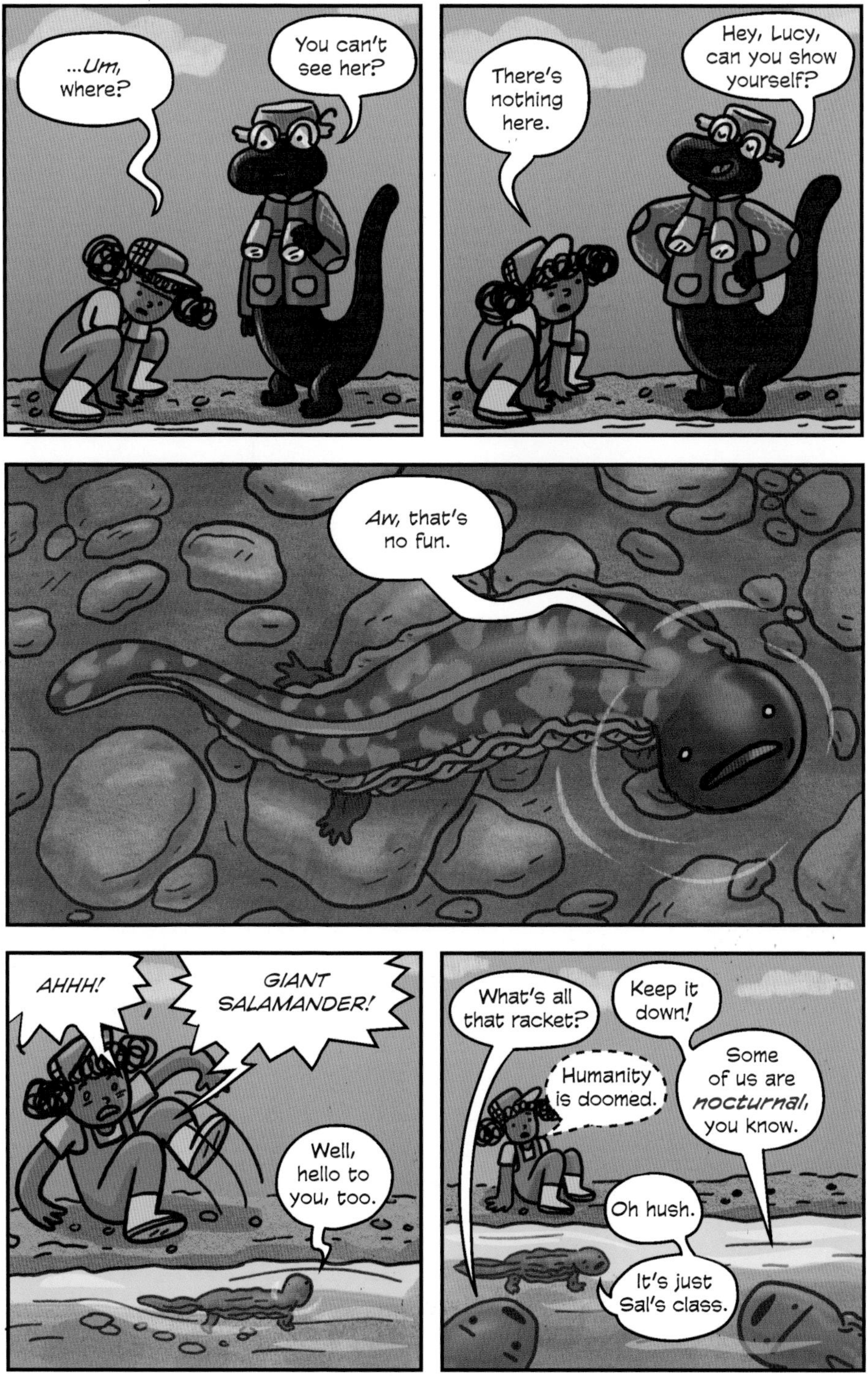
...*Um*, where?
You can't see her?
There's nothing here.
Hey, Lucy, can you show yourself?
Aw, that's no fun.
AHHH!
GIANT SALAMANDER!
Well, hello to you, too.
What's all that racket?
Keep it down!
Humanity is doomed.
Some of us are ***nocturnal***, you know.
Oh hush.
It's just Sal's class.

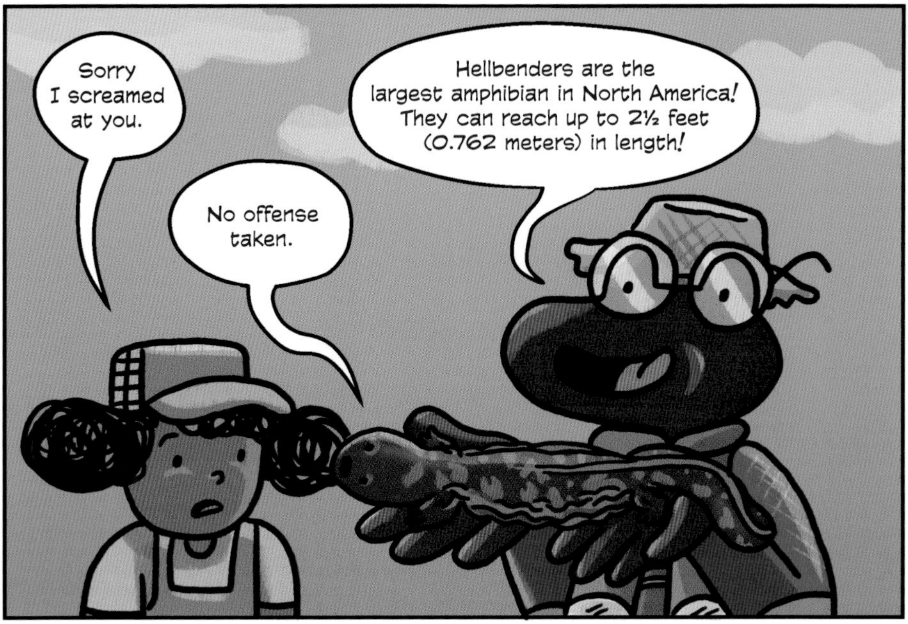
Sorry I screamed at you.
Hellbenders are the largest amphibian in North America! They can reach up to 2½ feet (0.762 meters) in length!
No offense taken.

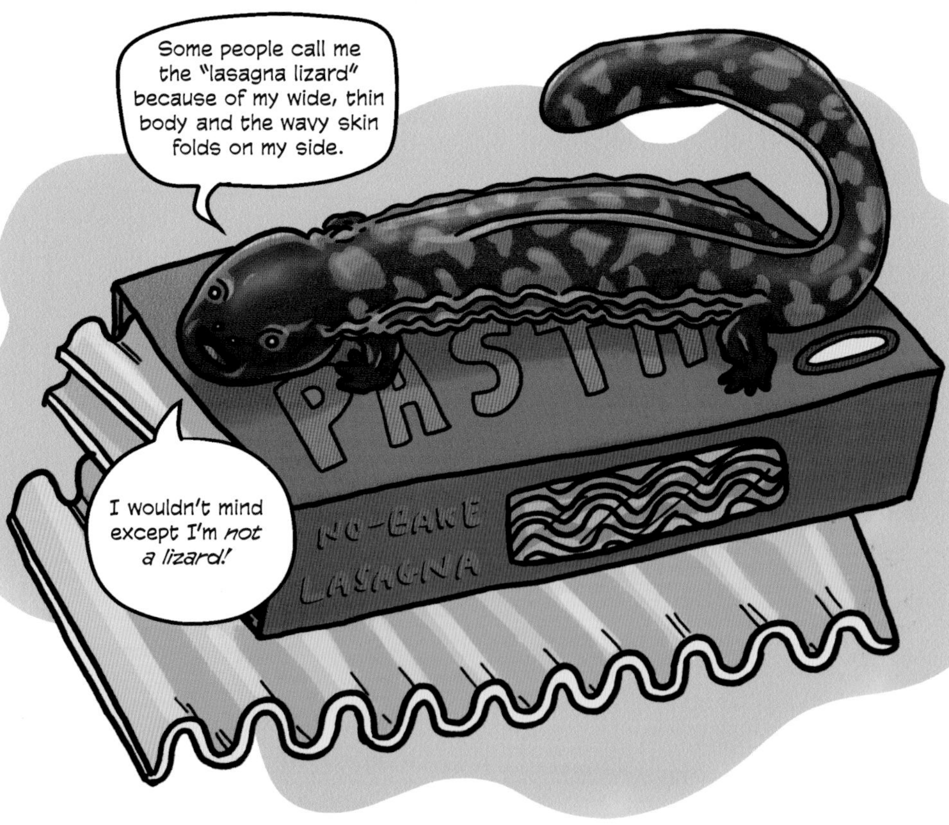
Some people call me the "lasagna lizard" because of my wide, thin body and the wavy skin folds on my side.
I wouldn't mind except I'm *not a lizard!*
NO-BAKE LASAGNA

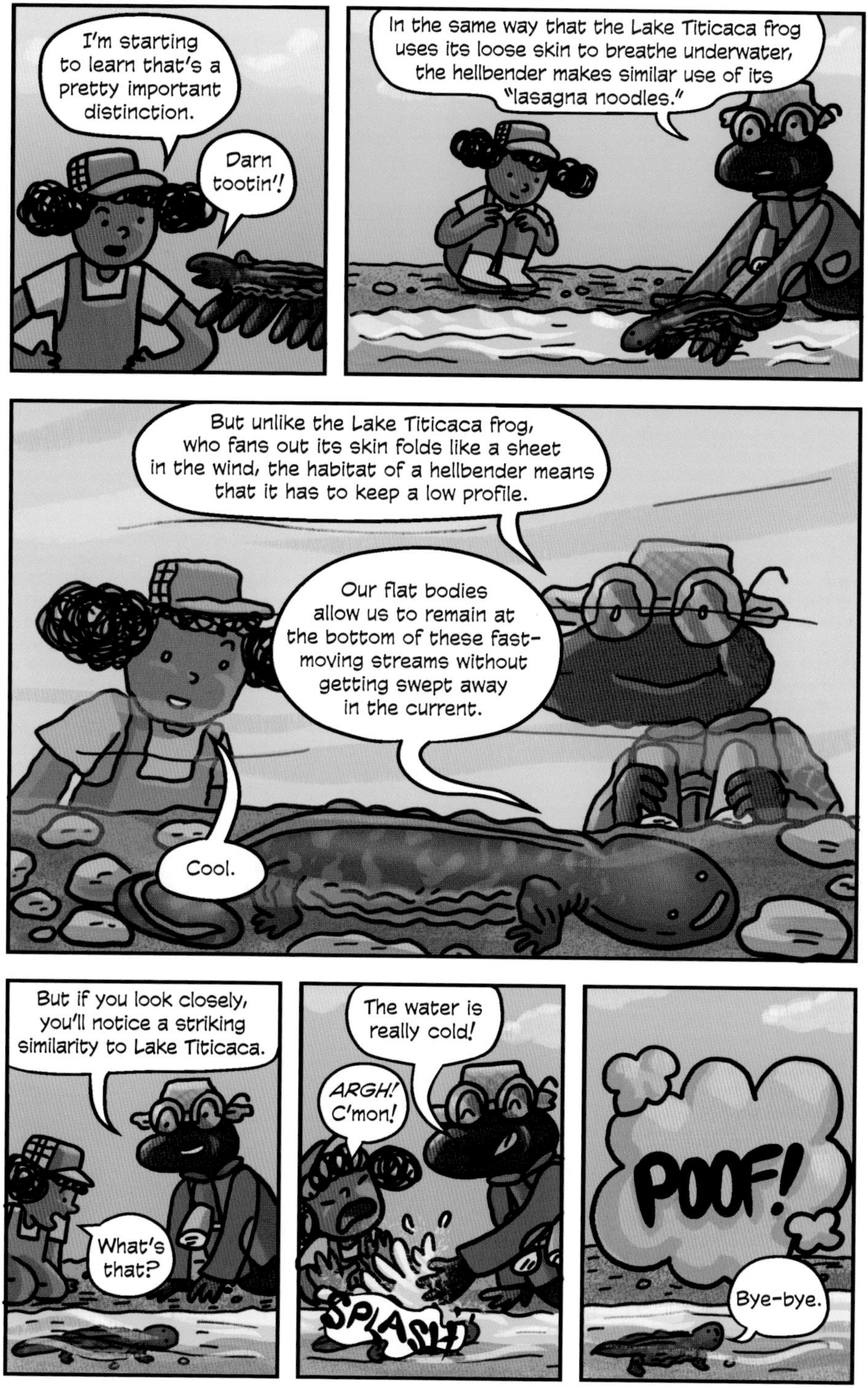

I'm starting to learn that's a pretty important distinction.
Darn tootin'!
In the same way that the Lake Titicaca frog uses its loose skin to breathe underwater, the hellbender makes similar use of its "lasagna noodles."
But unlike the Lake Titicaca frog, who fans out its skin folds like a sheet in the wind, the habitat of a hellbender means that it has to keep a low profile.
Our flat bodies allow us to remain at the bottom of these fast-moving streams without getting swept away in the current.
Cool.
But if you look closely, you'll notice a striking similarity to Lake Titicaca.
What's that?
The water is really cold!
ARGH! C'mon!
SPLASH!
POOF!
Bye-bye.

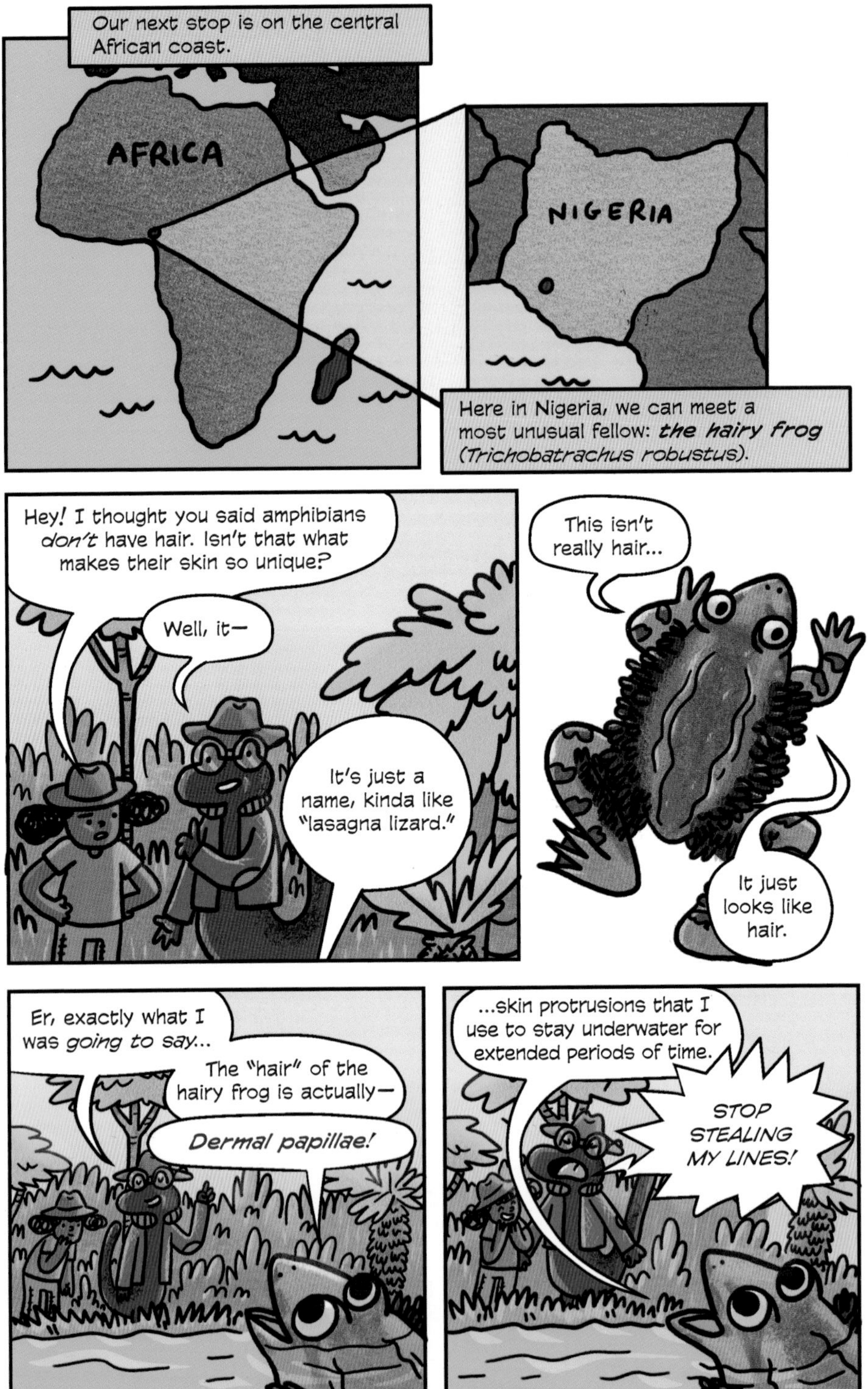

Our next stop is on the central African coast.
AFRICA
NIGERIA
Here in Nigeria, we can meet a most unusual fellow: ***the hairy frog*** *(Trichobatrachus robustus)*.
Hey! I thought you said amphibians *don't* have hair. Isn't that what makes their skin so unique?
Well, it—
It's just a name, kinda like "lasagna lizard."
This isn't really hair...
It just looks like hair.
Er, exactly what I was *going to say*...
The "hair" of the hairy frog is actually—
Dermal papillae!
...skin protrusions that I use to stay underwater for extended periods of time.
STOP STEALING MY LINES!

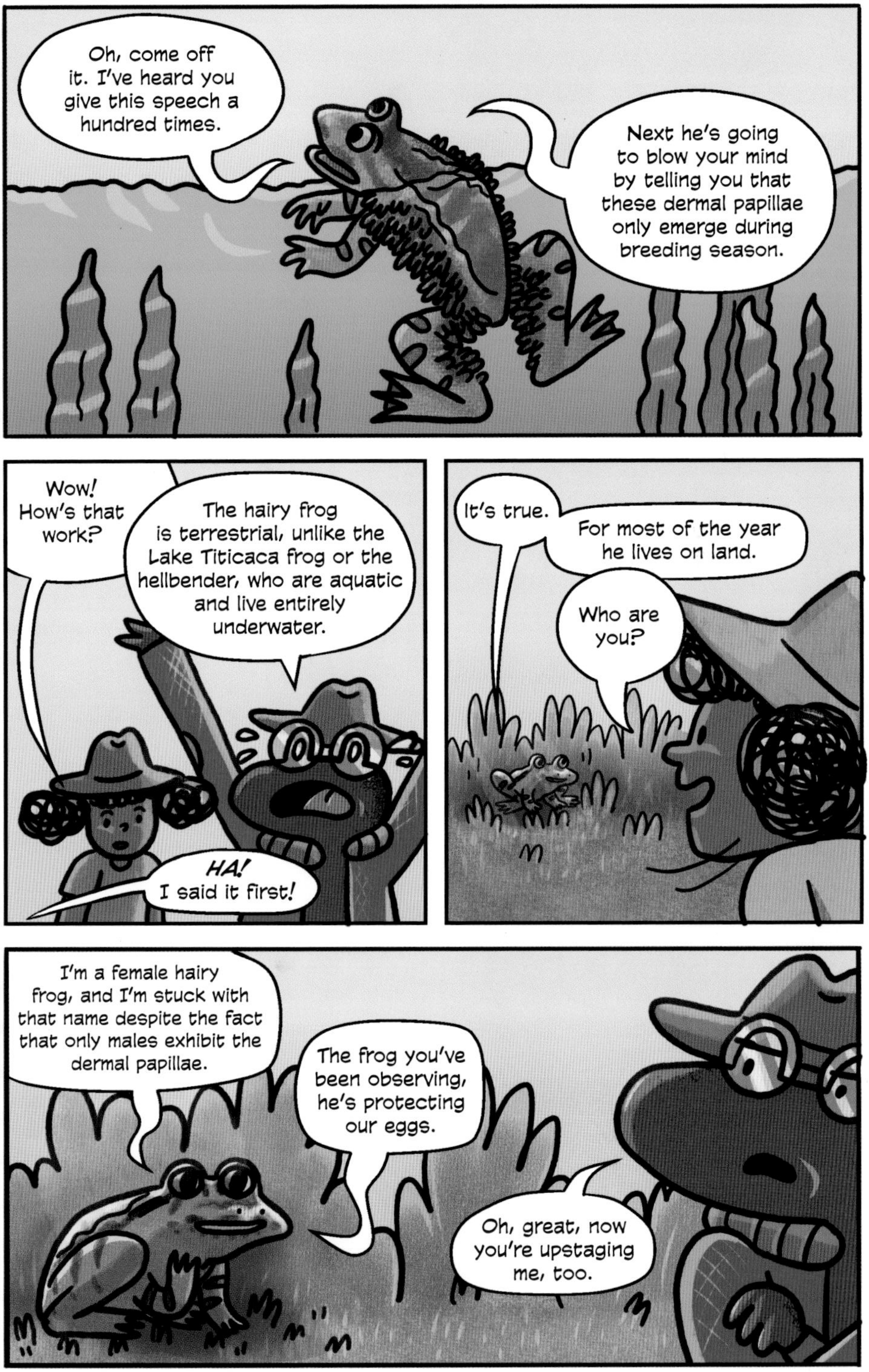
Oh, come off it. I've heard you give this speech a hundred times.
Next he's going to blow your mind by telling you that these dermal papillae only emerge during breeding season.
Wow! How's that work?
The hairy frog is terrestrial, unlike the Lake Titicaca frog or the hellbender, who are aquatic and live entirely underwater.
HA! I said it first!
It's true.
For most of the year he lives on land.
Who are you?
I'm a female hairy frog, and I'm stuck with that name despite the fact that only males exhibit the dermal papillae.
The frog you've been observing, he's protecting our eggs.
Oh, great, now you're upstaging me, too.

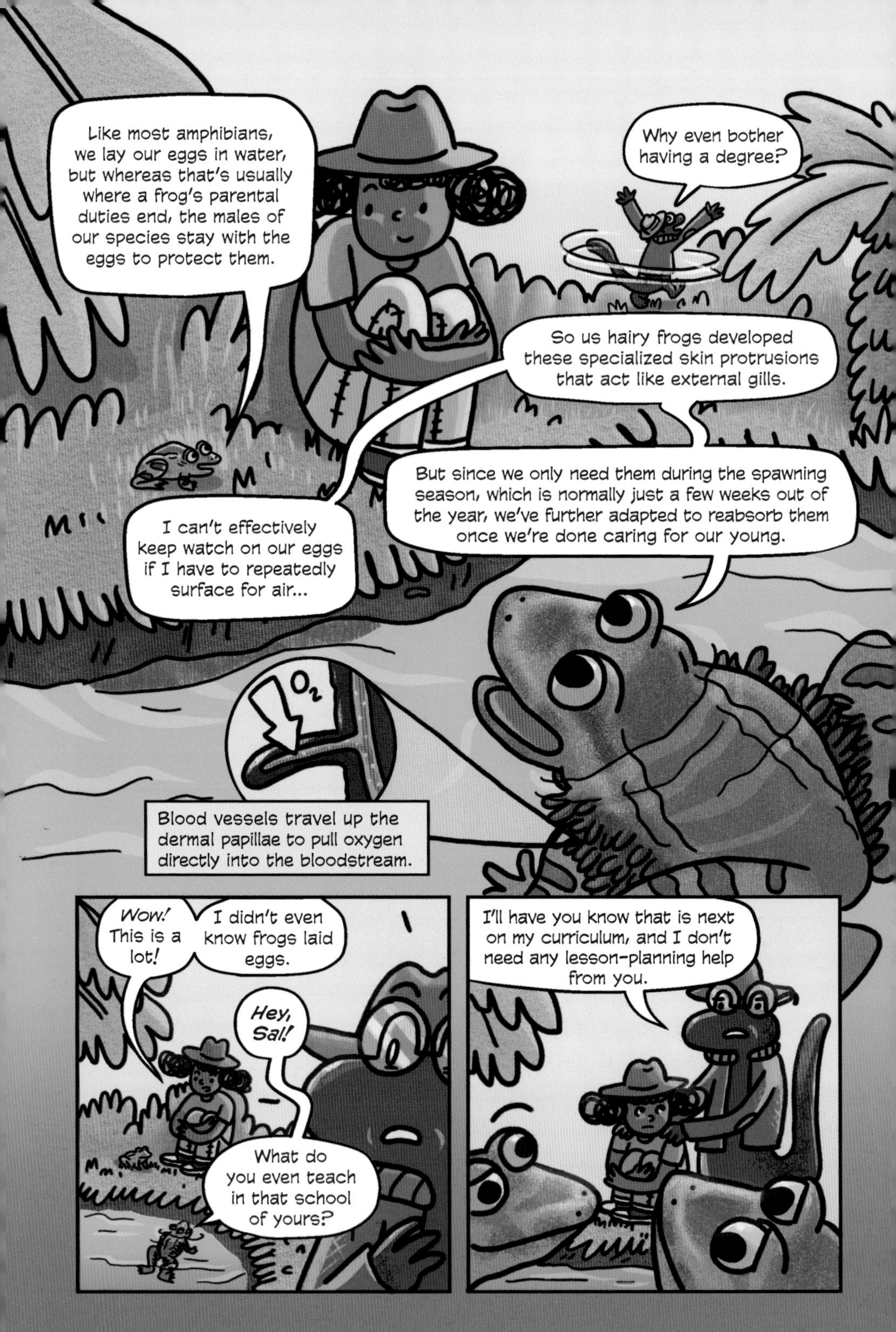
Like most amphibians, we lay our eggs in water, but whereas that's usually where a frog's parental duties end, the males of our species stay with the eggs to protect them.
Why even bother having a degree?
I can't effectively keep watch on our eggs if I have to repeatedly surface for air...
So us hairy frogs developed these specialized skin protrusions that act like external gills.
But since we only need them during the spawning season, which is normally just a few weeks out of the year, we've further adapted to reabsorb them once we're done caring for our young.
O2
Blood vessels travel up the dermal papillae to pull oxygen directly into the bloodstream.
Wow! This is a lot!
I didn't even know frogs laid eggs.
Hey, Sal!
What do you even teach in that school of yours?
I'll have you know that is next on my curriculum, and I don't need any lesson-planning help from you.

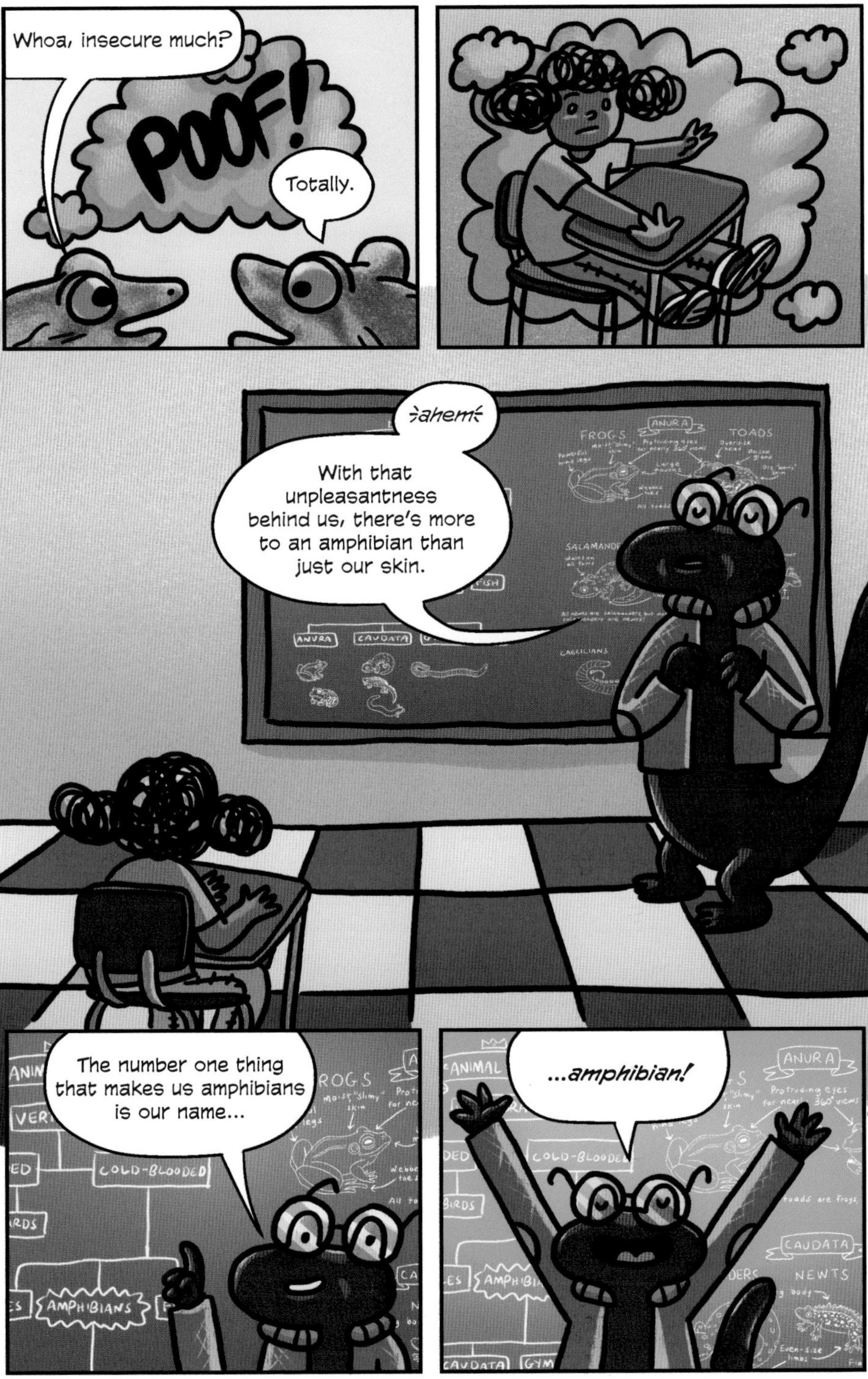
Whoa, insecure much?
POOF!
Totally.
ahem
With that unpleasantness behind us, there's more to an amphibian than just our skin.
FROGS
ANURA
TOADS
The number one thing that makes us amphibians is our name...
COLD-BLOODED
AMPHIBIANS
...amphibian!
ANURA
CAUDATA
NEWTS

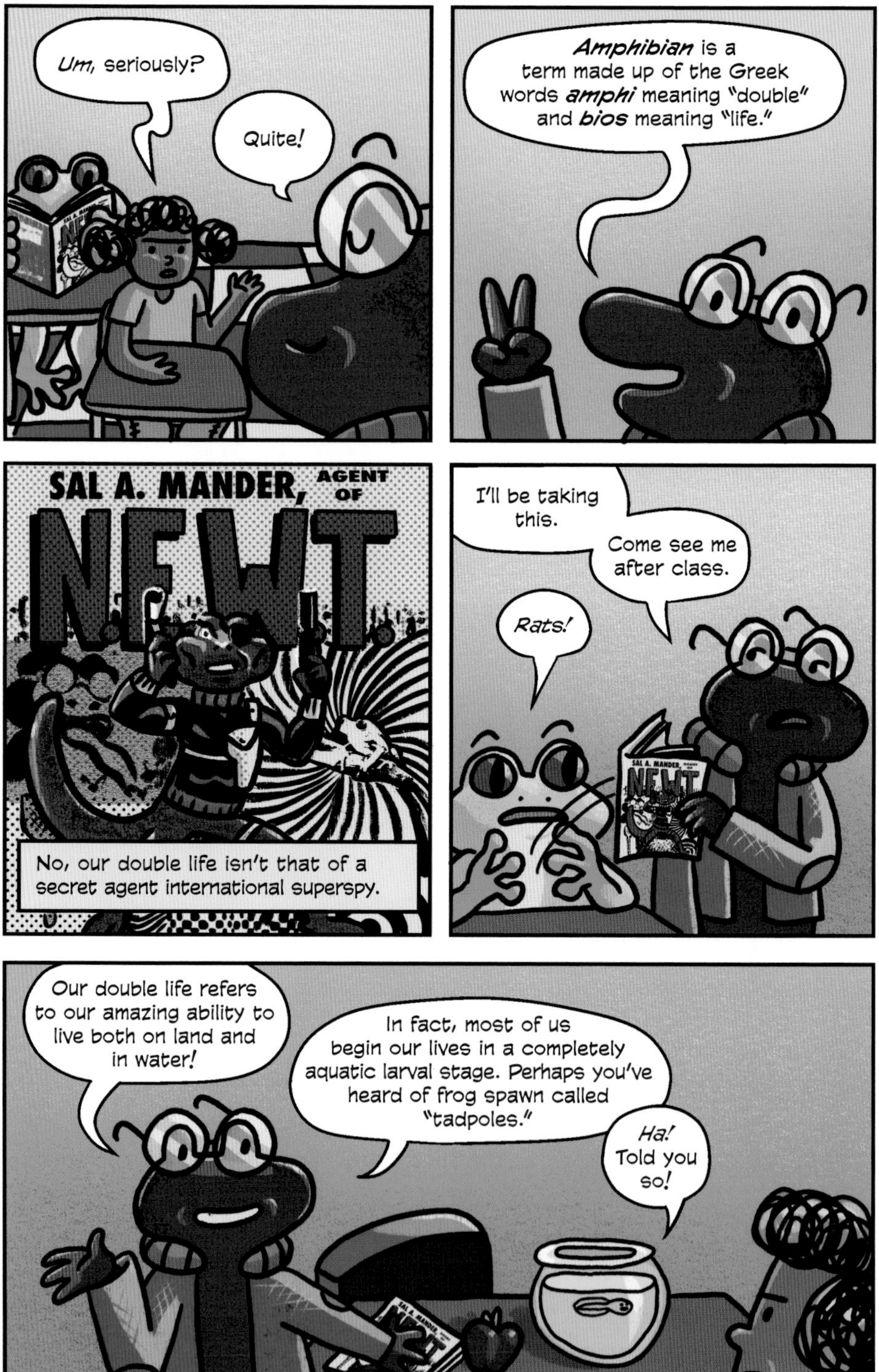

Um, seriously?
Quite!
Amphibian is a term made up of the Greek words ***amphi*** meaning "double" and ***bios*** meaning "life."
SAL A. MANDER, AGENT OF N.E.W.T.
No, our double life isn't that of a secret agent international superspy.
I'll be taking this.
Come see me after class.
Rats!
Our double life refers to our amazing ability to live both on land and in water!
In fact, most of us begin our lives in a completely aquatic larval stage. Perhaps you've heard of frog spawn called "tadpoles."
Ha! Told you so!

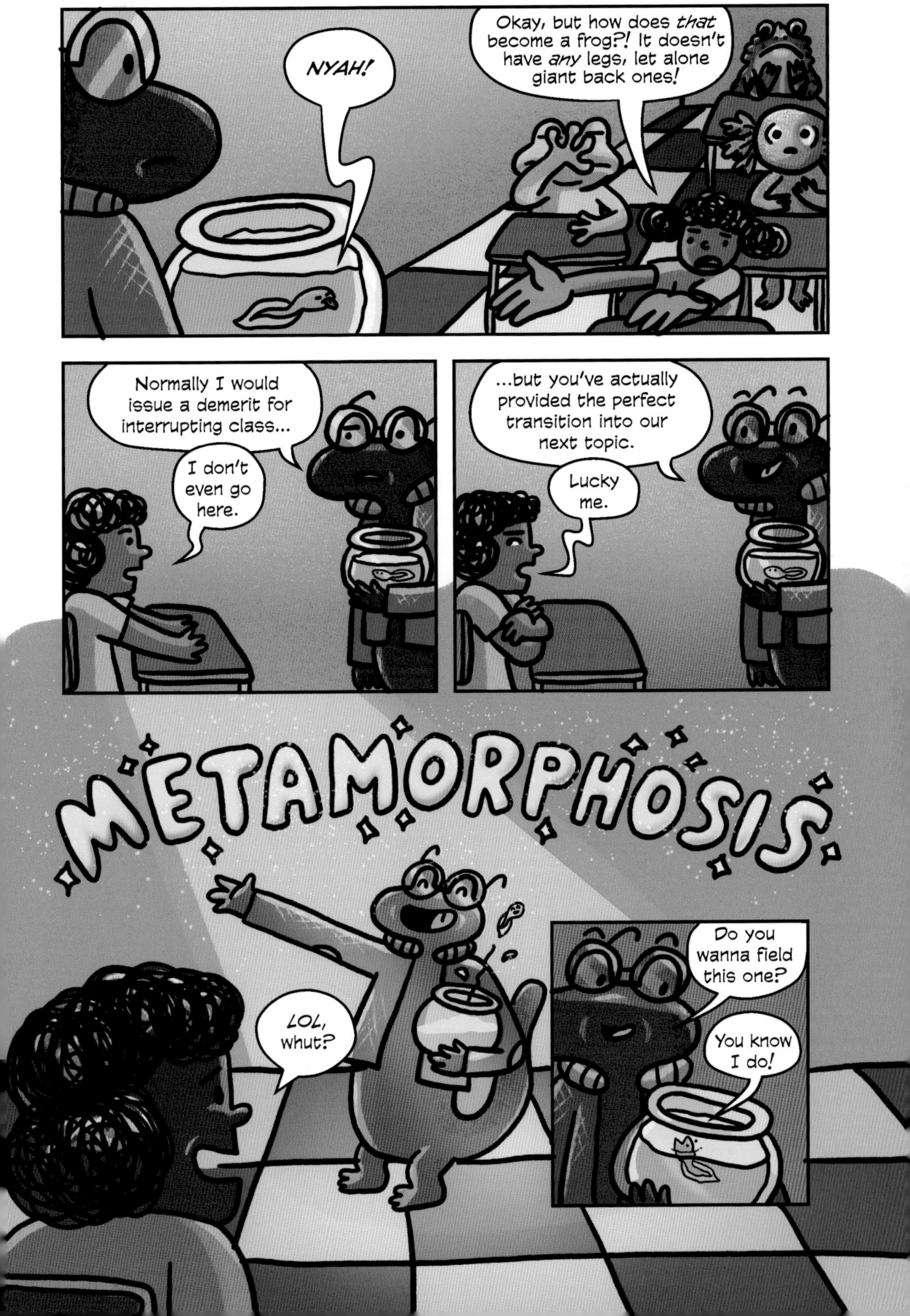
NYAH!
Okay, but how does *that* become a frog?! It doesn't have *any* legs, let alone giant back ones!
Normally I would issue a demerit for interrupting class...
I don't even go here.
...but you've actually provided the perfect transition into our next topic.
Lucky me.
METAMORPHOSIS
LOL, whut?
Do you wanna field this one?
You know I do!

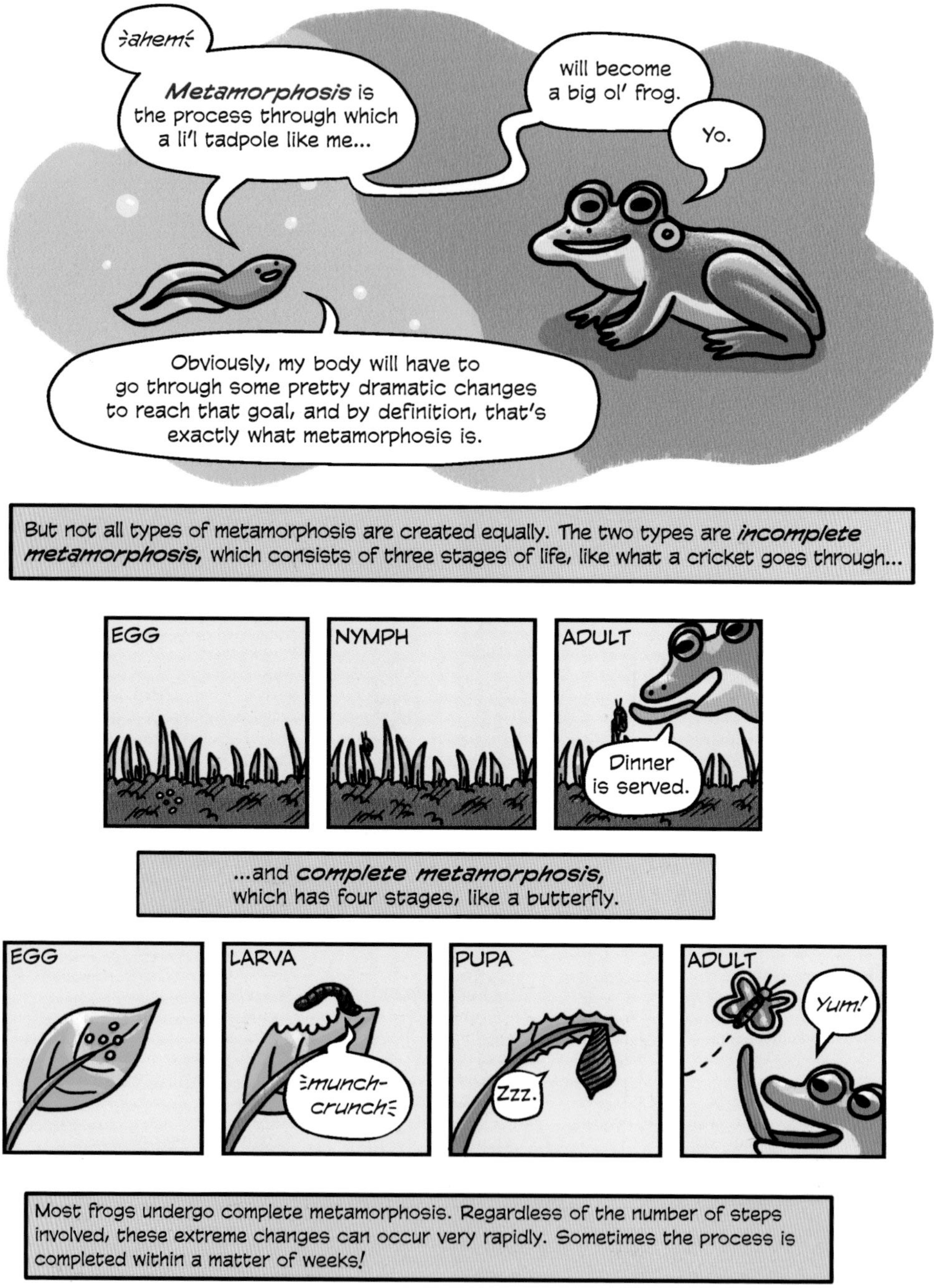

ahem
Metamorphosis is the process through which a li'l tadpole like me...
will become a big ol' frog.
Yo.
Obviously, my body will have to go through some pretty dramatic changes to reach that goal, and by definition, that's exactly what metamorphosis is.
But not all types of metamorphosis are created equally. The two types are incomplete metamorphosis, which consists of three stages of life, like what a cricket goes through...
EGG
NYMPH
ADULT
Dinner is served.
...and complete metamorphosis, which has four stages, like a butterfly.
EGG
LARVA
munch-crunch
PUPA
Zzz.
ADULT
Yum!
Most frogs undergo complete metamorphosis. Regardless of the number of steps involved, these extreme changes can occur very rapidly. Sometimes the process is completed within a matter of weeks!

STAGE 1: EGG

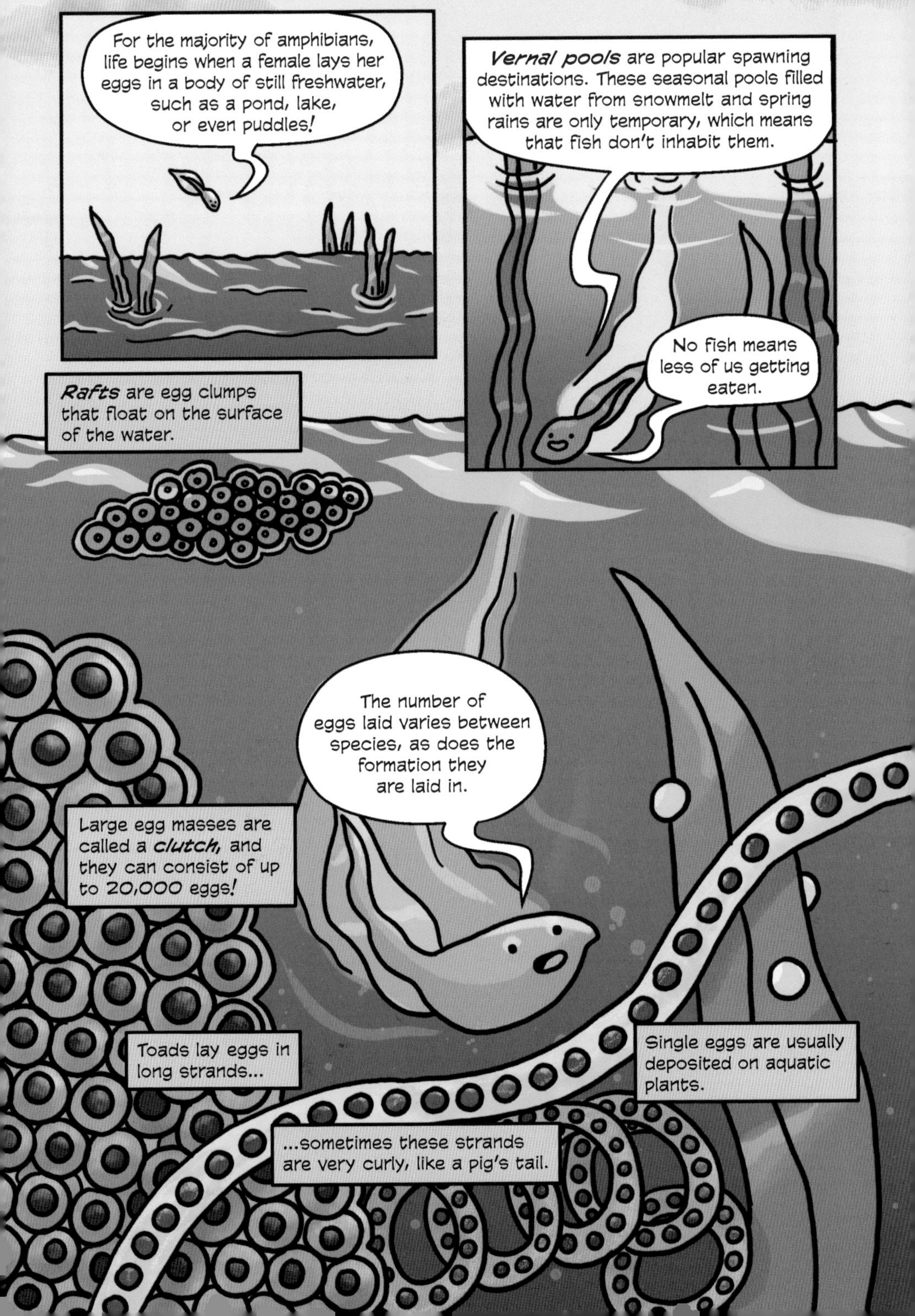
For the majority of amphibians, life begins when a female lays her eggs in a body of still freshwater, such as a pond, lake, or even puddles!
Vernal pools are popular spawning destinations. These seasonal pools filled with water from snowmelt and spring rains are only temporary, which means that fish don't inhabit them.
No fish means less of us getting eaten.
Rafts are egg clumps that float on the surface of the water.
The number of eggs laid varies between species, as does the formation they are laid in.
Large egg masses are called a clutch, and they can consist of up to 20,000 eggs!
Toads lay eggs in long strands...
...sometimes these strands are very curly, like a pig's tail.
Single eggs are usually deposited on aquatic plants.

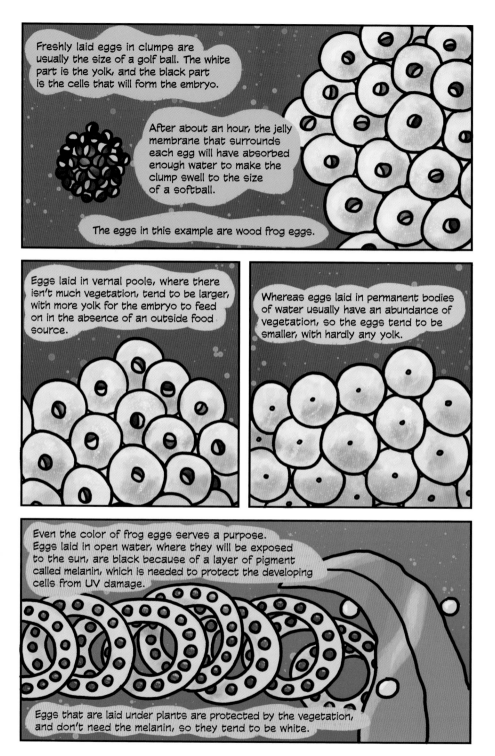

Freshly laid eggs in clumps are usually the size of a golf ball. The white part is the yolk, and the black part is the cells that will form the embryo.

After about an hour, the jelly membrane that surrounds each egg will have absorbed enough water to make the clump swell to the size of a softball.

The eggs in this example are wood frog eggs.

Eggs laid in vernal pools, where there isn't much vegetation, tend to be larger, with more yolk for the embryo to feed on in the absence of an outside food source.

Whereas eggs laid in permanent bodies of water usually have an abundance of vegetation, so the eggs tend to be smaller, with hardly any yolk.

Even the color of frog eggs serves a purpose. Eggs laid in open water, where they will be exposed to the sun, are black because of a layer of pigment called melanin, which is needed to protect the developing cells from UV damage.

Eggs that are laid under plants are protected by the vegetation, and don't need the melanin, so they tend to be white.

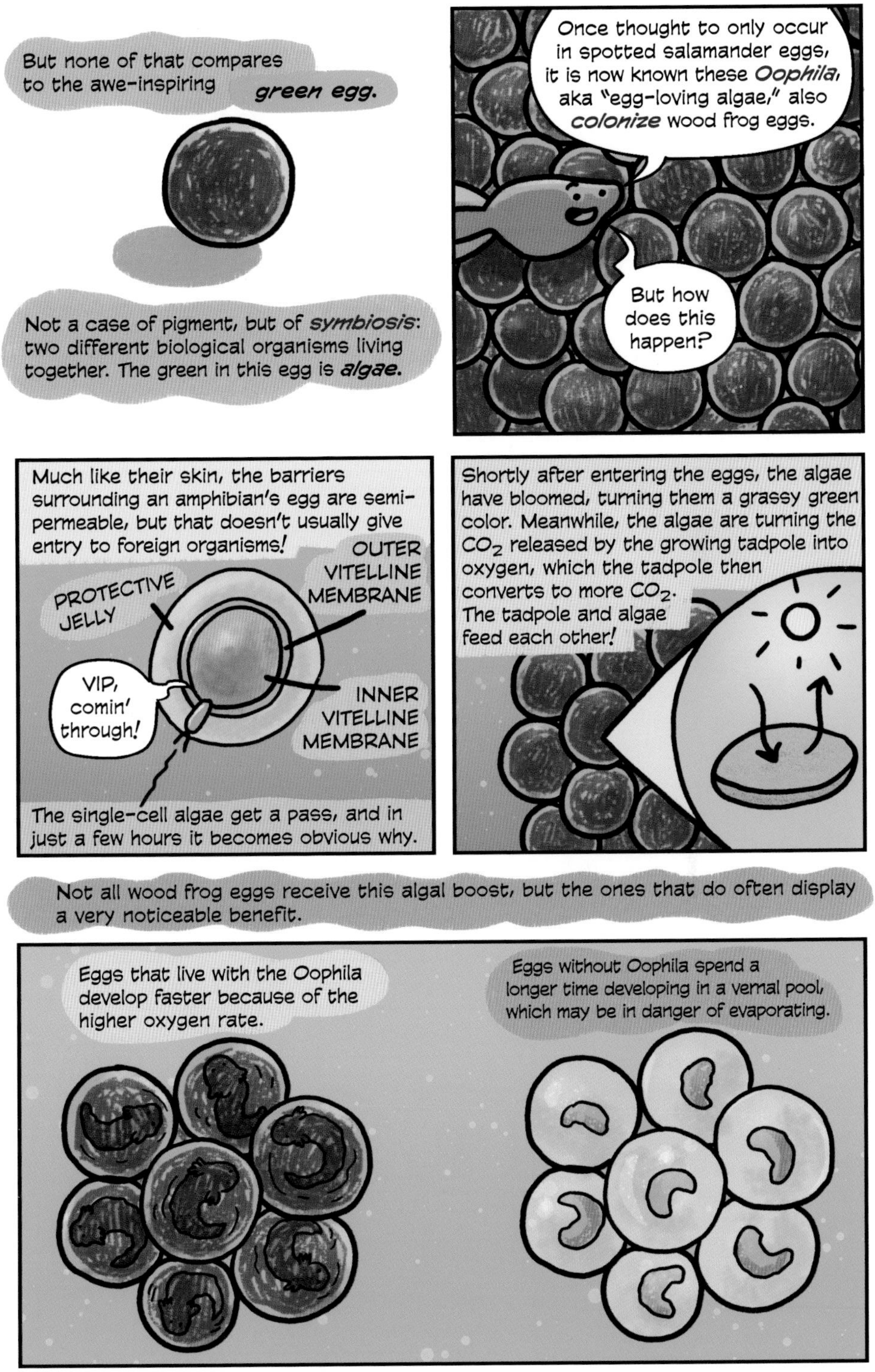

But none of that compares to the awe-inspiring *green egg.*
Not a case of pigment, but of *symbiosis*: two different biological organisms living together. The green in this egg is *algae.*
Once thought to only occur in spotted salamander eggs, it is now known these *Oophila,* aka "egg-loving algae," also *colonize* wood frog eggs.
But how does this happen?
Much like their skin, the barriers surrounding an amphibian's egg are semi-permeable, but that doesn't usually give entry to foreign organisms!
OUTER VITELLINE MEMBRANE
PROTECTIVE JELLY
VIP, comin' through!
INNER VITELLINE MEMBRANE
The single-cell algae get a pass, and in just a few hours it becomes obvious why.
Shortly after entering the eggs, the algae have bloomed, turning them a grassy green color. Meanwhile, the algae are turning the CO_2 released by the growing tadpole into oxygen, which the tadpole then converts to more CO_2. The tadpole and algae feed each other!
Not all wood frog eggs receive this algal boost, but the ones that do often display a very noticeable benefit.
Eggs that live with the Oophila develop faster because of the higher oxygen rate.
Eggs without Oophila spend a longer time developing in a vernal pool, which may be in danger of evaporating.

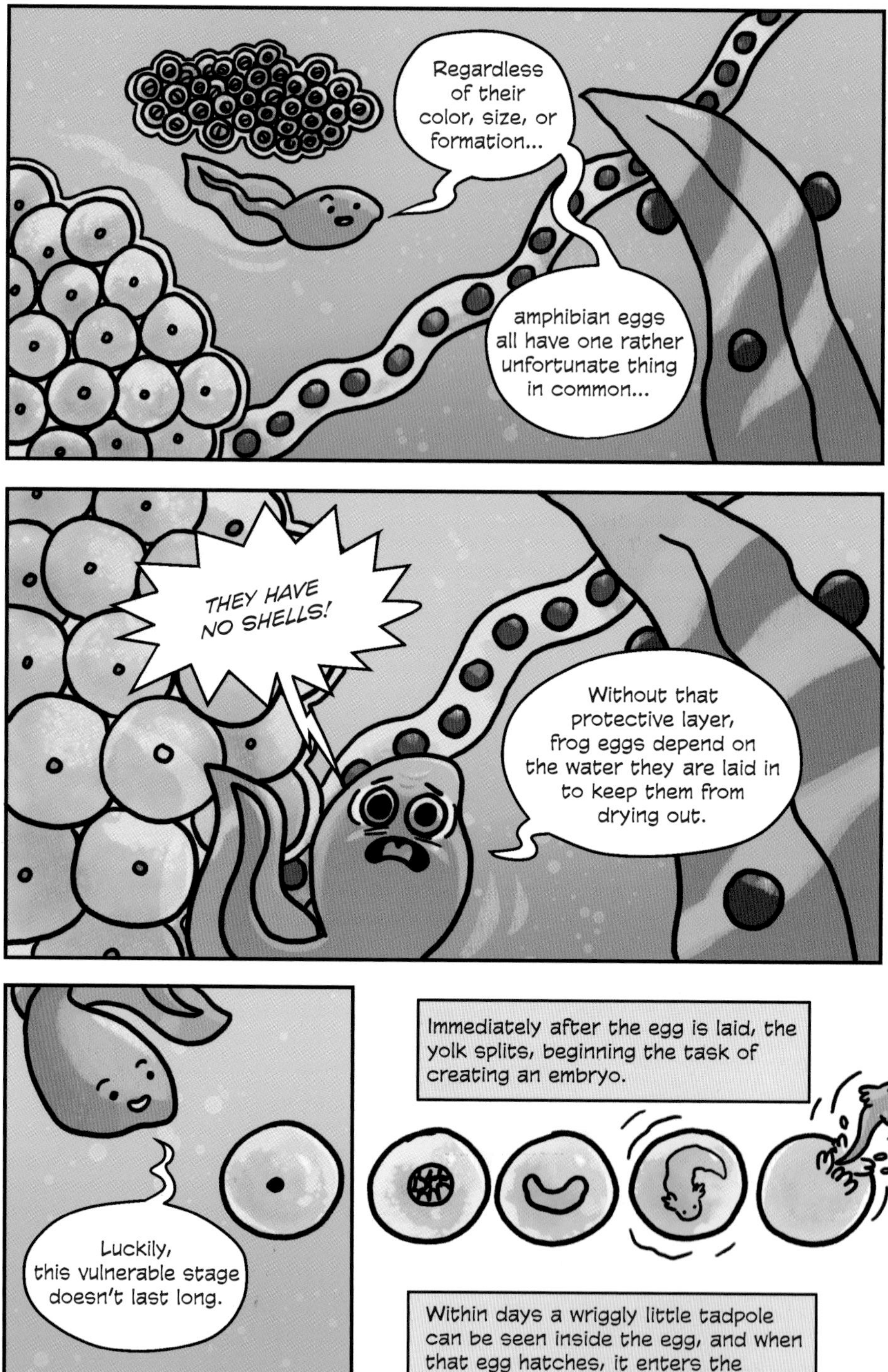
Regardless of their color, size, or formation...
amphibian eggs all have one rather unfortunate thing in common...
THEY HAVE NO SHELLS!
Without that protective layer, frog eggs depend on the water they are laid in to keep them from drying out.
Immediately after the egg is laid, the yolk splits, beginning the task of creating an embryo.
Luckily, this vulnerable stage doesn't last long.
Within days a wriggly little tadpole can be seen inside the egg, and when that egg hatches, it enters the second stage of its life cycle.

STAGE 2: TADPOLE

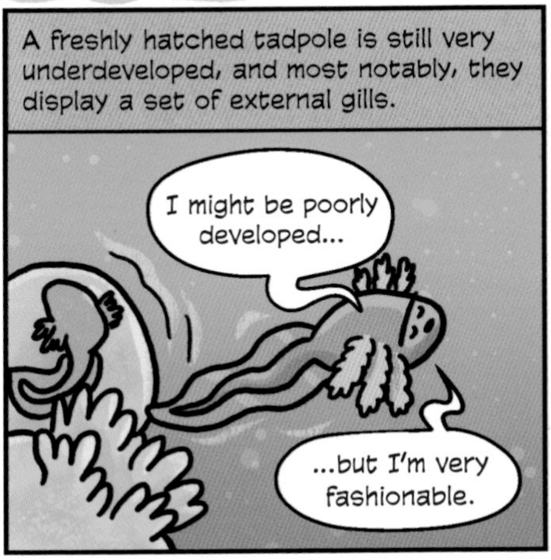
A freshly hatched tadpole is still very underdeveloped, and most notably, they display a set of external gills.
I might be poorly developed...
...but I'm very fashionable.

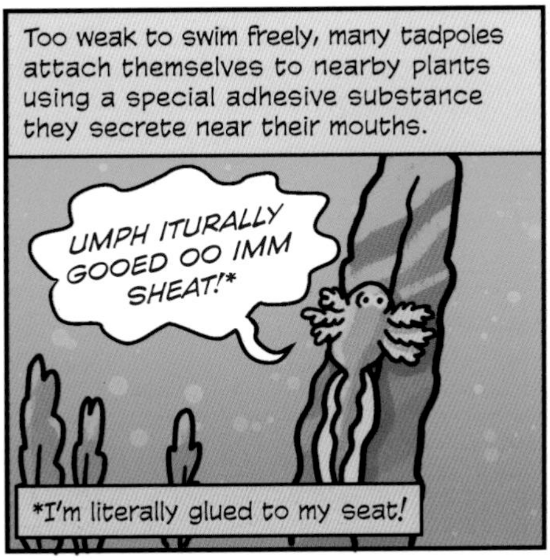
Too weak to swim freely, many tadpoles attach themselves to nearby plants using a special adhesive substance they secrete near their mouths.
UMPH ITURALLY GOOED OO IMM SHEAT!*
*I'm literally glued to my seat!

During this time, the tadpole builds up strength by digesting the last of their egg's yolk. Their gills then begin to recede and are covered by a flap of skin called an *operculum*, or "gill pouch."

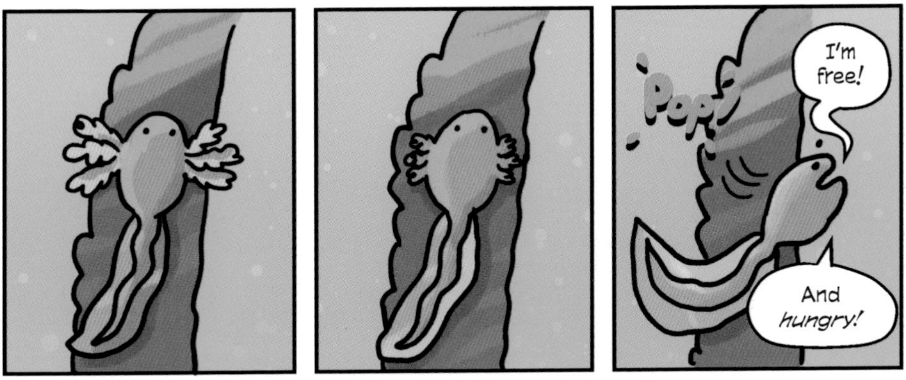
POP!
I'm free!
And *hungry!*

By the end of the tadpole phase, the gills will disappear completely, being replaced by lungs, but that kind of transformation requires a lot of fuel.

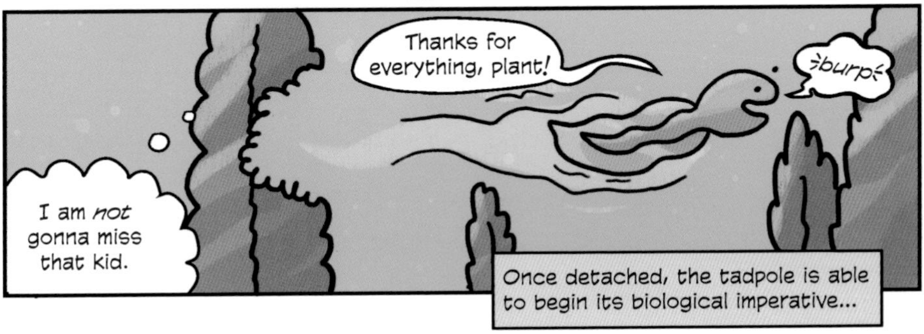
Thanks for everything, plant!
burp
I am *not* gonna miss that kid.
Once detached, the tadpole is able to begin its biological imperative...

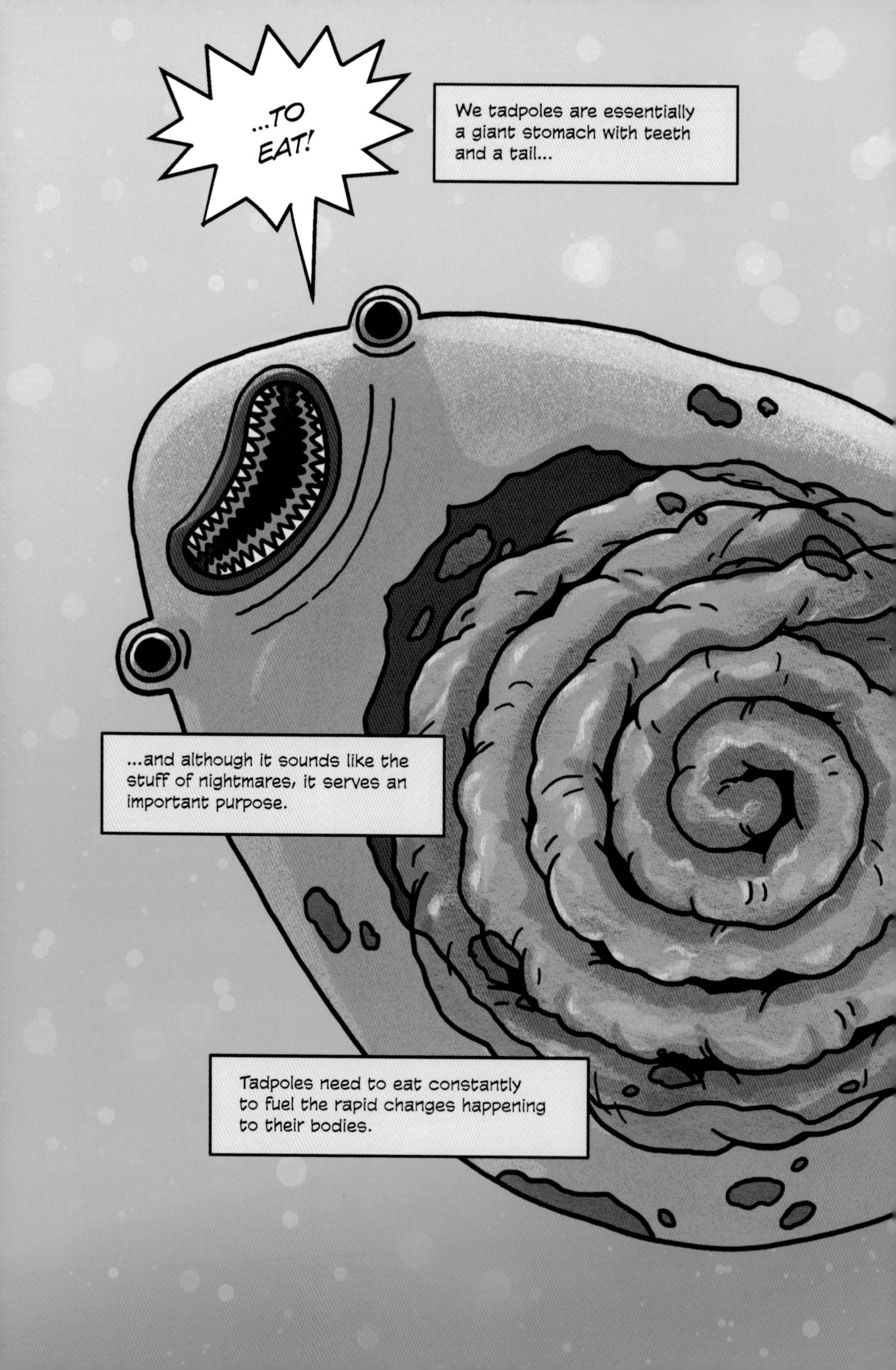
...TO EAT!
We tadpoles are essentially a giant stomach with teeth and a tail...
...and although it sounds like the stuff of nightmares, it serves an important purpose.
Tadpoles need to eat constantly to fuel the rapid changes happening to their bodies.

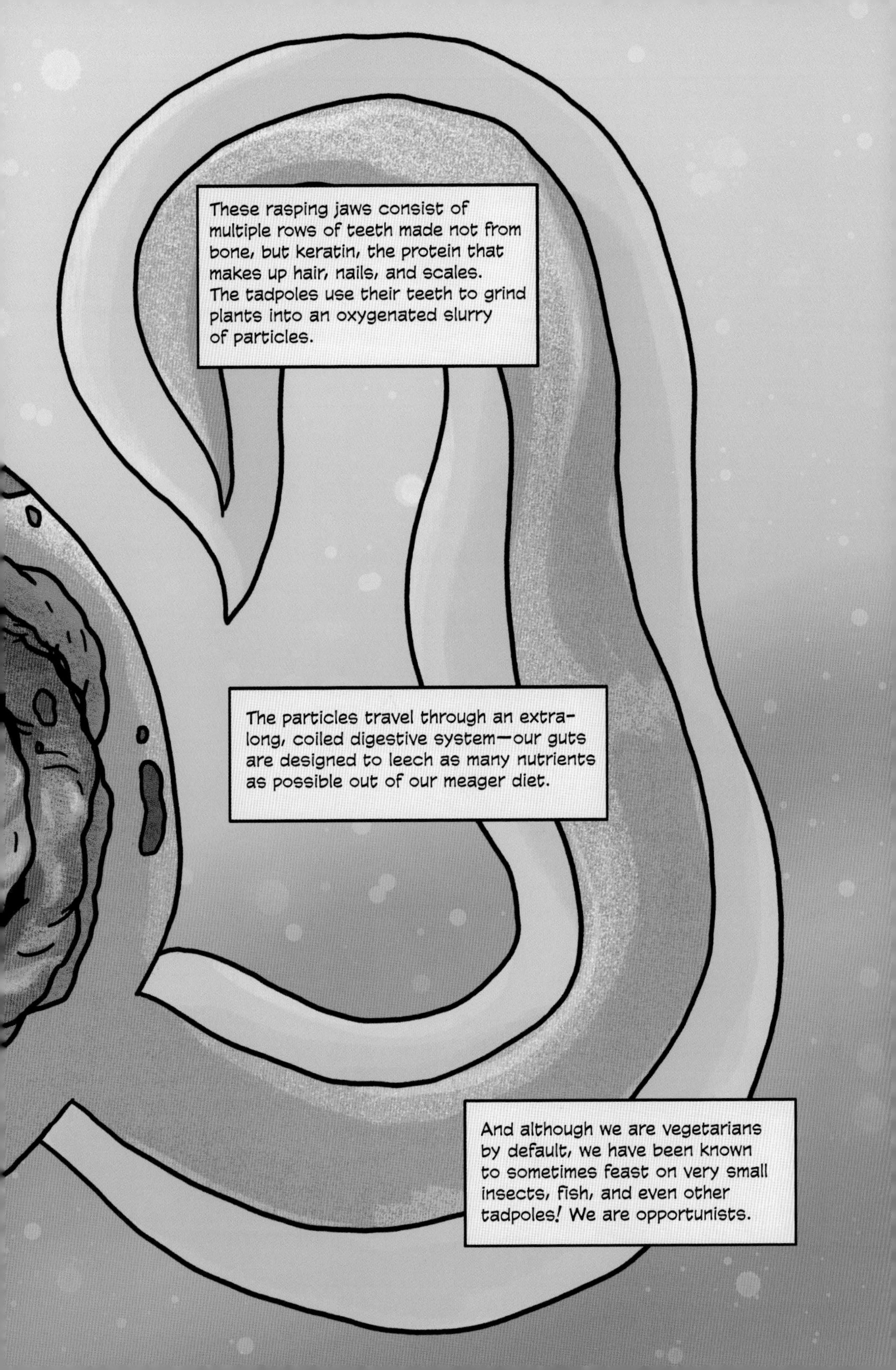
These rasping jaws consist of multiple rows of teeth made not from bone, but keratin, the protein that makes up hair, nails, and scales. The tadpoles use their teeth to grind plants into an oxygenated slurry of particles.
The particles travel through an extra-long, coiled digestive system—our guts are designed to leech as many nutrients as possible out of our meager diet.
And although we are vegetarians by default, we have been known to sometimes feast on very small insects, fish, and even other tadpoles! We are opportunists.

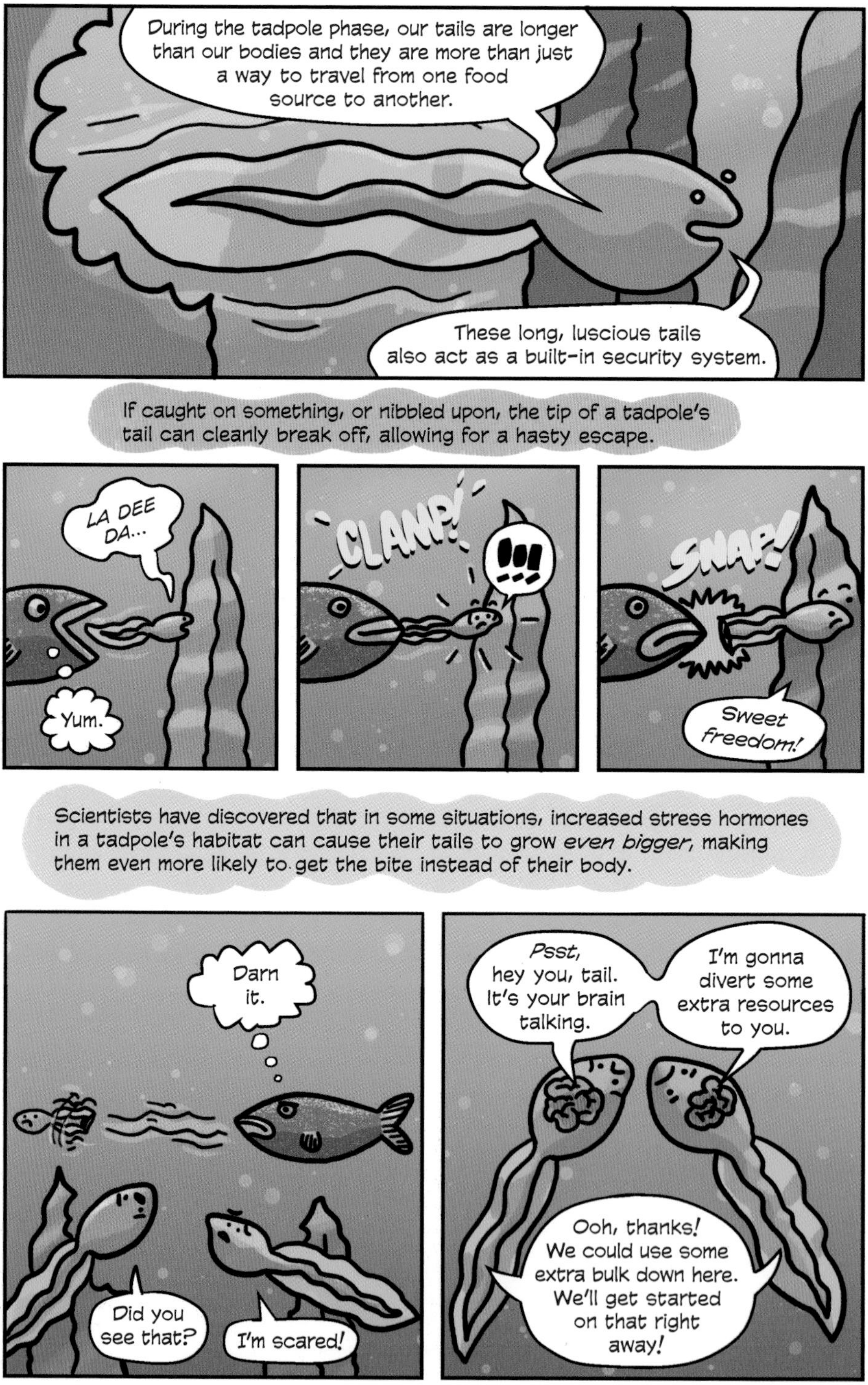
During the tadpole phase, our tails are longer than our bodies and they are more than just a way to travel from one food source to another.
These long, luscious tails also act as a built-in security system.
If caught on something, or nibbled upon, the tip of a tadpole's tail can cleanly break off, allowing for a hasty escape.
LA DEE DA...
Yum.
CLAMP!
!!!
SNAP!
Sweet freedom!
Scientists have discovered that in some situations, increased stress hormones in a tadpole's habitat can cause their tails to grow *even bigger*, making them even more likely to get the bite instead of their body.
Darn it.
Did you see that?
I'm scared!
Psst, hey you, tail. It's your brain talking.
I'm gonna divert some extra resources to you.
Ooh, thanks! We could use some extra bulk down here. We'll get started on that right away!

Tadpoles that survive will start to develop hind legs while their body begins to elongate and their head becomes more defined.

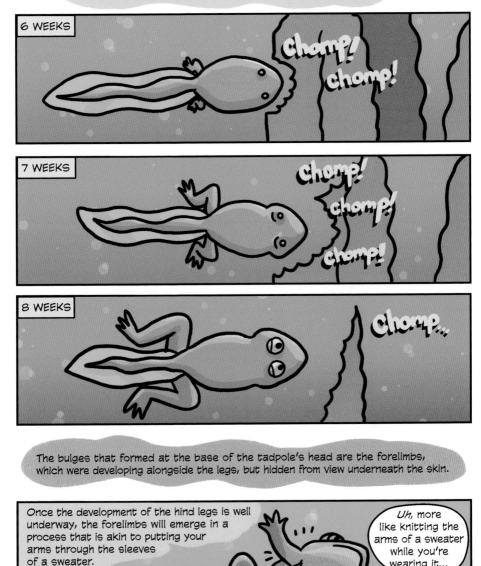

6 WEEKS

chomp!
chomp!

7 WEEKS

chomp!
chomp!
chomp!

8 WEEKS

chomp...

The bulges that formed at the base of the tadpole's head are the forelimbs, which were developing alongside the legs, but hidden from view underneath the skin.

Once the development of the hind legs is well underway, the forelimbs will emerge in a process that is akin to putting your arms through the sleeves of a sweater.

Uh, more like knitting the arms of a sweater while you're wearing it...

...but okay.

STAGE 3: METAMORPH

Now that the tadpole has developed all four legs, it is called a *metamorph*, and although it is finally starting to resemble an adult frog, it still has some major changes in store.

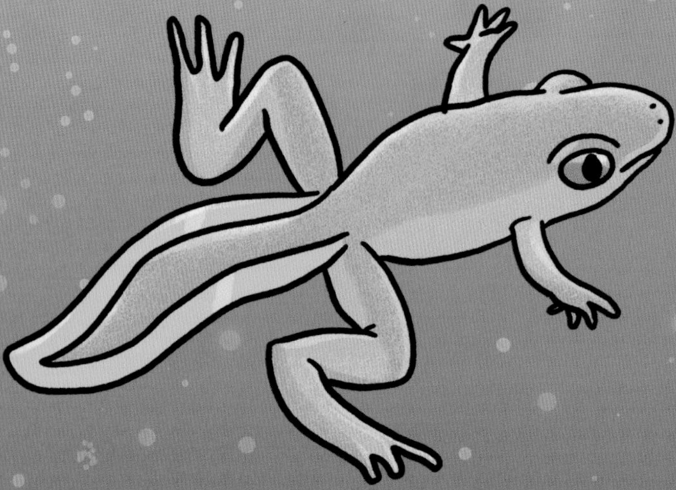

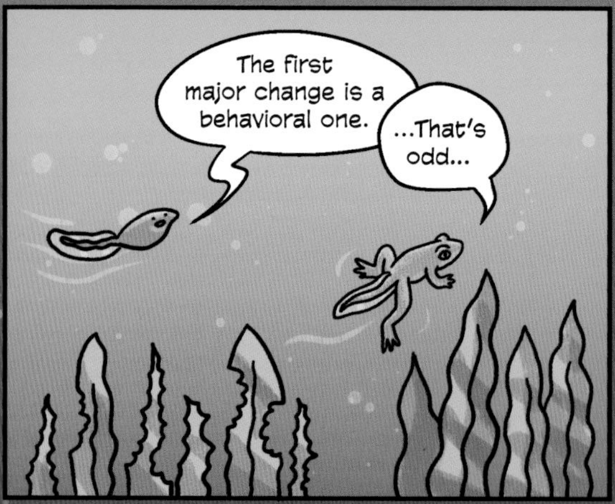
The first major change is a behavioral one.
...That's odd...

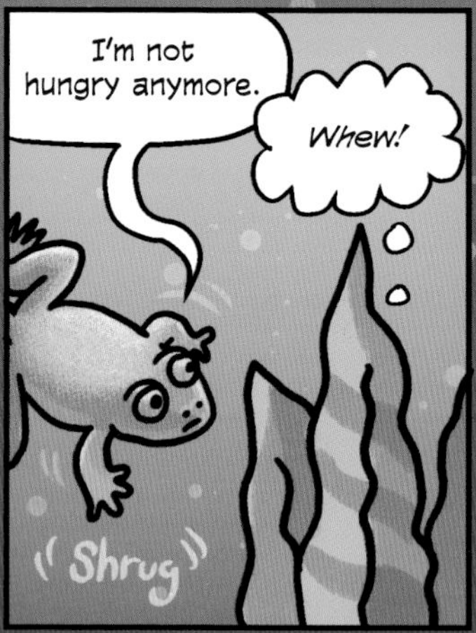
I'm not hungry anymore.
Whew!
Shrug

All of that voracious eating during the tadpole phase was to not only grow their limbs, but to also build up a significant store of fat.

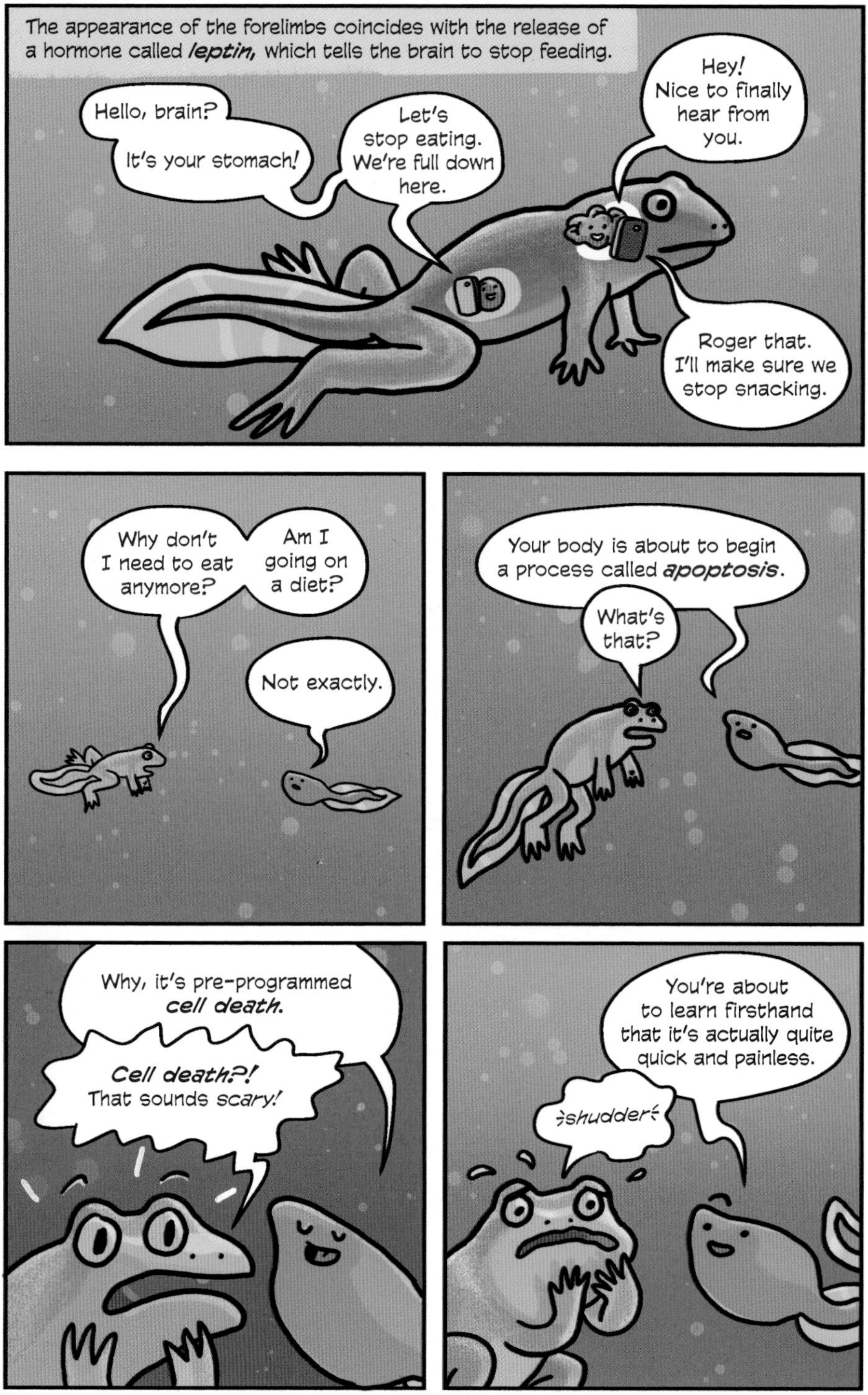
The appearance of the forelimbs coincides with the release of a hormone called *leptin,* which tells the brain to stop feeding.
Hello, brain? It's your stomach!
Let's stop eating. We're full down here.
Hey! Nice to finally hear from you.
Roger that. I'll make sure we stop snacking.
Why don't I need to eat anymore?
Am I going on a diet?
Not exactly.
Your body is about to begin a process called ***apoptosis***.
What's that?
Why, it's pre-programmed ***cell death***.
Cell death?! That sounds *scary!*
You're about to learn firsthand that it's actually quite quick and painless.
shudder

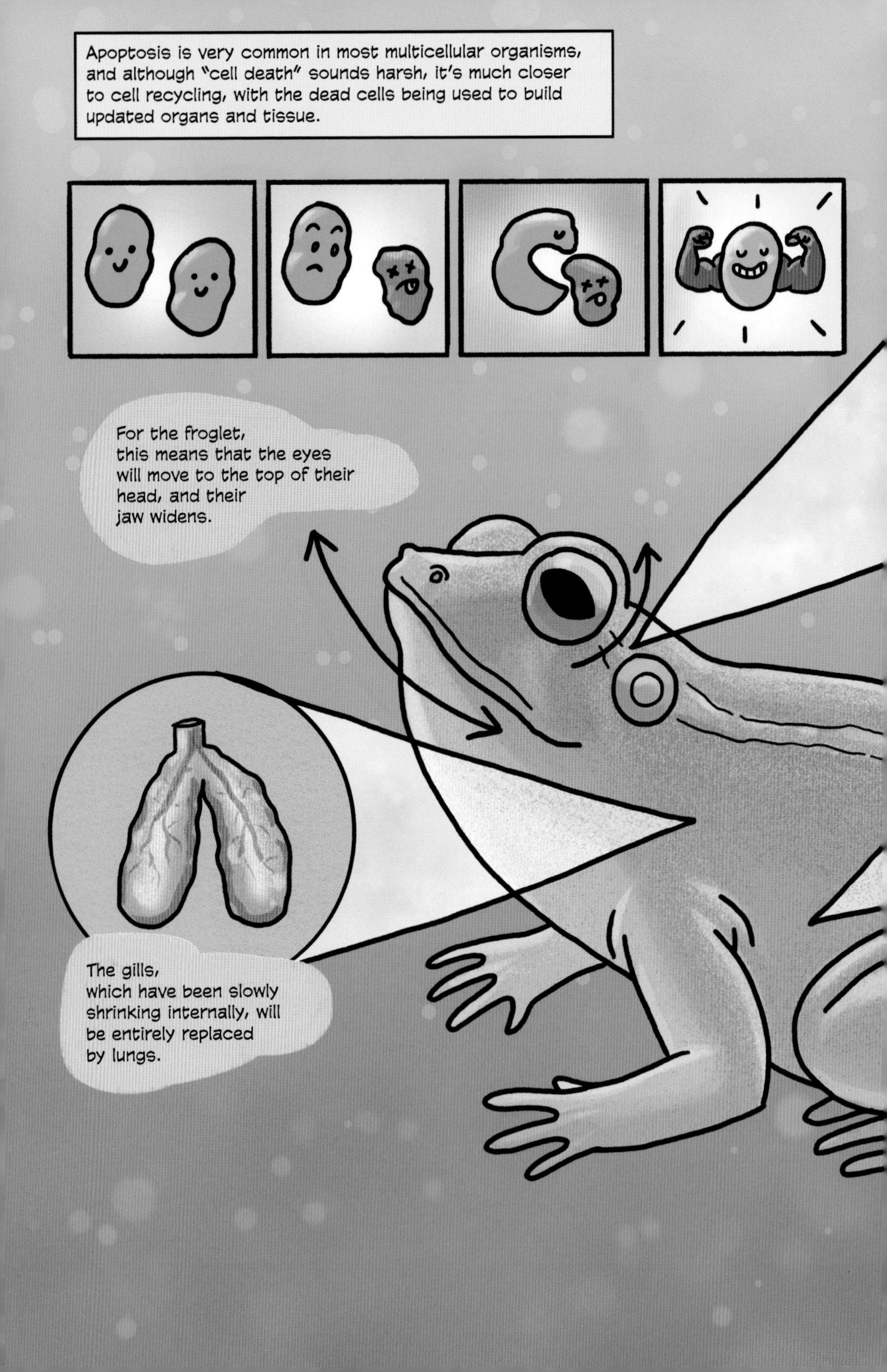

Apoptosis is very common in most multicellular organisms, and although "cell death" sounds harsh, it's much closer to cell recycling, with the dead cells being used to build updated organs and tissue.

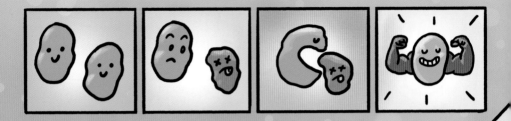

For the froglet, this means that the eyes will move to the top of their head, and their jaw widens.

The gills, which have been slowly shrinking internally, will be entirely replaced by lungs.

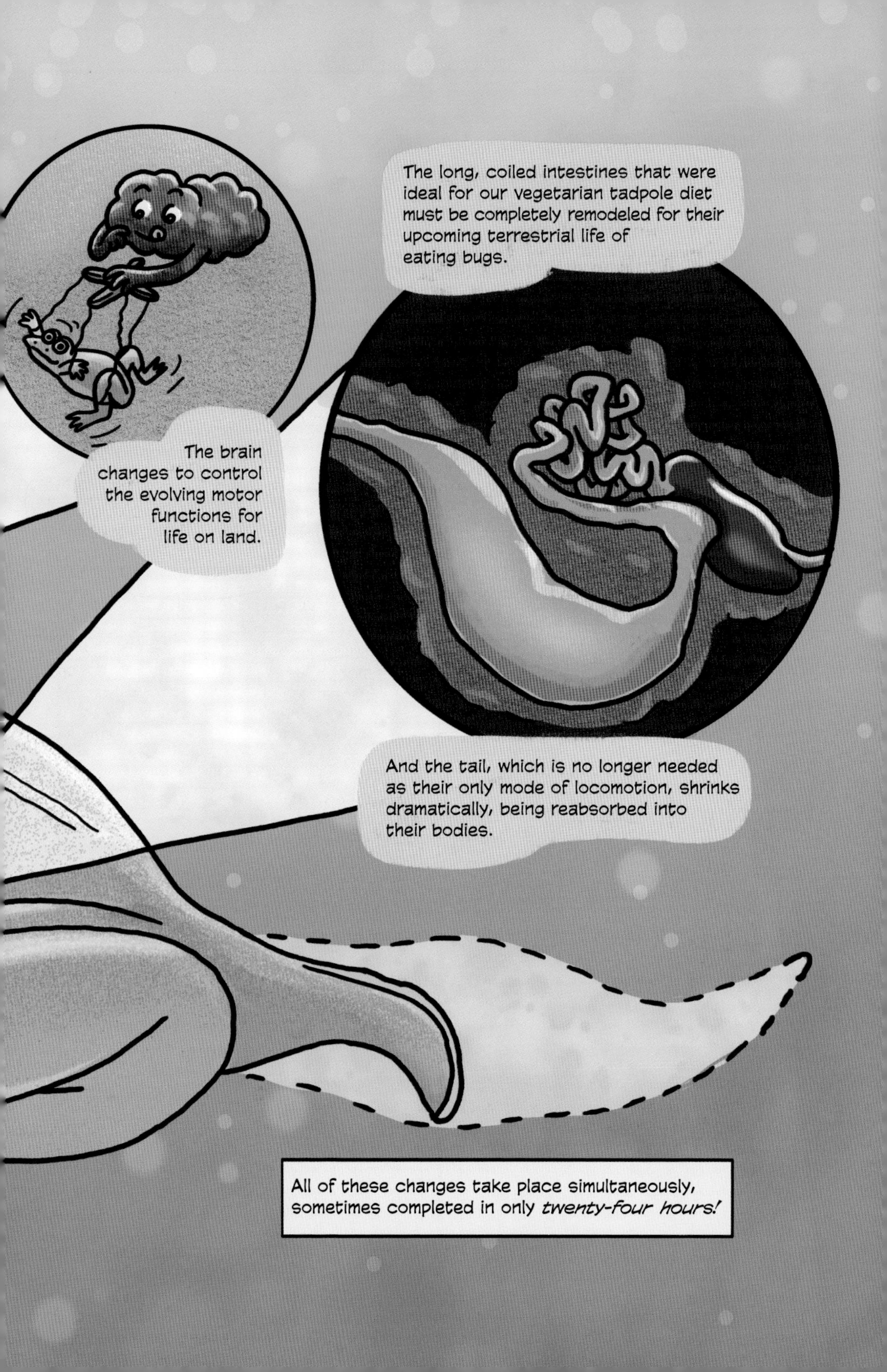
The brain changes to control the evolving motor functions for life on land.
The long, coiled intestines that were ideal for our vegetarian tadpole diet must be completely remodeled for their upcoming terrestrial life of eating bugs.
And the tail, which is no longer needed as their only mode of locomotion, shrinks dramatically, being reabsorbed into their bodies.
All of these changes take place simultaneously, sometimes completed in only *twenty-four hours!*

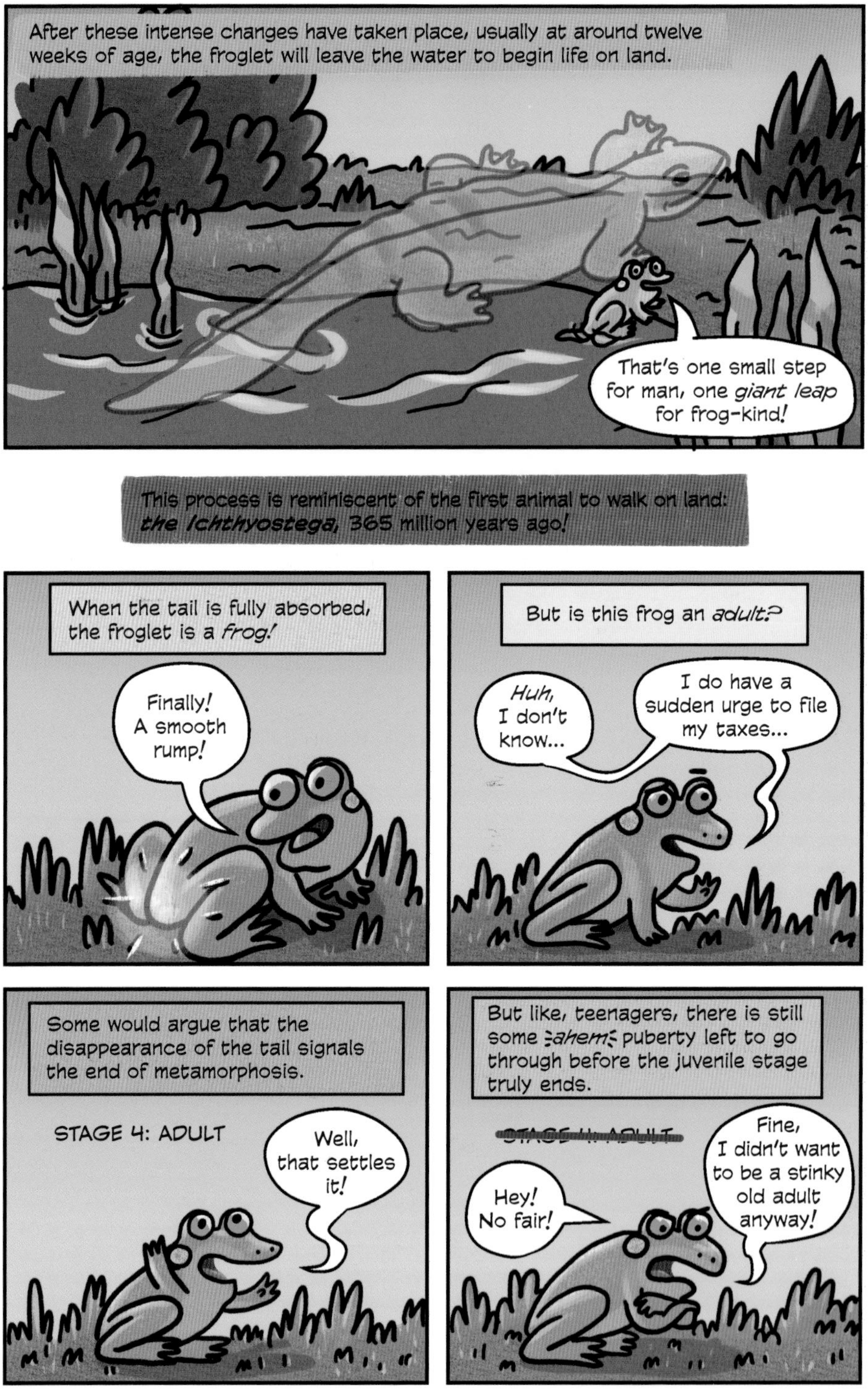

After these intense changes have taken place, usually at around twelve weeks of age, the froglet will leave the water to begin life on land.
That's one small step for man, one *giant leap* for frog-kind!
This process is reminiscent of the first animal to walk on land: *the Ichthyostega,* 365 million years ago!
When the tail is fully absorbed, the froglet is a *frog!*
Finally! A smooth rump!
But is this frog an *adult?*
Huh, I don't know...
I do have a sudden urge to file my taxes...
Some would argue that the disappearance of the tail signals the end of metamorphosis.
STAGE 4: ADULT
Well, that settles it!
But like, teenagers, there is still some *ahem* puberty left to go through before the juvenile stage truly ends.
~~STAGE 4: ADULT~~
Hey! No fair!
Fine, I didn't want to be a stinky old adult anyway!

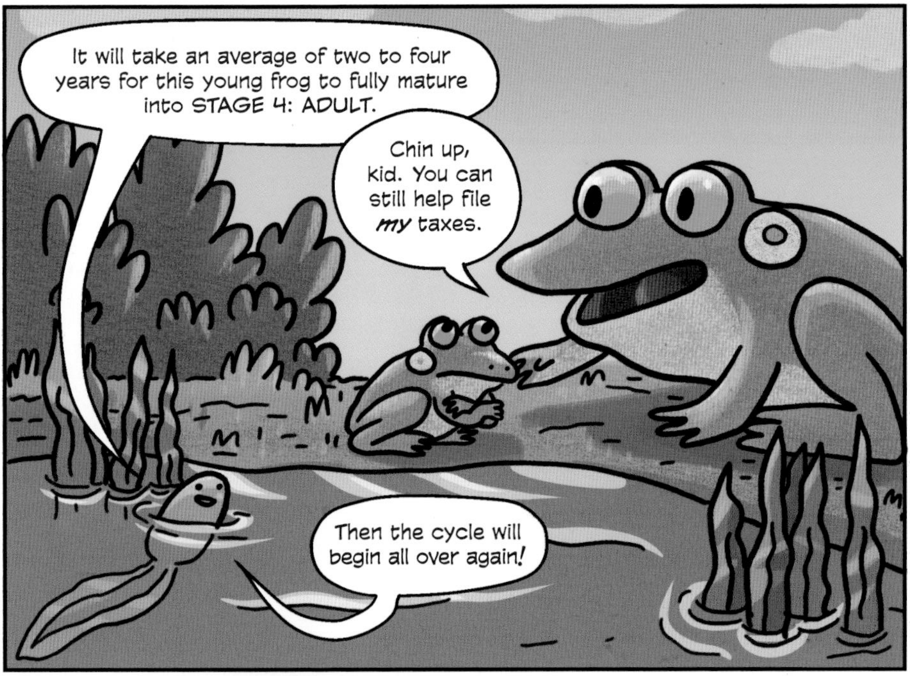
It will take an average of two to four years for this young frog to fully mature into STAGE 4: ADULT.
Chin up, kid. You can still help file *my* taxes.
Then the cycle will begin all over again!

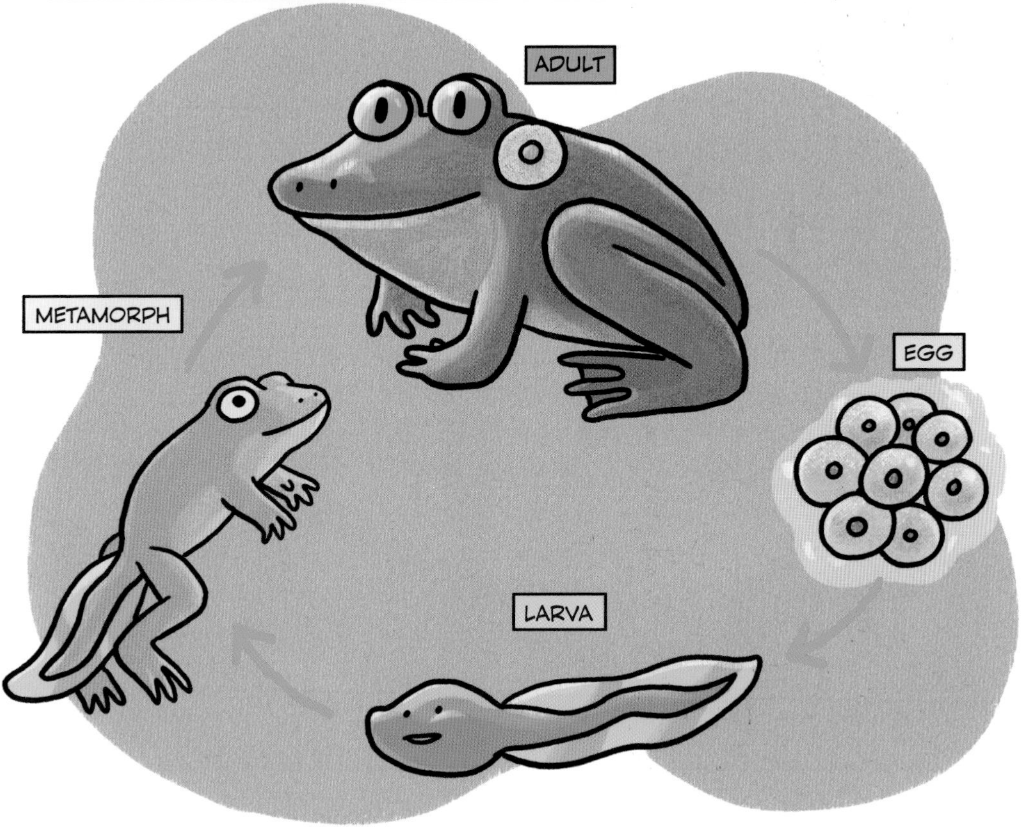
ADULT
EGG
LARVA
METAMORPH

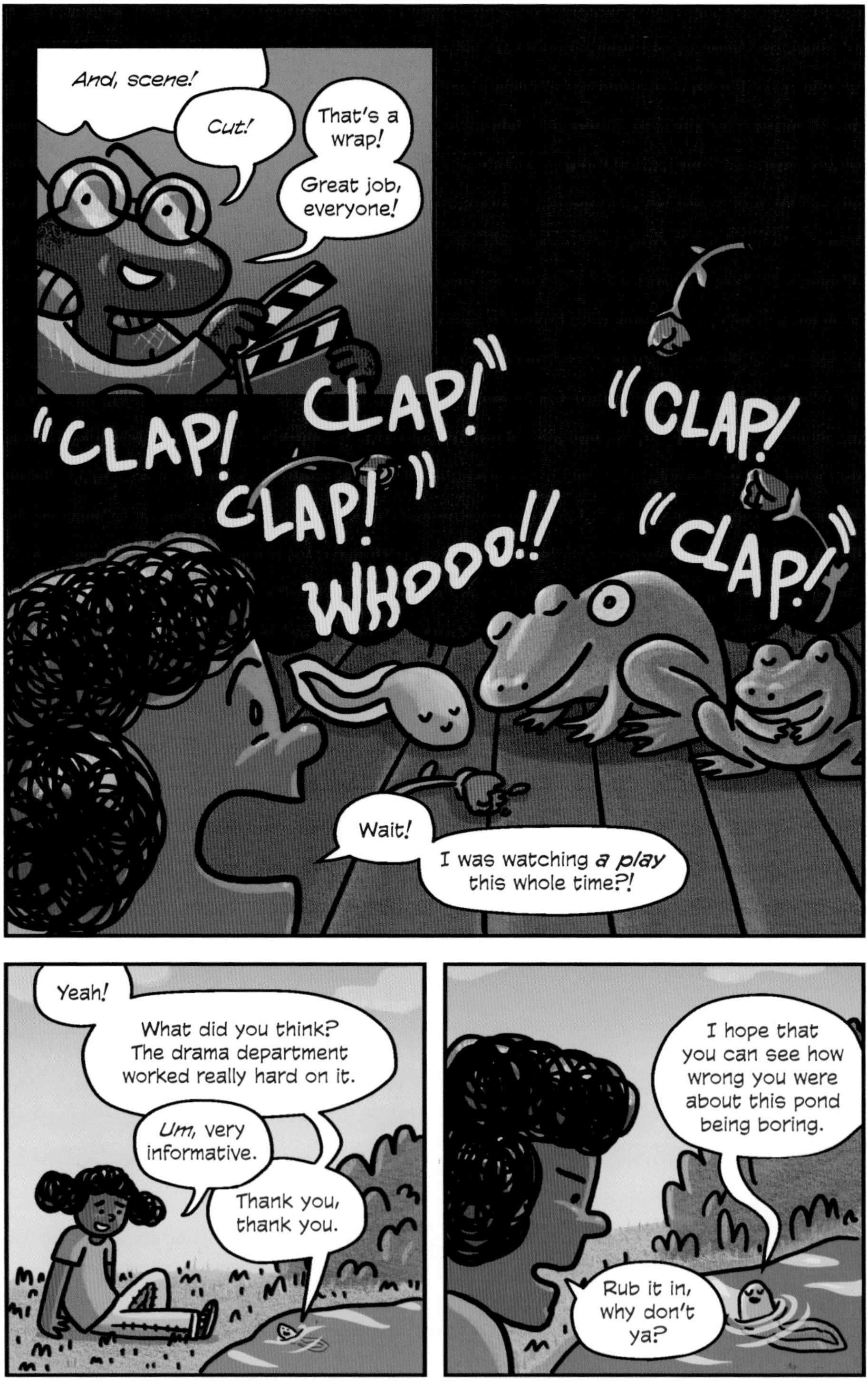
And, scene!
Cut!
That's a wrap!
Great job, everyone!
"CLAP!
CLAP!"
CLAP!"
WHOOO!!
"CLAP!
"CLAP!"
Wait!
I was watching *a play* this whole time?!
Yeah!
What did you think? The drama department worked really hard on it.
Um, very informative.
Thank you, thank you.
I hope that you can see how wrong you were about this pond being boring.
Rub it in, why don't ya?

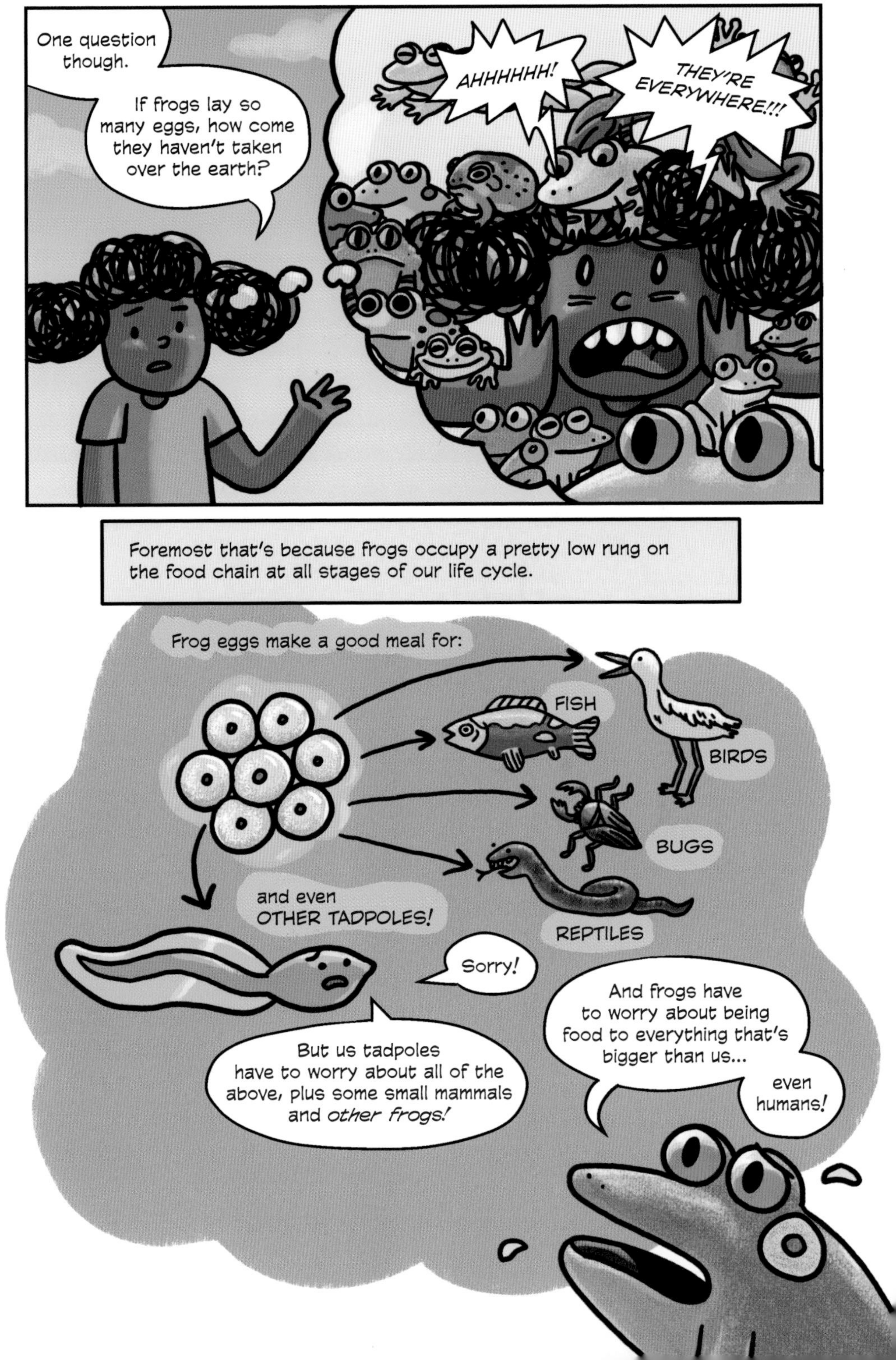
One question though.
If frogs lay so many eggs, how come they haven't taken over the earth?
AHHHHHH!
THEY'RE EVERYWHERE!!!
Foremost that's because frogs occupy a pretty low rung on the food chain at all stages of our life cycle.
Frog eggs make a good meal for:
FISH
BIRDS
BUGS
REPTILES
and even OTHER TADPOLES!
Sorry!
But us tadpoles have to worry about all of the above, plus some small mammals and *other frogs!*
And frogs have to worry about being food to everything that's bigger than us...
even humans!

Combine our palatability with all the environmental changes we're vulnerable to, and you'll be surprised that frogs aren't entirely extinct!

Too cold and we can freeze to death.

Too hot and our water or skin can dry up.

And pollution can poison us.

MOTOR OIL

It is estimated that out of 2,000 eggs, only around five will make it to adulthood.

In fact, a spawn is considered successful if the mom and dad manage to replace themselves with just one adult male and one adult female, because they are all that's needed to create the next generation of their species.

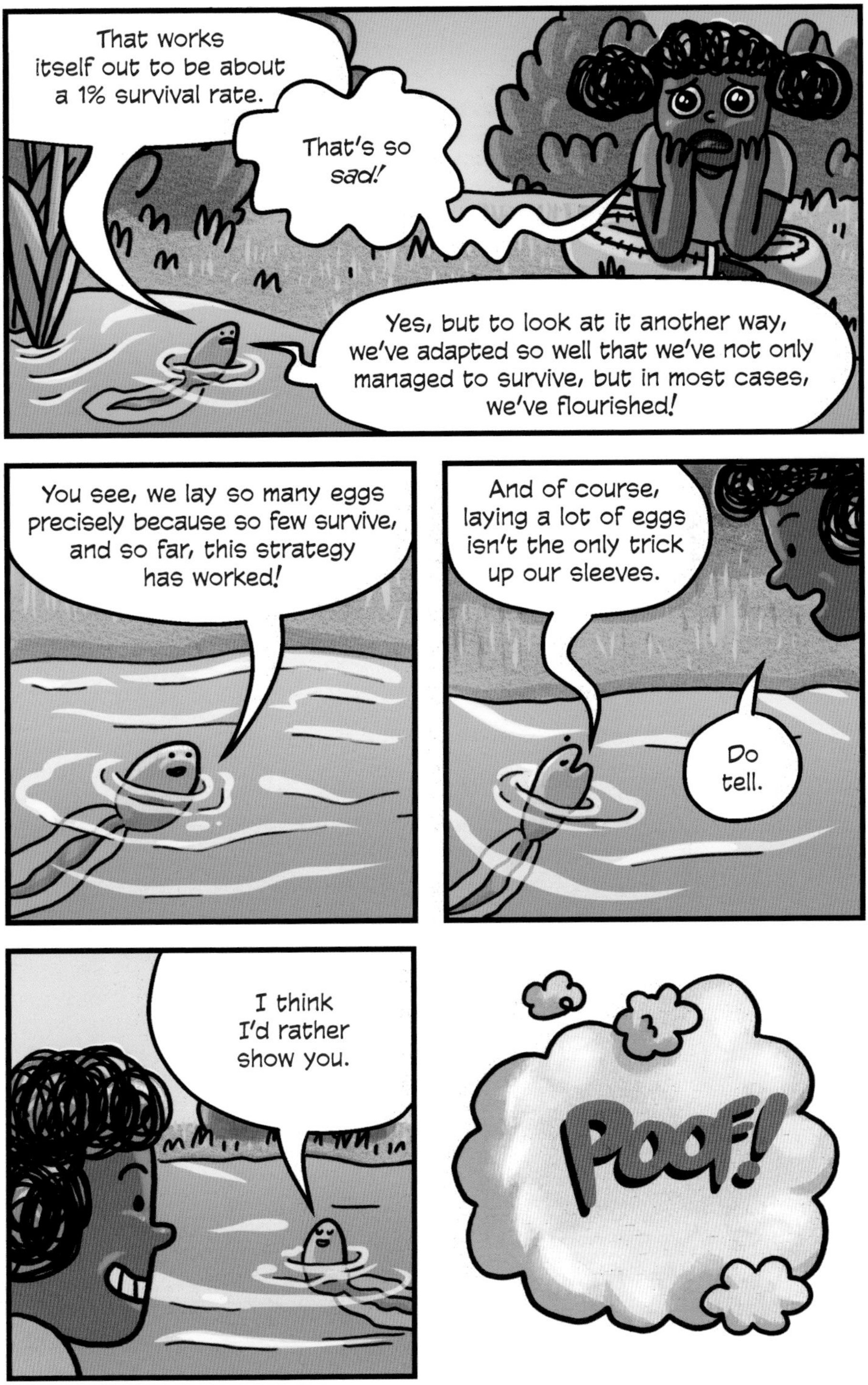
That works itself out to be about a 1% survival rate.
That's so *sad!*
Yes, but to look at it another way, we've adapted so well that we've not only managed to survive, but in most cases, we've flourished!
You see, we lay so many eggs precisely because so few survive, and so far, this strategy has worked!
And of course, laying a lot of eggs isn't the only trick up our sleeves.
Do tell.
I think I'd rather show you.
POOF!

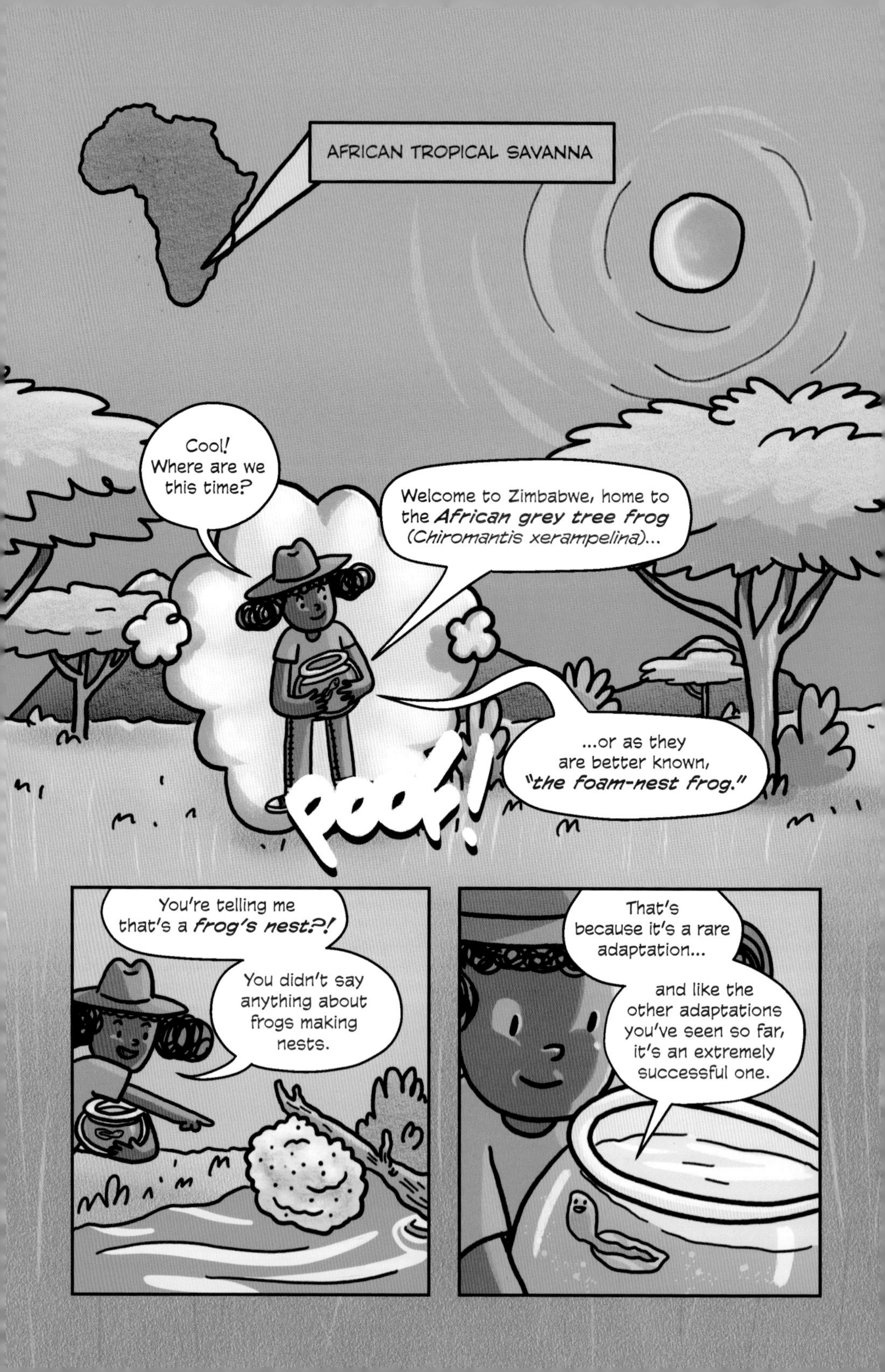

AFRICAN TROPICAL SAVANNA
Cool! Where are we this time?
Welcome to Zimbabwe, home to the *African grey tree frog* (*Chiromantis xerampelina*)...
...or as they are better known, *"the foam-nest frog."*
POOF!
You're telling me that's a *frog's nest?!*
You didn't say anything about frogs making nests.
That's because it's a rare adaptation...
and like the other adaptations you've seen so far, it's an extremely successful one.

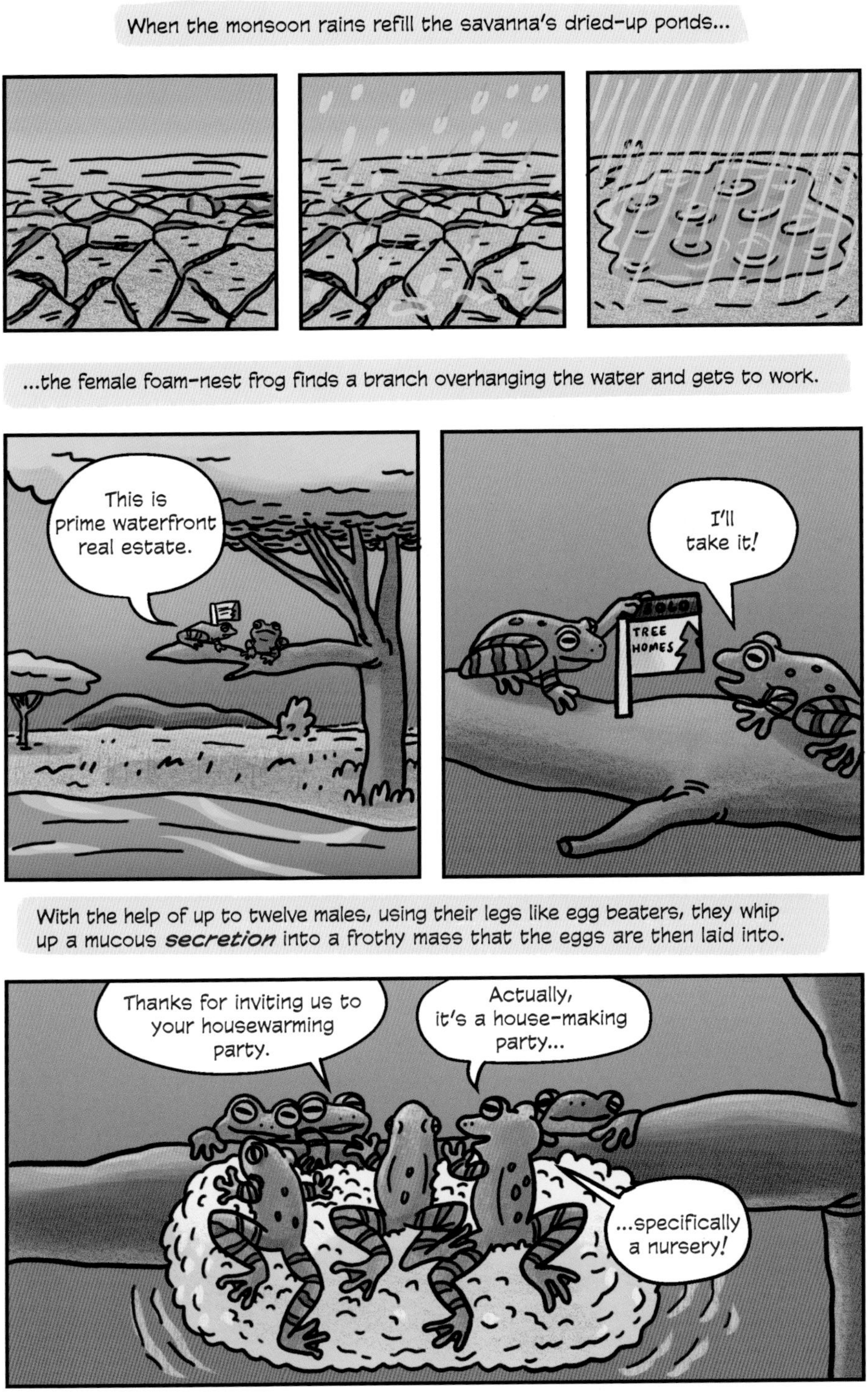
When the monsoon rains refill the savanna's dried-up ponds...
...the female foam-nest frog finds a branch overhanging the water and gets to work.
This is prime waterfront real estate.
I'll take it!
TREE HOMES
With the help of up to twelve males, using their legs like egg beaters, they whip up a mucous ***secretion*** into a frothy mass that the eggs are then laid into.
Thanks for inviting us to your housewarming party.
Actually, it's a house-making party...
...specifically a nursery!

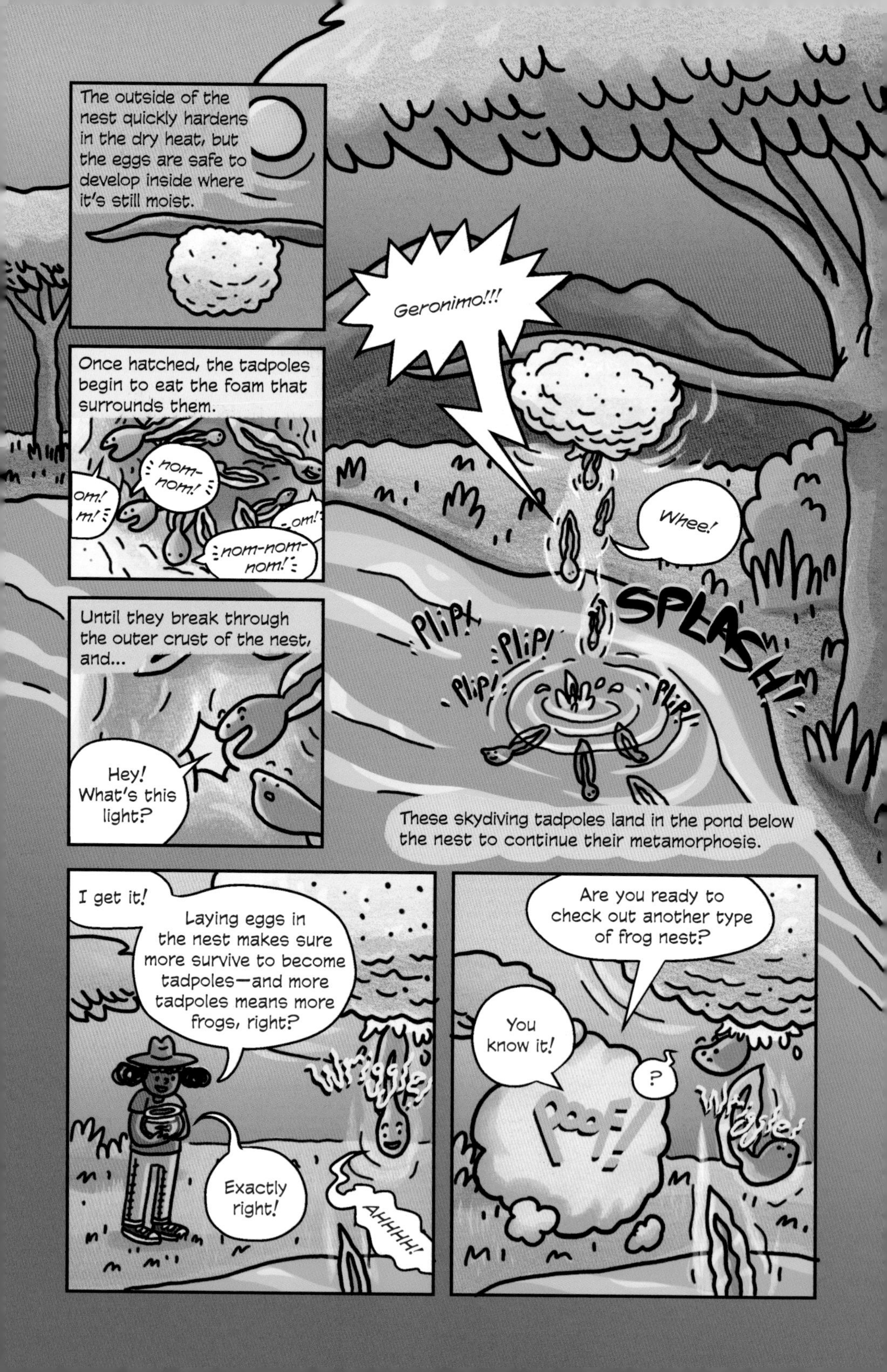
The outside of the nest quickly hardens in the dry heat, but the eggs are safe to develop inside where it's still moist.
Once hatched, the tadpoles begin to eat the foam that surrounds them.
nom-nom!
om! m!
om!
nom-nom-nom!
Until they break through the outer crust of the nest, and...
Hey! What's this light?
Geronimo!!!
Whee!
SPLASH!
Plip!
Plip!
Plip!
Plip!
These skydiving tadpoles land in the pond below the nest to continue their metamorphosis.
I get it!
Laying eggs in the nest makes sure more survive to become tadpoles—and more tadpoles means more frogs, right?
Exactly right!
AHHHH!
Are you ready to check out another type of frog nest?
You know it!
?
Poof!

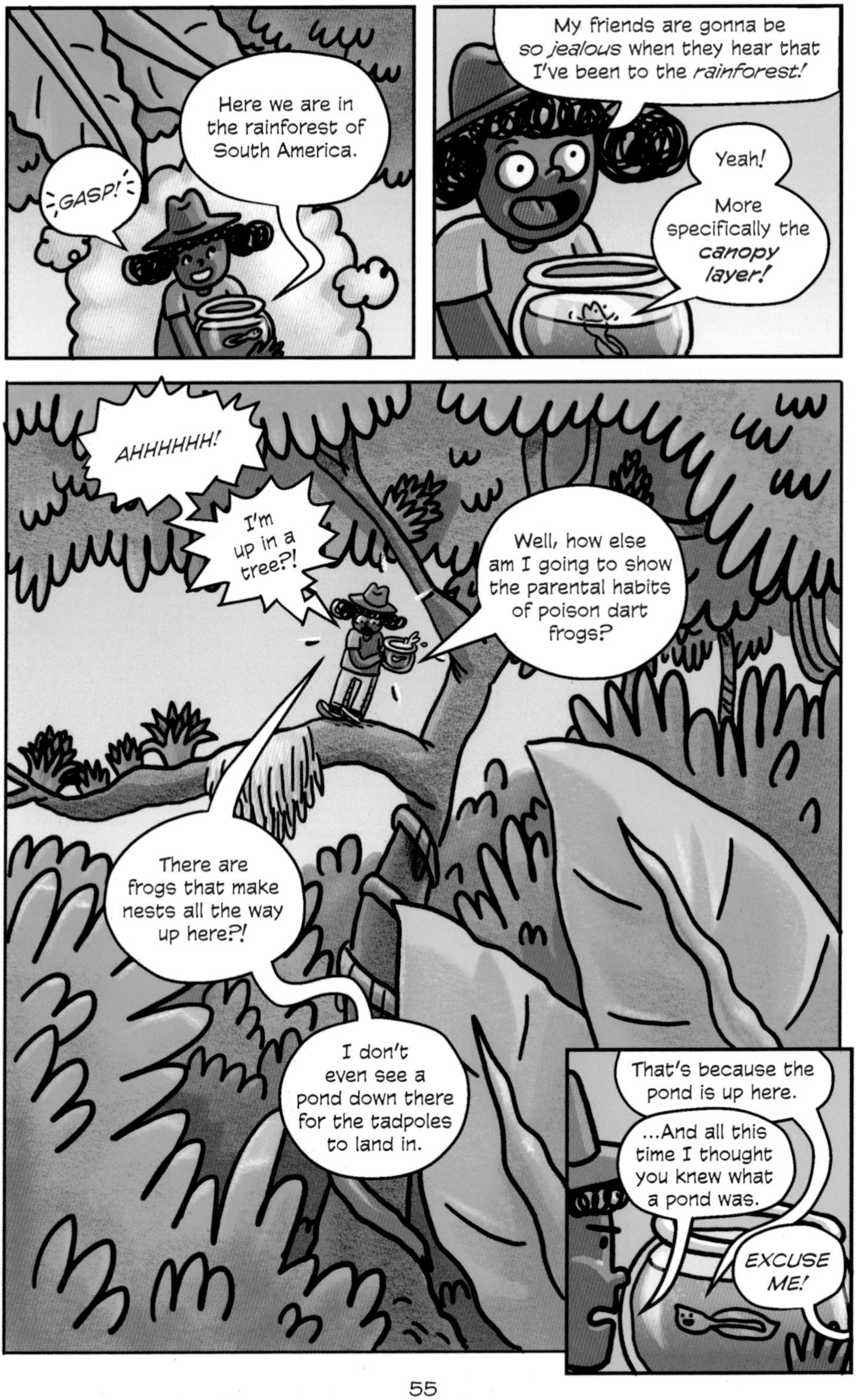
GASP!
Here we are in the rainforest of South America.
My friends are gonna be so *jealous* when they hear that I've been to the *rainforest!*
Yeah!
More specifically the **canopy layer!**
AHHHHHH!
I'm up in a tree?!
Well, how else am I going to show the parental habits of poison dart frogs?
There are frogs that make nests all the way up here?!
I don't even see a pond down there for the tadpoles to land in.
That's because the pond is up here.
...And all this time I thought you knew what a pond was.
EXCUSE ME!

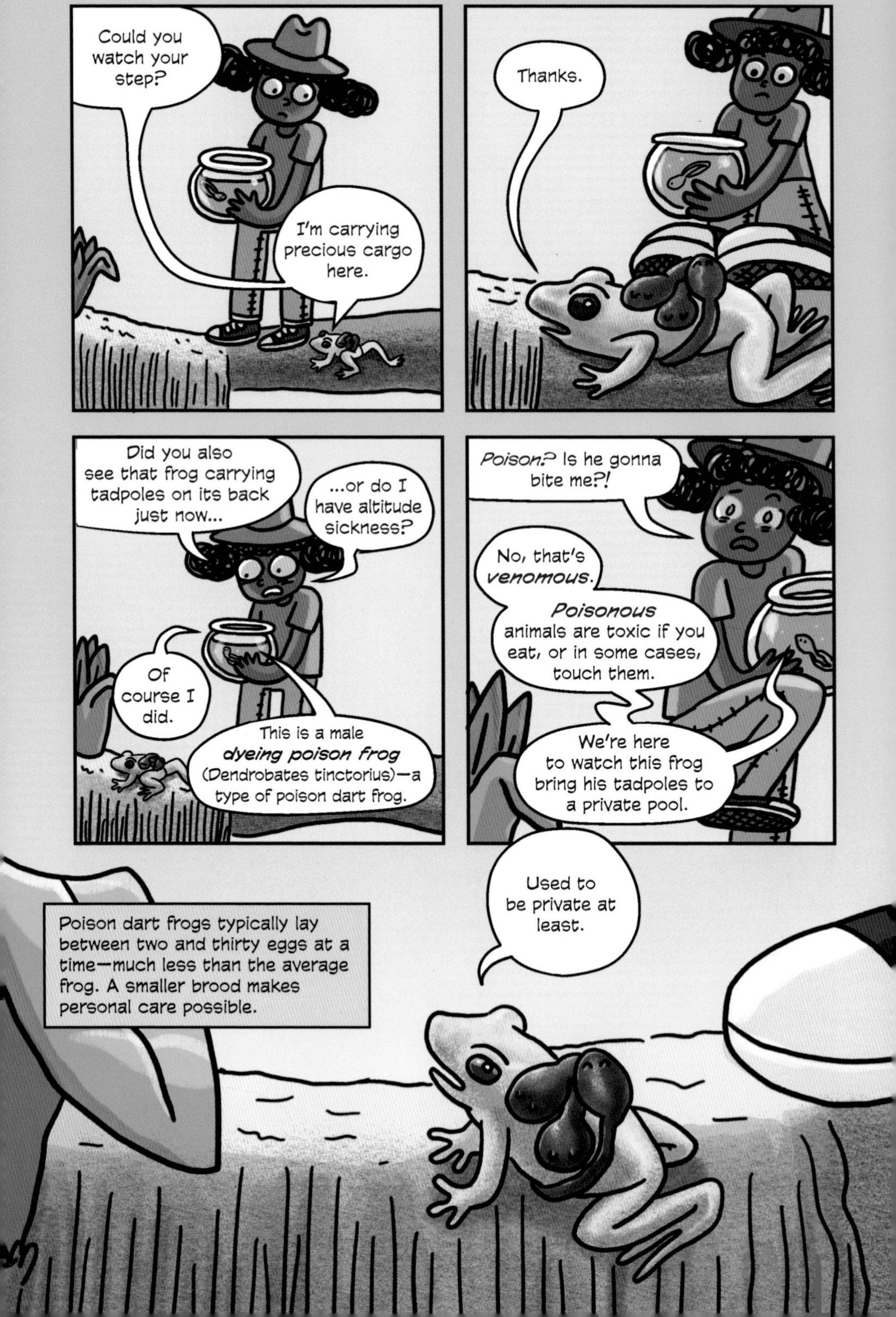
Could you watch your step?
I'm carrying precious cargo here.
Thanks.
Did you also see that frog carrying tadpoles on its back just now...
...or do I have altitude sickness?
Of course I did.
This is a male *dyeing poison frog* (Dendrobates tinctorius)—a type of poison dart frog.
Poison? Is he gonna bite me?!
No, that's ***venomous***.
Poisonous animals are toxic if you eat, or in some cases, touch them.
We're here to watch this frog bring his tadpoles to a private pool.
Poison dart frogs typically lay between two and thirty eggs at a time—much less than the average frog. A smaller brood makes personal care possible.
Used to be private at least.

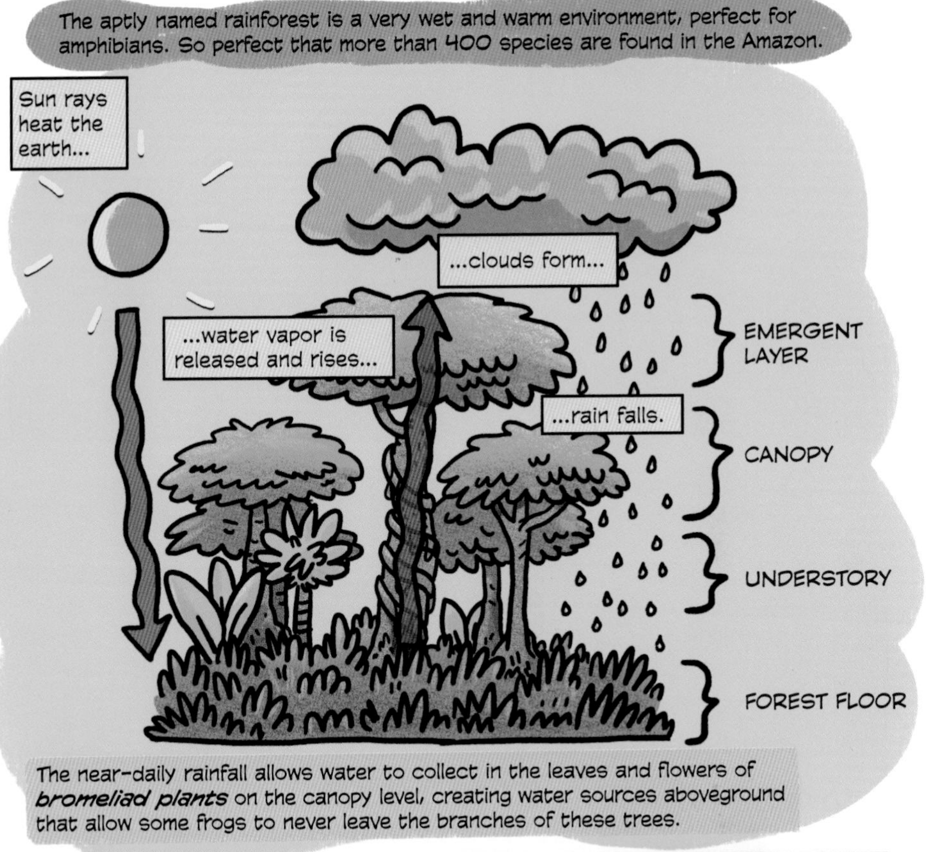
The aptly named rainforest is a very wet and warm environment, perfect for amphibians. So perfect that more than 400 species are found in the Amazon.
Sun rays heat the earth...
...water vapor is released and rises...
...clouds form...
...rain falls.
EMERGENT LAYER
CANOPY
UNDERSTORY
FOREST FLOOR
The near-daily rainfall allows water to collect in the leaves and flowers of *bromeliad plants* on the canopy level, creating water sources aboveground that allow some frogs to never leave the branches of these trees.

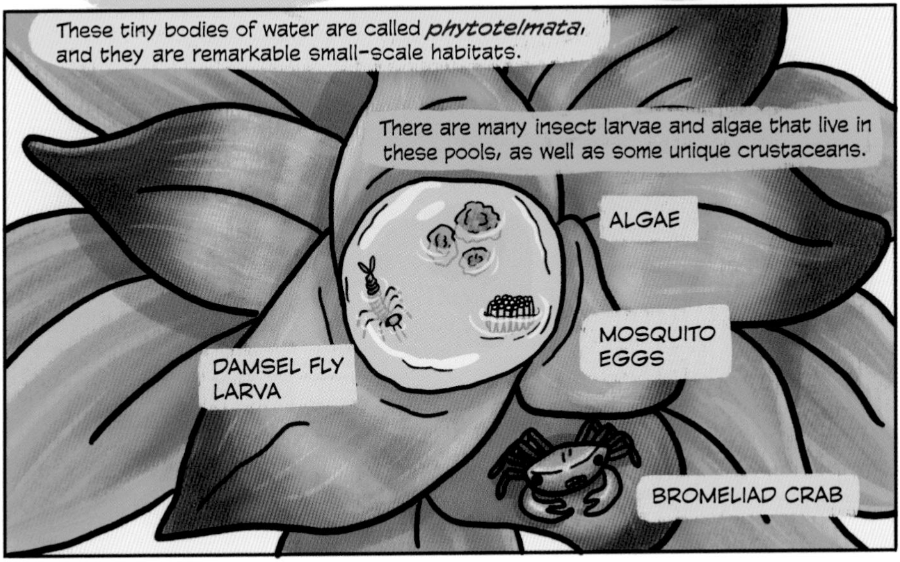
These tiny bodies of water are called *phytotelmata*, and they are remarkable small-scale habitats.
There are many insect larvae and algae that live in these pools, as well as some unique crustaceans.
ALGAE
MOSQUITO EGGS
DAMSEL FLY LARVA
BROMELIAD CRAB

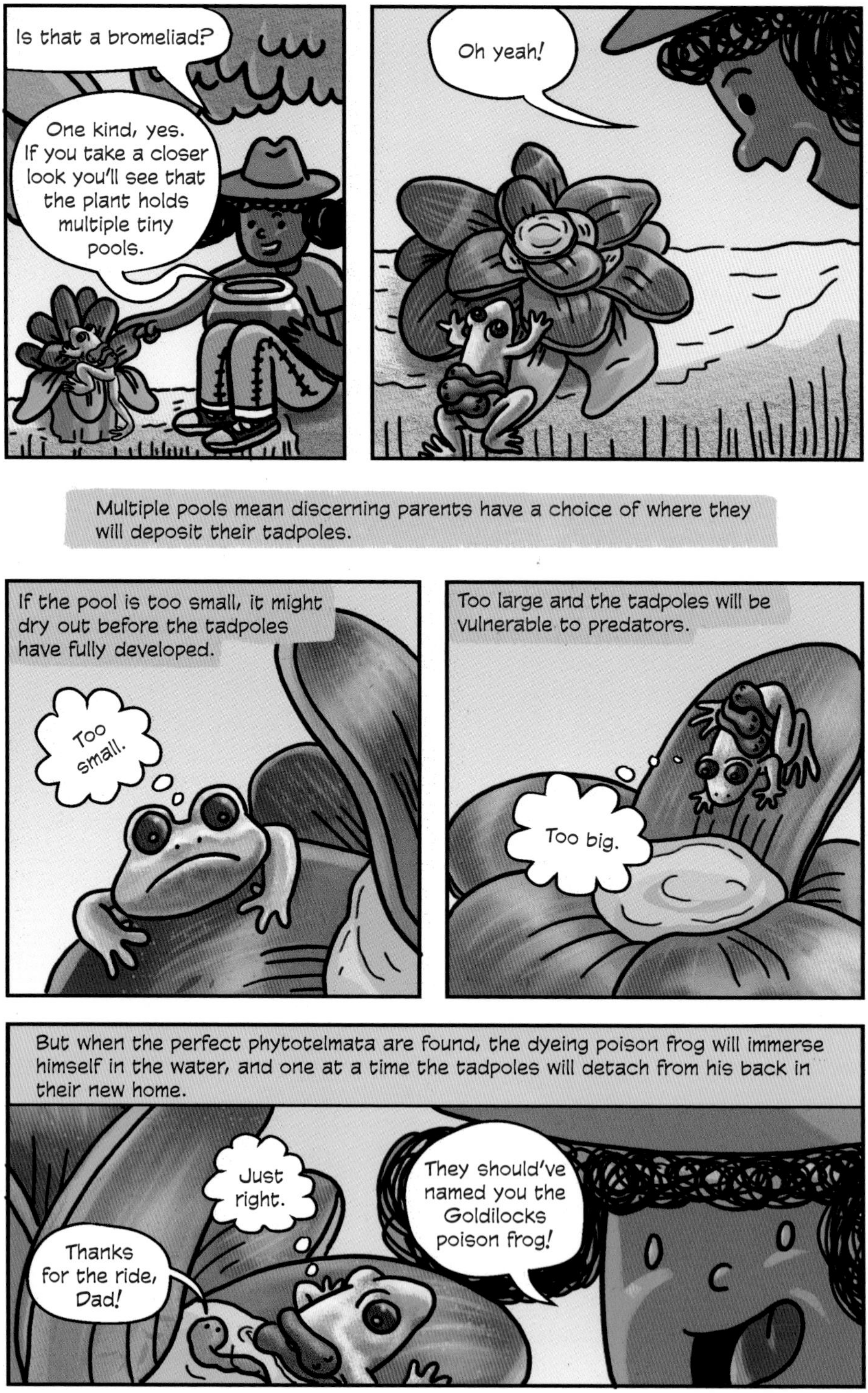

Is that a bromeliad?
One kind, yes. If you take a closer look you'll see that the plant holds multiple tiny pools.
Oh yeah!
Multiple pools mean discerning parents have a choice of where they will deposit their tadpoles.
If the pool is too small, it might dry out before the tadpoles have fully developed.
Too small.
Too large and the tadpoles will be vulnerable to predators.
Too big.
But when the perfect phytotelmata are found, the dyeing poison frog will immerse himself in the water, and one at a time the tadpoles will detach from his back in their new home.
Just right.
They should've named you the Goldilocks poison frog!
Thanks for the ride, Dad!

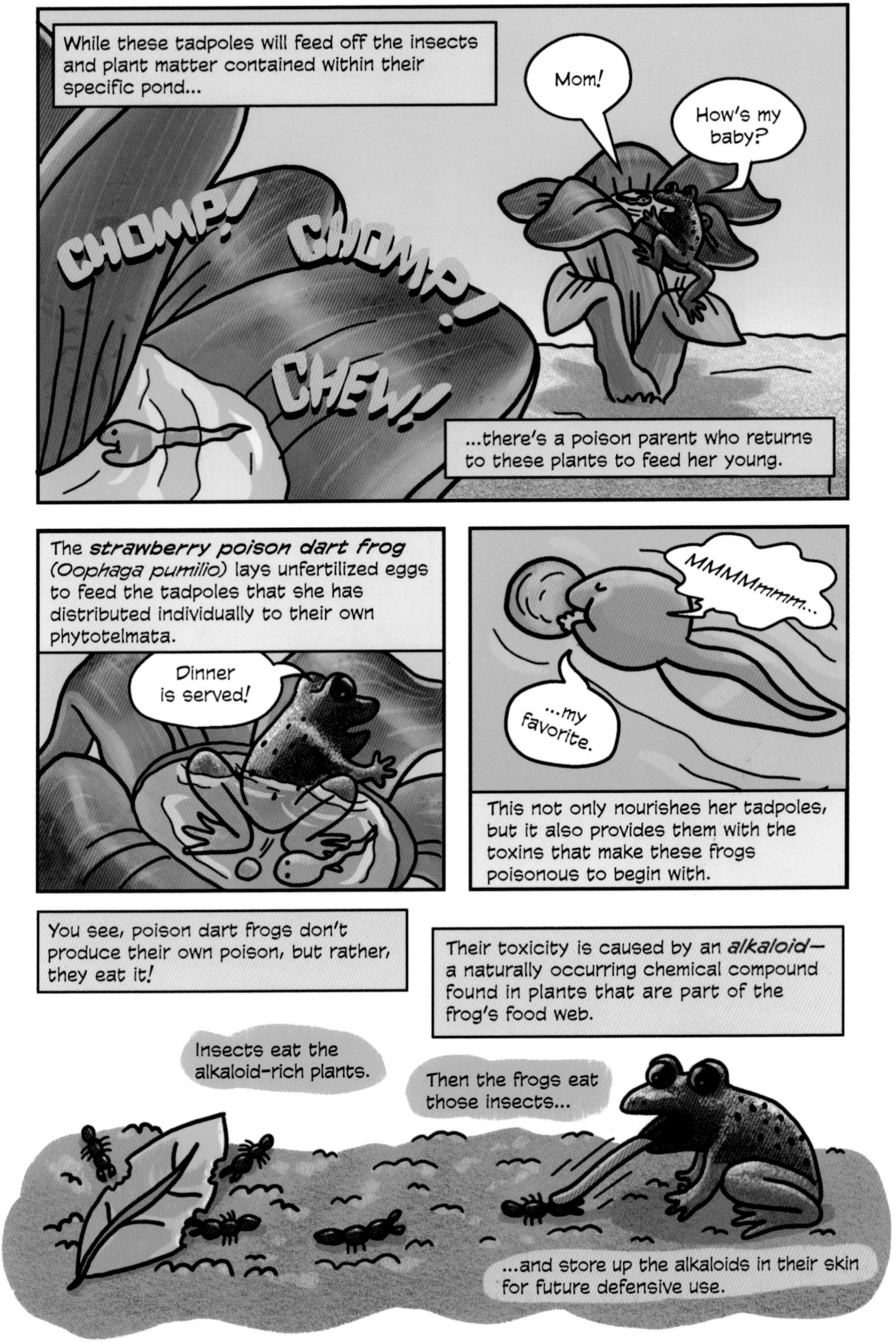
While these tadpoles will feed off the insects and plant matter contained within their specific pond...
Mom!
How's my baby?
CHOMP!
CHOMP!
CHEW!
...there's a poison parent who returns to these plants to feed her young.
The *strawberry poison dart frog* (*Oophaga pumilio*) lays unfertilized eggs to feed the tadpoles that she has distributed individually to their own phytotelmata.
Dinner is served!
MMMMmmmm...
...my favorite.
This not only nourishes her tadpoles, but it also provides them with the toxins that make these frogs poisonous to begin with.
You see, poison dart frogs don't produce their own poison, but rather, they eat it!
Their toxicity is caused by an *alkaloid*—a naturally occurring chemical compound found in plants that are part of the frog's food web.
Insects eat the alkaloid-rich plants.
Then the frogs eat those insects...
...and store up the alkaloids in their skin for future defensive use.

Poison frogs raised in captivity lack their eponymous poison because their diet doesn't include the bugs that feed on the toxin.

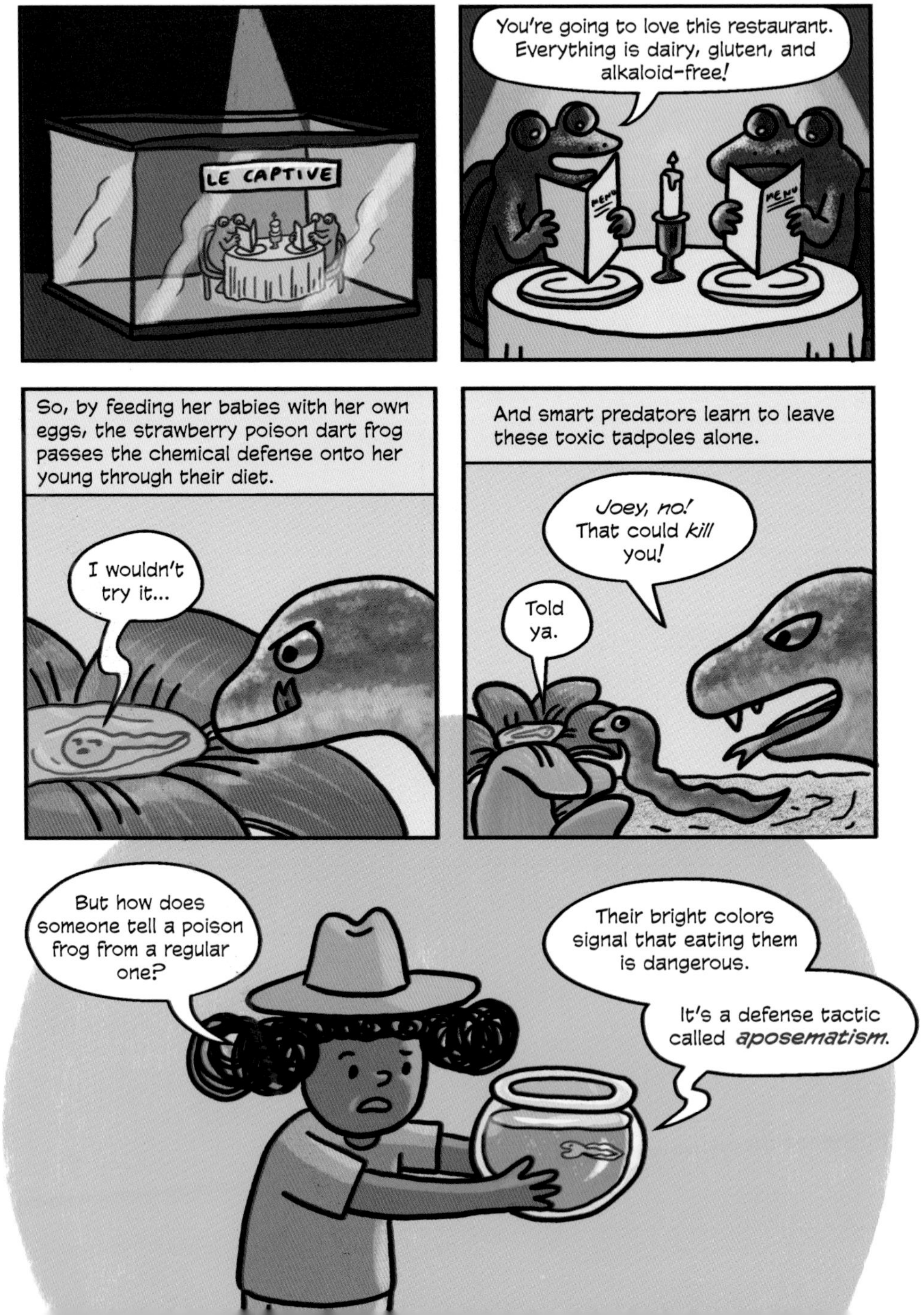
LE CAPTIVE
You're going to love this restaurant. Everything is dairy, gluten, and alkaloid-free!
MENU
MENU
So, by feeding her babies with her own eggs, the strawberry poison dart frog passes the chemical defense onto her young through their diet.
I wouldn't try it...
And smart predators learn to leave these toxic tadpoles alone.
Joey, no! That could *kill* you!
Told ya.
But how does someone tell a poison frog from a regular one?
Their bright colors signal that eating them is dangerous.
It's a defense tactic called ***aposematism***.

Most frogs rely on earthy hues of greens and browns in combination with highly specialized skin markings matched to their habitats in order to *camouflage*.

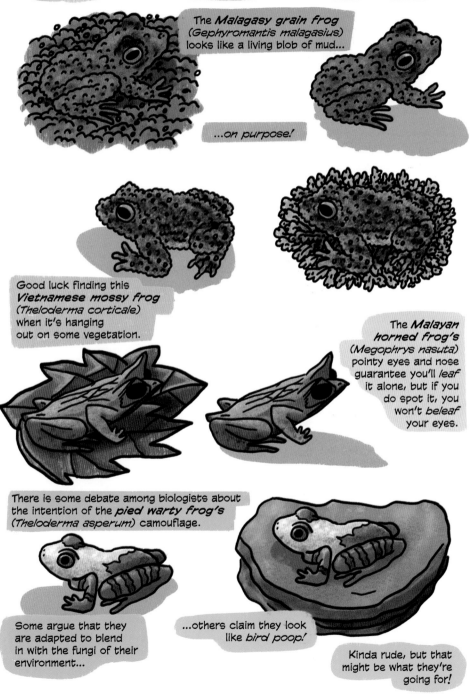

The *Malagasy grain frog* (Gephyromantis malagasius) looks like a living blob of mud...

...on purpose!

Good luck finding this *Vietnamese mossy frog* (Theloderma corticale) when it's hanging out on some vegetation.

The *Malayan horned frog's* (Megophrys nasuta) pointy eyes and nose guarantee you'll *leaf* it alone, but if you do spot it, you won't *beleaf* your eyes.

There is some debate among biologists about the intention of the *pied warty frog's* (Theloderma asperum) camouflage.

Some argue that they are adapted to blend in with the fungi of their environment...

...others claim they look like *bird poop!*

Kinda rude, but that might be what they're going for!

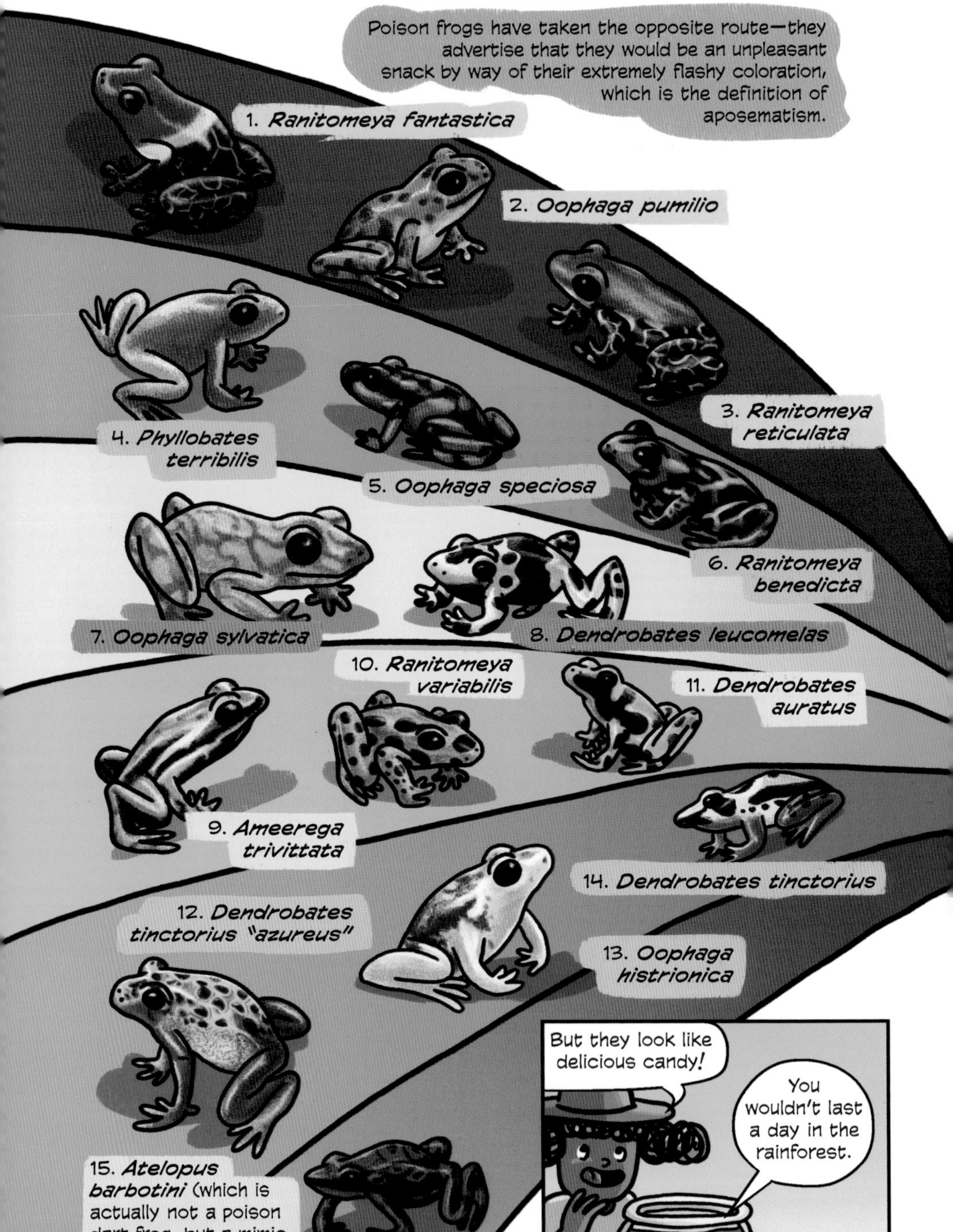
Poison frogs have taken the opposite route—they advertise that they would be an unpleasant snack by way of their extremely flashy coloration, which is the definition of aposematism.
1. Ranitomeya fantastica
2. Oophaga pumilio
3. Ranitomeya reticulata
4. Phyllobates terribilis
5. Oophaga speciosa
6. Ranitomeya benedicta
7. Oophaga sylvatica
8. Dendrobates leucomelas
10. Ranitomeya variabilis
11. Dendrobates auratus
9. Ameerega trivittata
14. Dendrobates tinctorius
12. Dendrobates tinctorius "azureus"
13. Oophaga histrionica
15. Atelopus barbotini (which is actually not a poison dart frog, but a mimic. We couldn't have a proper rainbow without violet!)
But they look like delicious candy!
You wouldn't last a day in the rainforest.

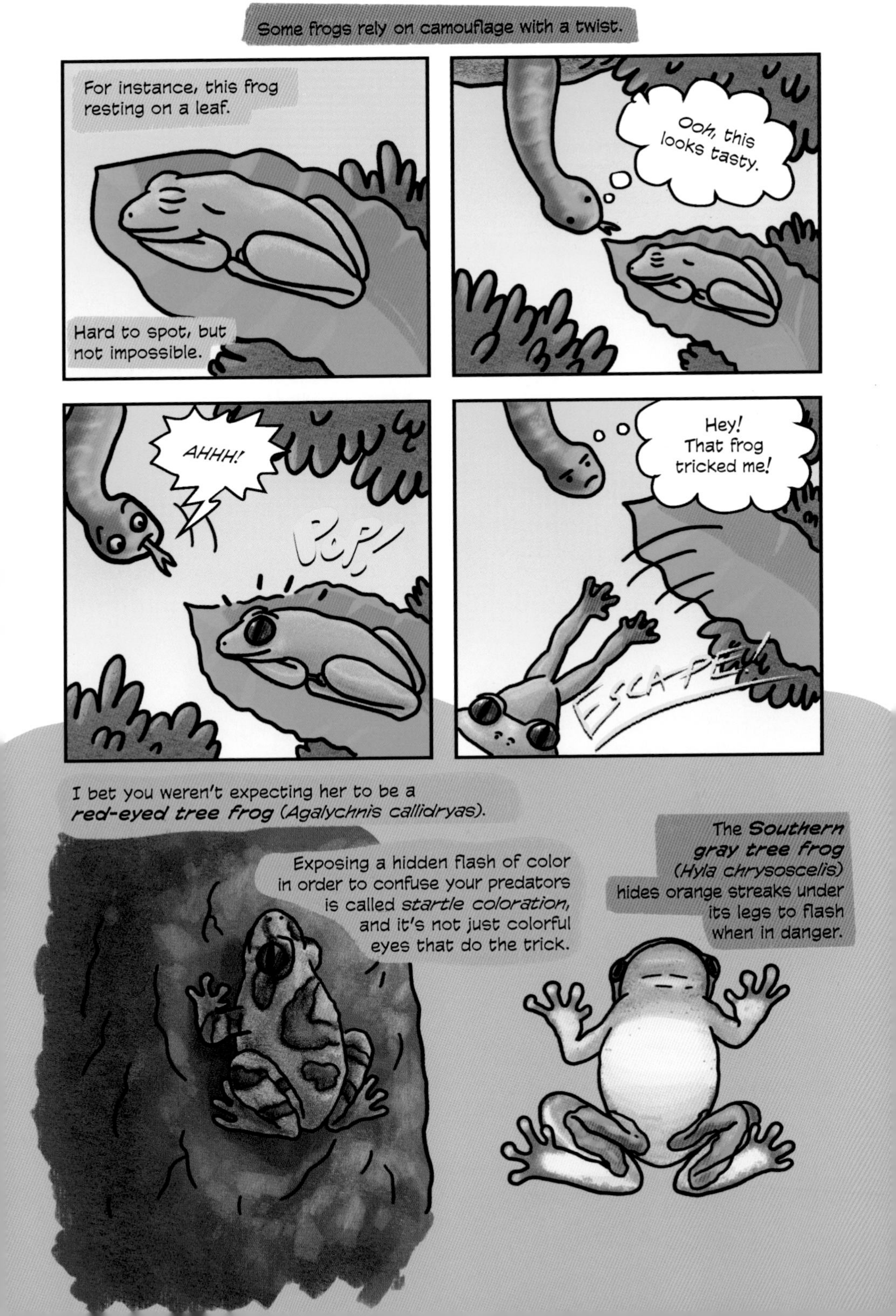

Some frogs rely on camouflage with a twist.
For instance, this frog resting on a leaf.
Hard to spot, but not impossible.
Ooh, this looks tasty.
AHHH!
POP!
Hey! That frog tricked me!
ESCA-PE!
I bet you weren't expecting her to be a *red-eyed tree frog* (*Agalychnis callidryas*).
Exposing a hidden flash of color in order to confuse your predators is called *startle coloration*, and it's not just colorful eyes that do the trick.
The *Southern gray tree frog* (*Hyla chrysoscelis*) hides orange streaks under its legs to flash when in danger.

Frogs and toads also come in an array of shapes of sizes.

The largest frog is the ***Goliath frog*** (*Conraua goliath*) from Africa—it can be up to 12 in (30.48 cm) and weigh 6 lb (2.72 kg)!

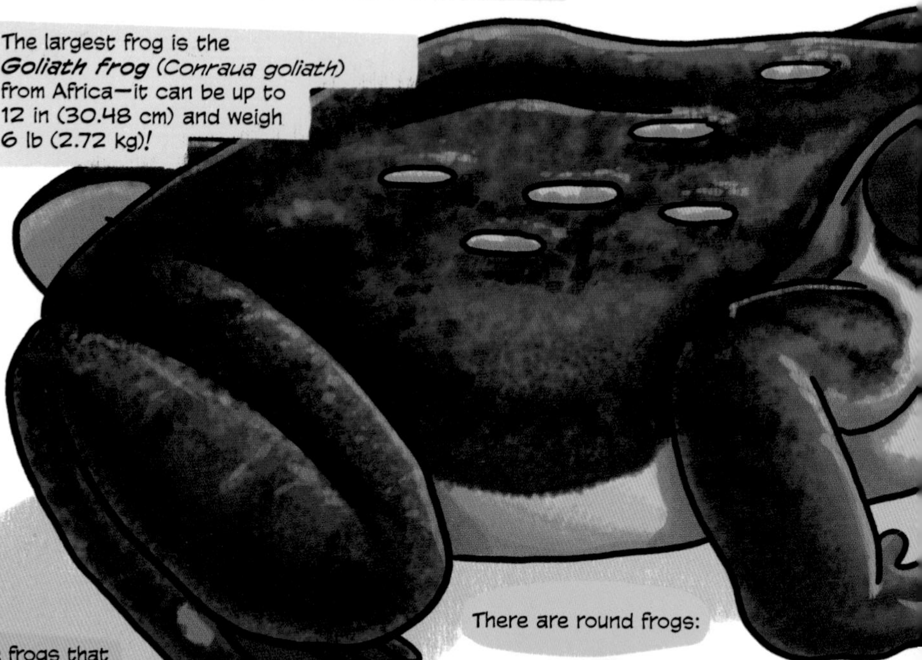

There are frogs that don't really look like frogs at all:

Purple frog
(*Nasikabatrachus sahyadrensis*),
or the "Indian pig-nosed frog"

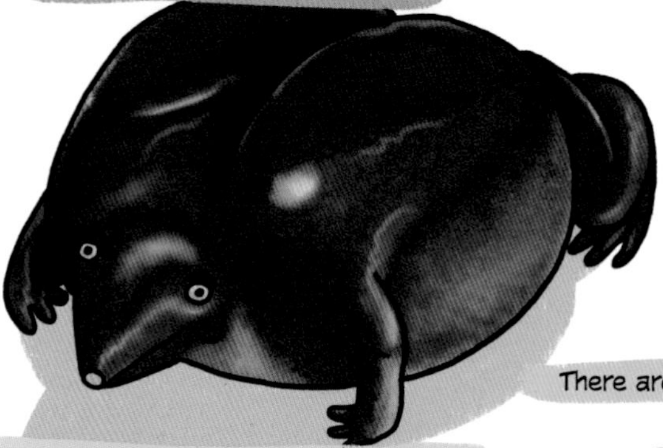

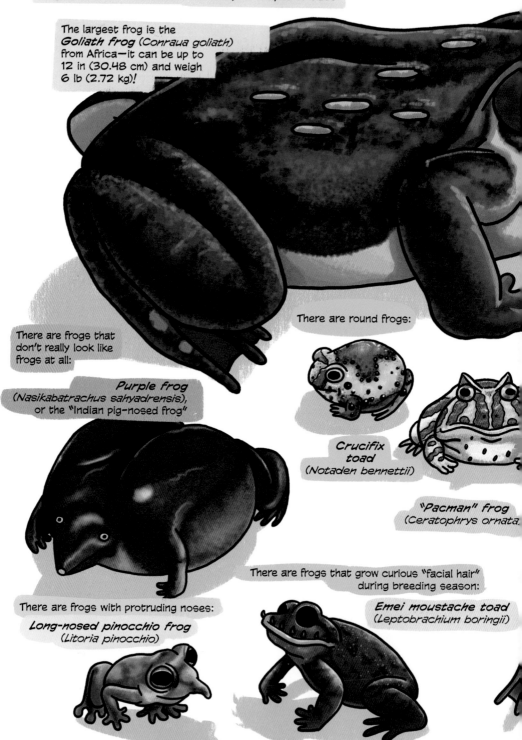

There are round frogs:

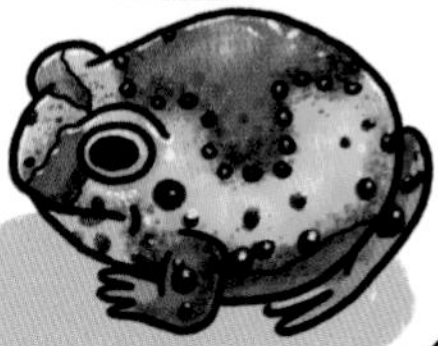

Crucifix toad
(*Notaden bennettii*)

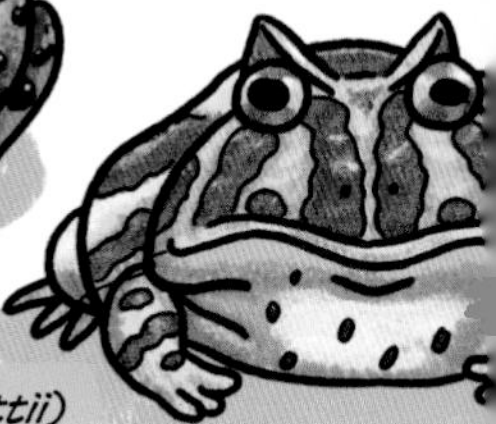

"Pacman" frog
(*Ceratophrys ornata*)

There are frogs with protruding noses:

Long-nosed pinocchio frog
(*Litoria pinocchio*)

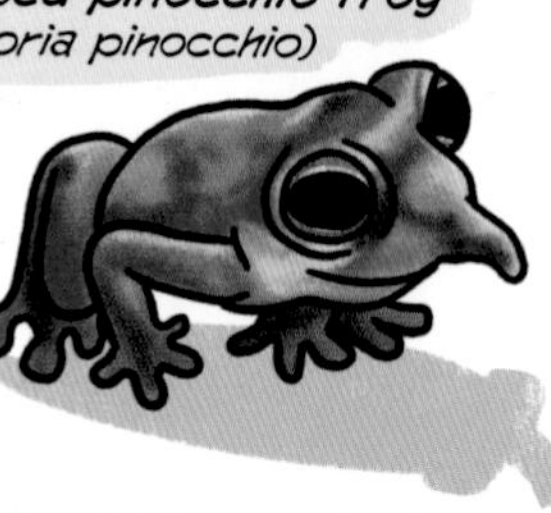

There are frogs that grow curious "facial hair" during breeding season:

Emei moustache toad
(*Leptobrachium boringii*)

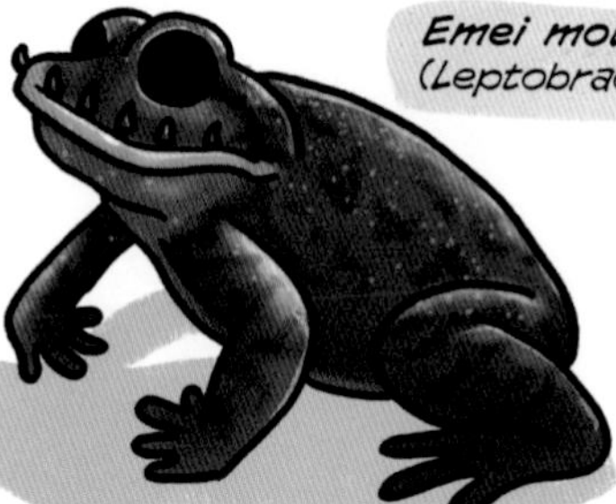

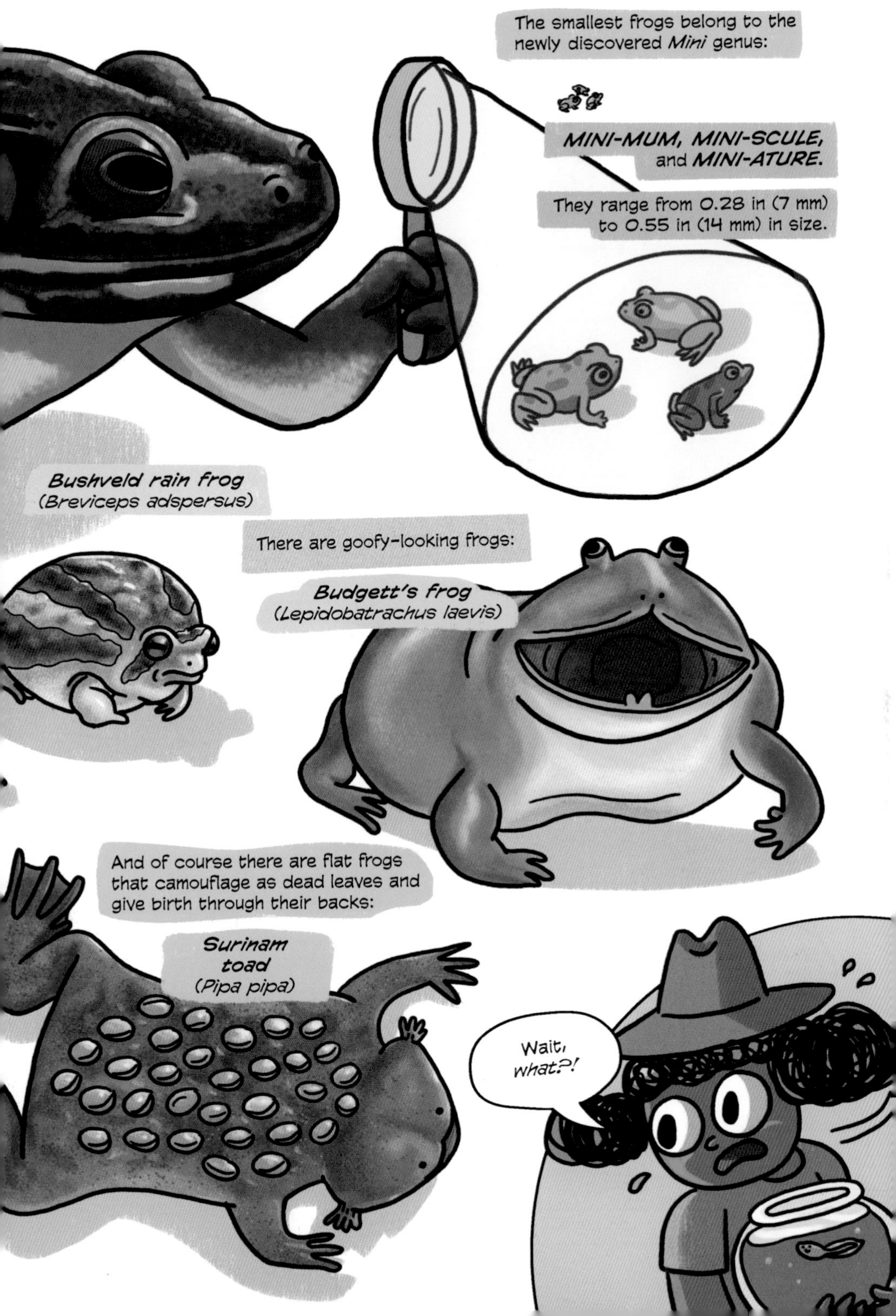
The smallest frogs belong to the newly discovered *Mini* genus:
MINI-MUM, MINI-SCULE, and *MINI-ATURE.*
They range from 0.28 in (7 mm) to 0.55 in (14 mm) in size.
Bushveld rain frog (*Breviceps adspersus*)
There are goofy-looking frogs:
Budgett's frog (*Lepidobatrachus laevis*)
And of course there are flat frogs that camouflage as dead leaves and give birth through their backs:
Surinam toad (*Pipa pipa*)
Wait, *what?!*

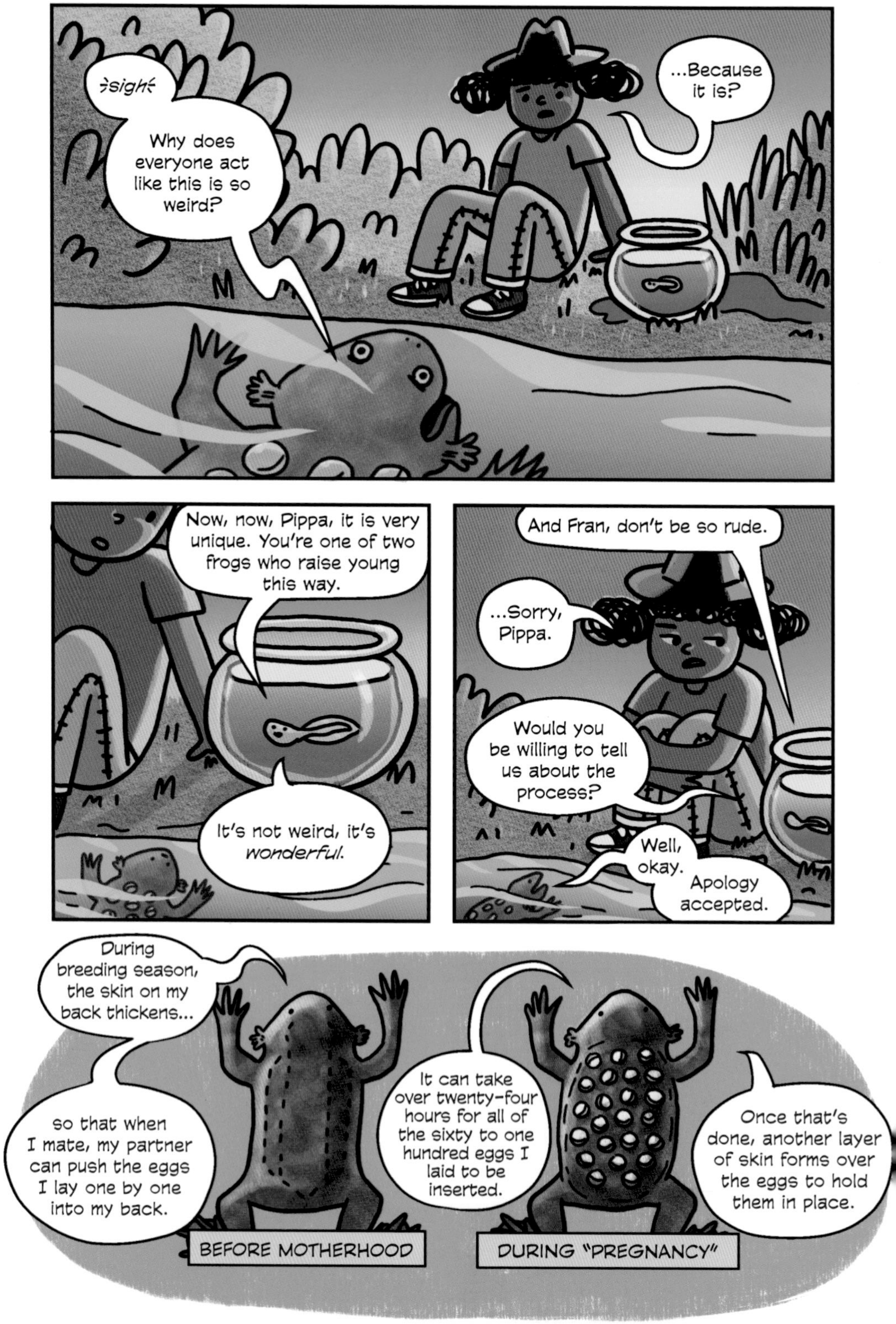

≯sigh≮
Why does everyone act like this is so weird?
...Because it is?
Now, now, Pippa, it is very unique. You're one of two frogs who raise young this way.
It's not weird, it's *wonderful*.
And Fran, don't be so rude.
...Sorry, Pippa.
Would you be willing to tell us about the process?
Well, okay.
Apology accepted.
During breeding season, the skin on my back thickens...
so that when I mate, my partner can push the eggs I lay one by one into my back.
It can take over twenty-four hours for all of the sixty to one hundred eggs I laid to be inserted.
Once that's done, another layer of skin forms over the eggs to hold them in place.
BEFORE MOTHERHOOD
DURING "PREGNANCY"

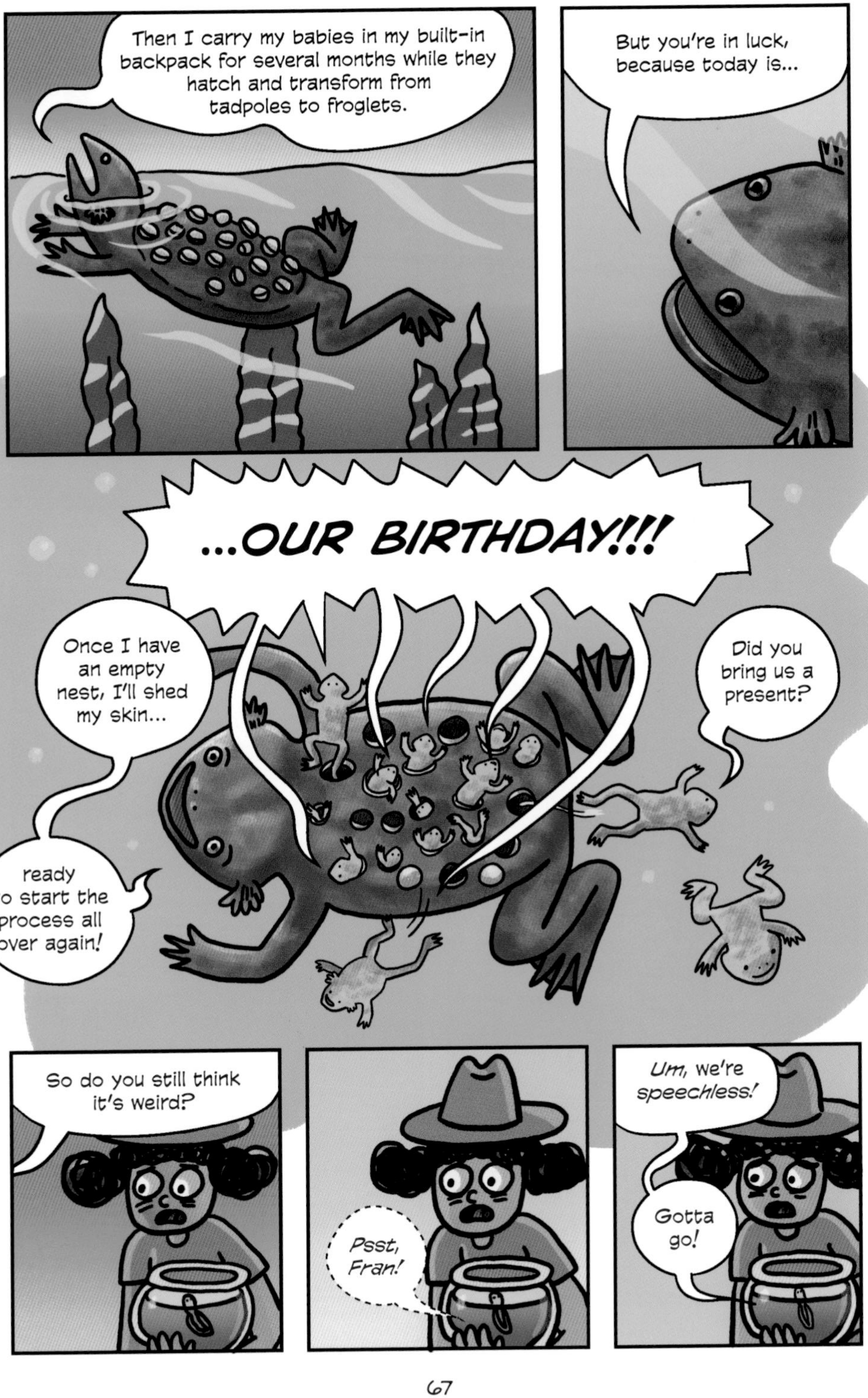

Then I carry my babies in my built-in backpack for several months while they hatch and transform from tadpoles to froglets.
But you're in luck, because today is...
...OUR BIRTHDAY!!!
Once I have an empty nest, I'll shed my skin...
ready to start the process all over again!
Did you bring us a present?
So do you still think it's weird?
Psst, Fran!
Um, we're speechless!
Gotta go!

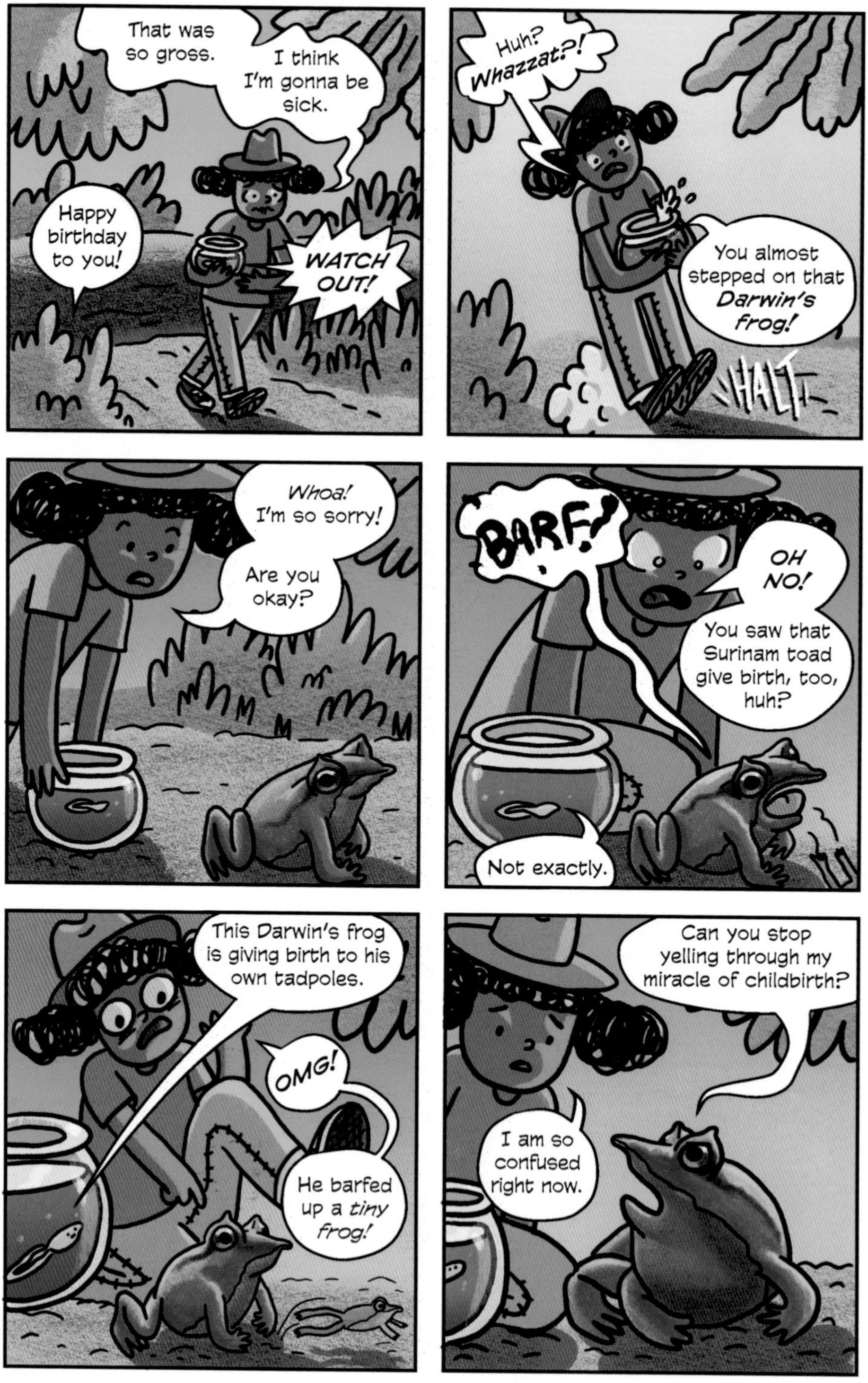
That was so gross.
I think I'm gonna be sick.
Happy birthday to you!
WATCH OUT!
Huh? Whazzat?!
You almost stepped on that Darwin's frog!
HALT
Whoa! I'm so sorry!
Are you okay?
BARF!
OH NO!
You saw that Surinam toad give birth, too, huh?
Not exactly.
This Darwin's frog is giving birth to his own tadpoles.
OMG!
He barfed up a tiny frog!
Can you stop yelling through my miracle of childbirth?
I am so confused right now.

The Darwin's frog was once a genus with two species: the Northern Darwin's frog and the Southern Darwin's frog—named for the regions of Chile and Argentina that they inhabited.

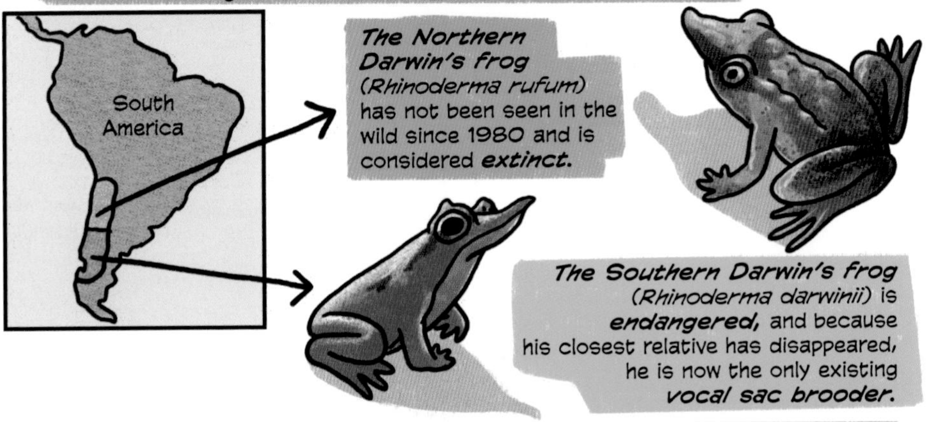
South America
The Northern Darwin's frog (*Rhinoderma rufum*) has not been seen in the wild since 1980 and is considered ***extinct***.
The Southern Darwin's frog (*Rhinoderma darwinii*) is ***endangered***, and because his closest relative has disappeared, he is now the only existing ***vocal sac brooder***.

When the female Darwin's frog lays her small clutch of four to seven eggs on the forest floor, the male stays with them until the tadpoles are developed enough to hatch.

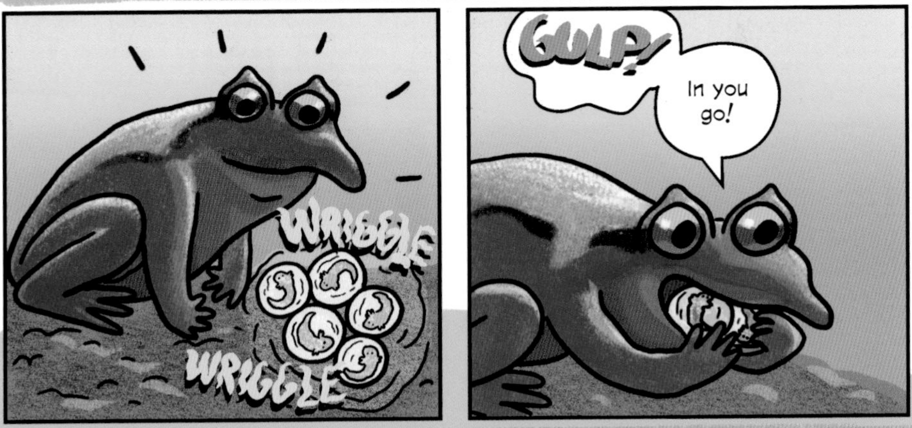
WRIGGLE
WRIGGLE
GULP!
In you go!

The tadpoles remain inside their dad's vocal sac until they have fully metamorphosed into froglets. This can take up to seventy days, after which the father regurgitates his offspring.

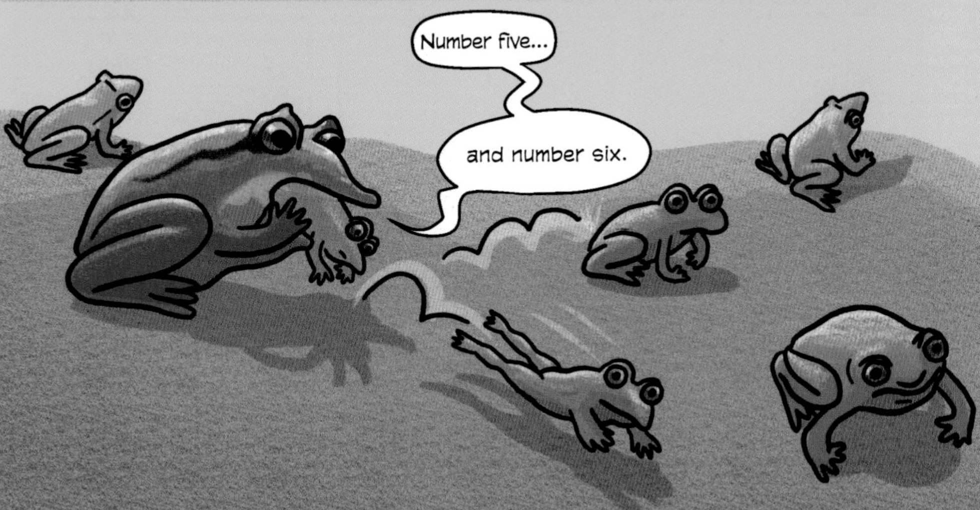
Number five...
and number six.

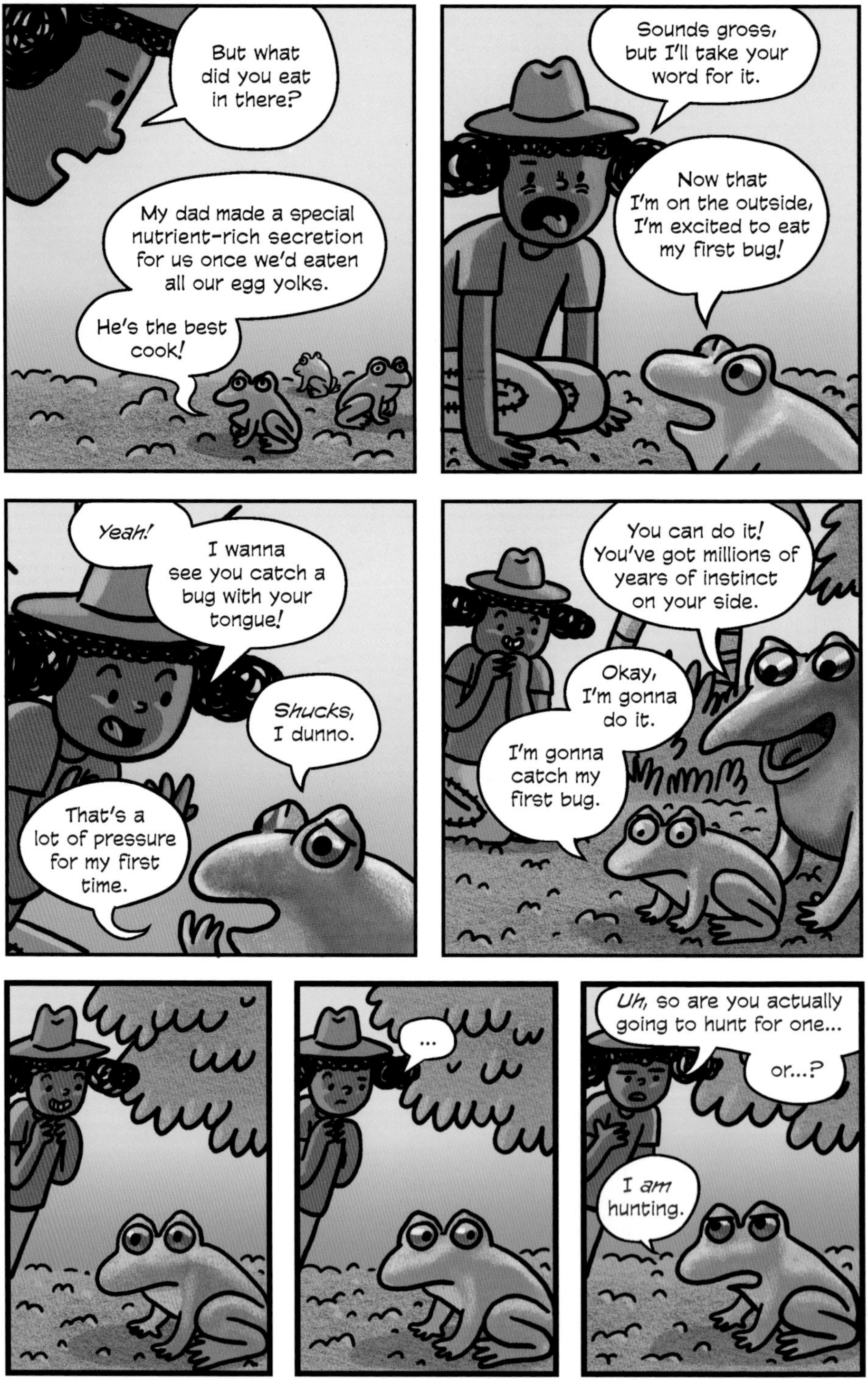
But what did you eat in there?
My dad made a special nutrient-rich secretion for us once we'd eaten all our egg yolks.
He's the best cook!
Sounds gross, but I'll take your word for it.
Now that I'm on the outside, I'm excited to eat my first bug!
Yeah!
I wanna see you catch a bug with your tongue!
Shucks, I dunno.
That's a lot of pressure for my first time.
You can do it! You've got millions of years of instinct on your side.
Okay, I'm gonna do it.
I'm gonna catch my first bug.
...
Uh, so are you actually going to hunt for one...
or...?
I *am* hunting.

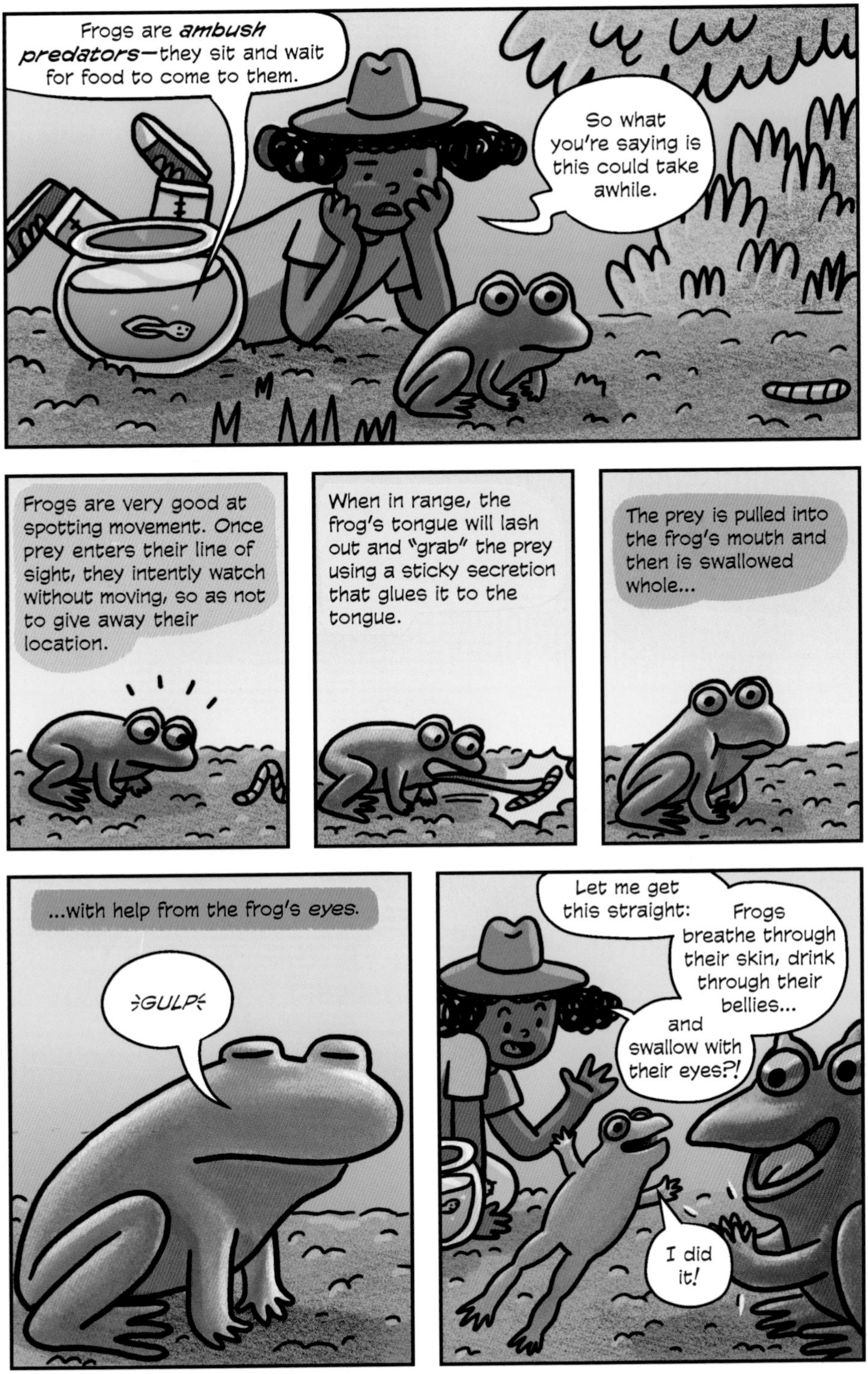

Frogs are *ambush predators*—they sit and wait for food to come to them.
So what you're saying is this could take awhile.
Frogs are very good at spotting movement. Once prey enters their line of sight, they intently watch without moving, so as not to give away their location.
When in range, the frog's tongue will lash out and "grab" the prey using a sticky secretion that glues it to the tongue.
The prey is pulled into the frog's mouth and then is swallowed whole...
...with help from the frog's *eyes*.
GULP
Let me get this straight:
Frogs breathe through their skin, drink through their bellies...
and swallow with their eyes?!
I did it!

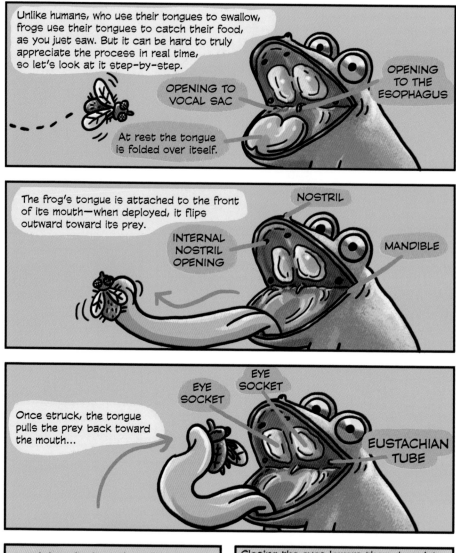

Unlike humans, who use their tongues to swallow, frogs use their tongues to catch their food, as you just saw. But it can be hard to truly appreciate the process in real time, so let's look at it step-by-step.

OPENING TO VOCAL SAC

OPENING TO THE ESOPHAGUS

At rest the tongue is folded over itself.

The frog's tongue is attached to the front of its mouth—when deployed, it flips outward toward its prey.

NOSTRIL

INTERNAL NOSTRIL OPENING

MANDIBLE

Once struck, the tongue pulls the prey back toward the mouth...

EYE SOCKET

EYE SOCKET

EUSTACHIAN TUBE

...and deposits it at the gullet opening.

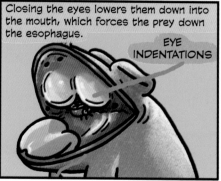

Closing the eyes lowers them down into the mouth, which forces the prey down the esophagus.

EYE INDENTATIONS

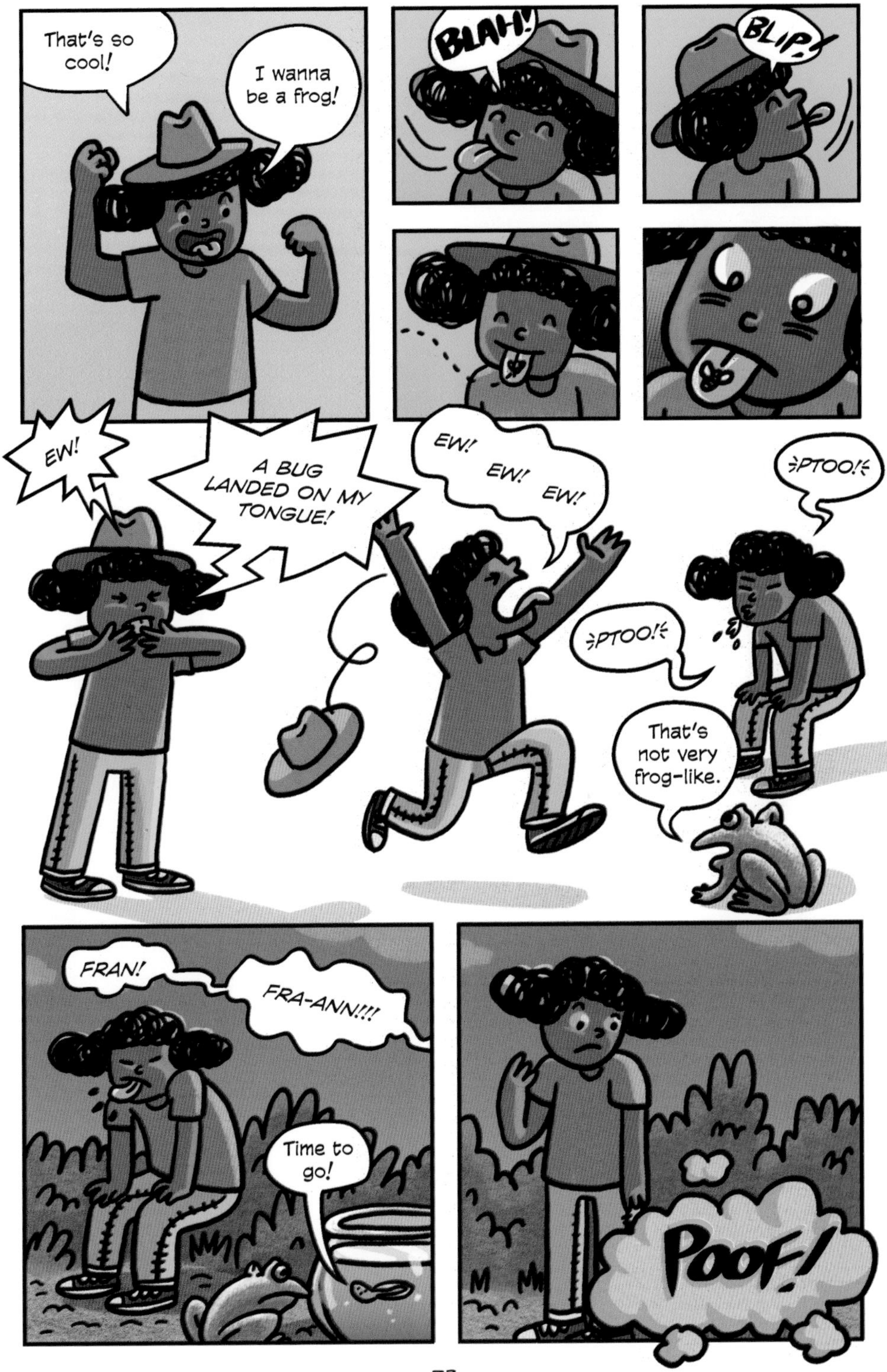
That's so cool!
I wanna be a frog!
BLAH!
BLIP!
EW!
A BUG LANDED ON MY TONGUE!
EW! EW! EW!
PTOO!
PTOO!
That's not very frog-like.
FRAN!
FRA-ANN!!!
Time to go!
POOF!

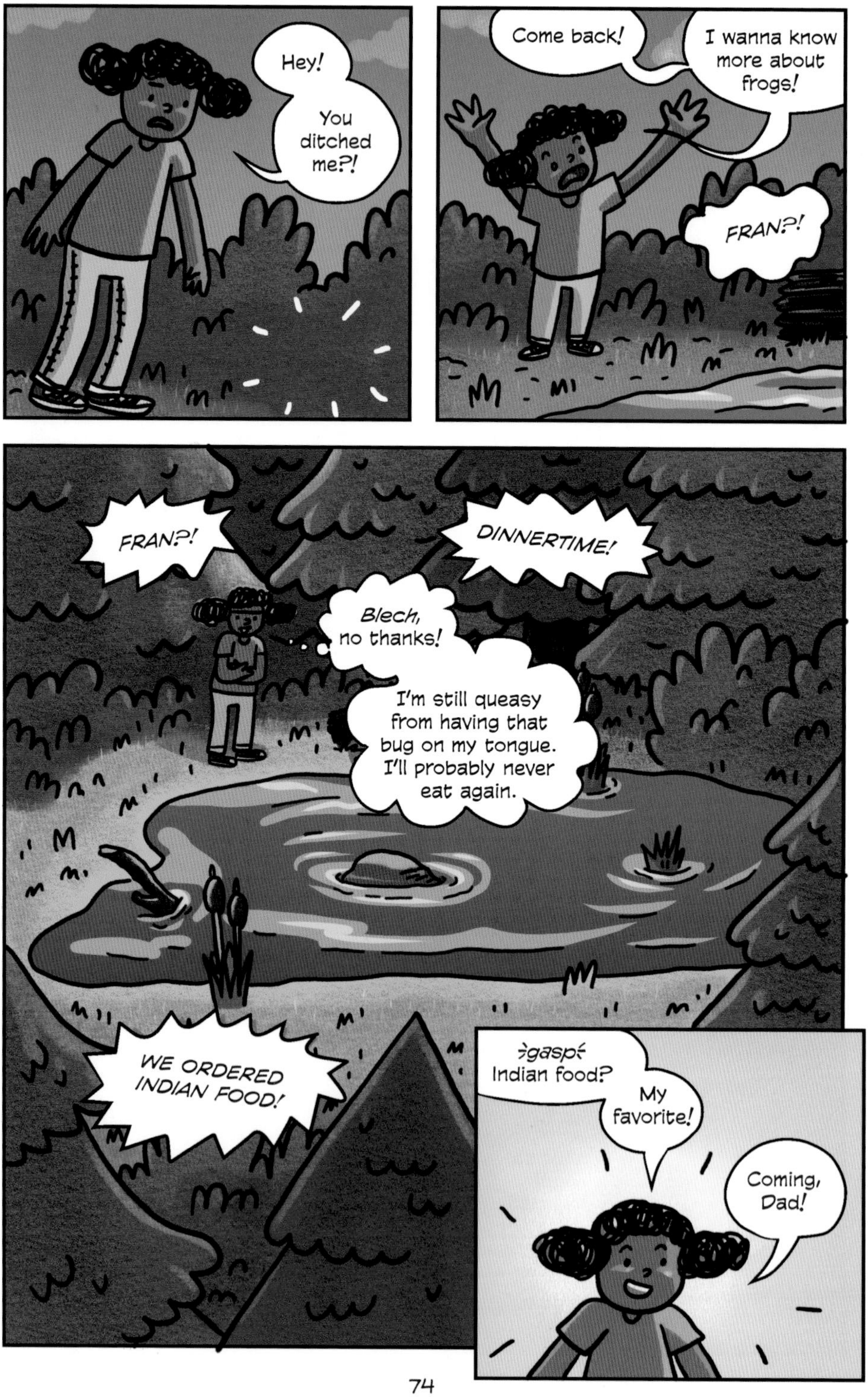
Hey!
You ditched me?!
Come back!
I wanna know more about frogs!
FRAN?!
FRAN?!
DINNERTIME!
Blech, no thanks!
I'm still queasy from having that bug on my tongue. I'll probably never eat again.
WE ORDERED INDIAN FOOD!
gasp Indian food?
My favorite!
Coming, Dad!

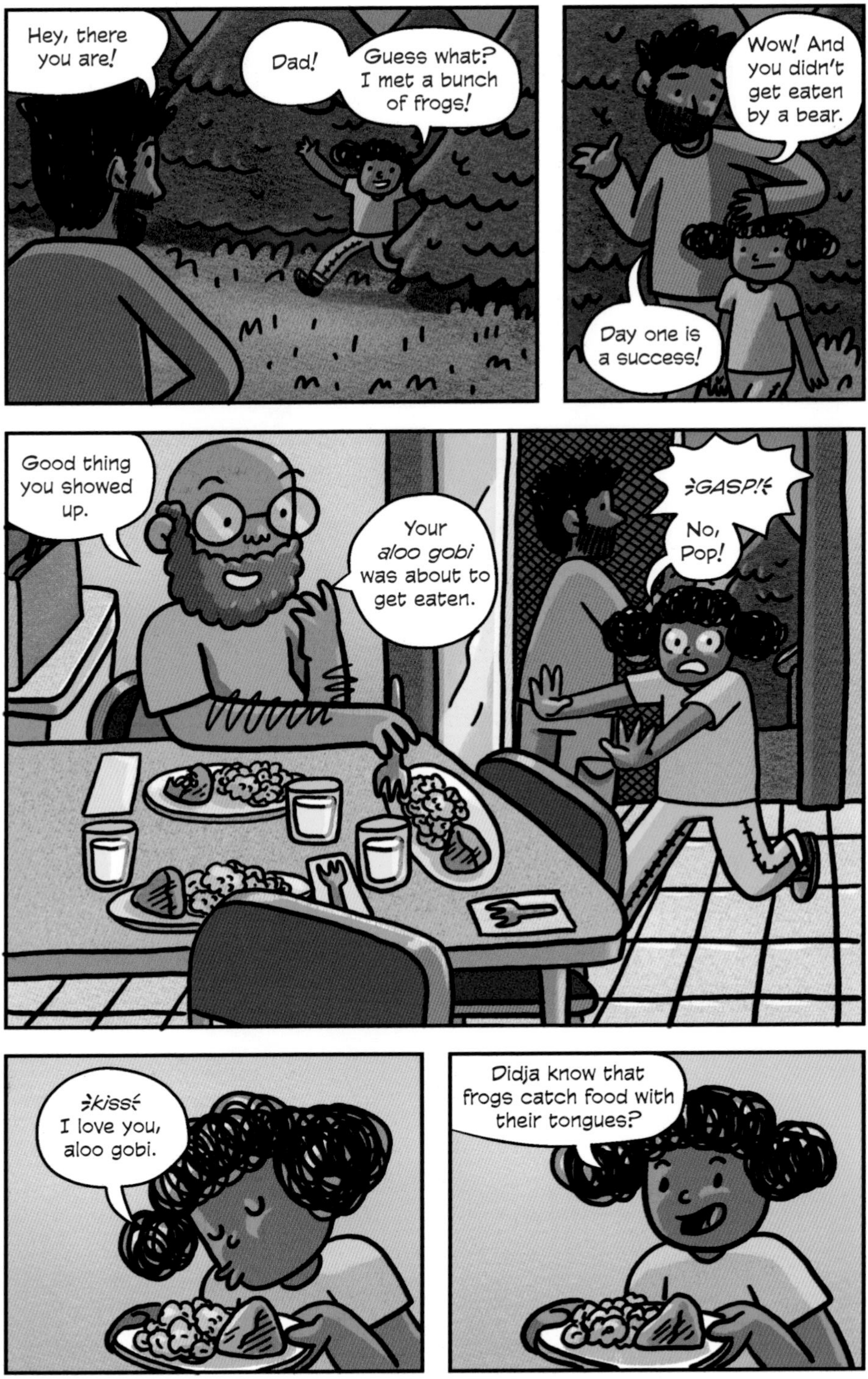
Hey, there you are!
Dad!
Guess what? I met a bunch of frogs!
Wow! And you didn't get eaten by a bear.
Day one is a success!
Good thing you showed up.
Your *aloo gobi* was about to get eaten.
GASP!
No, Pop!
kiss
I love you, aloo gobi.
Didja know that frogs catch food with their tongues?

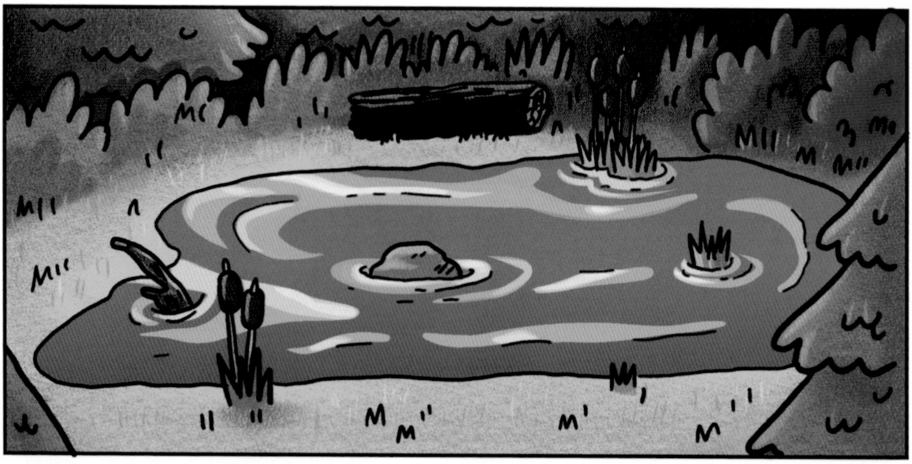

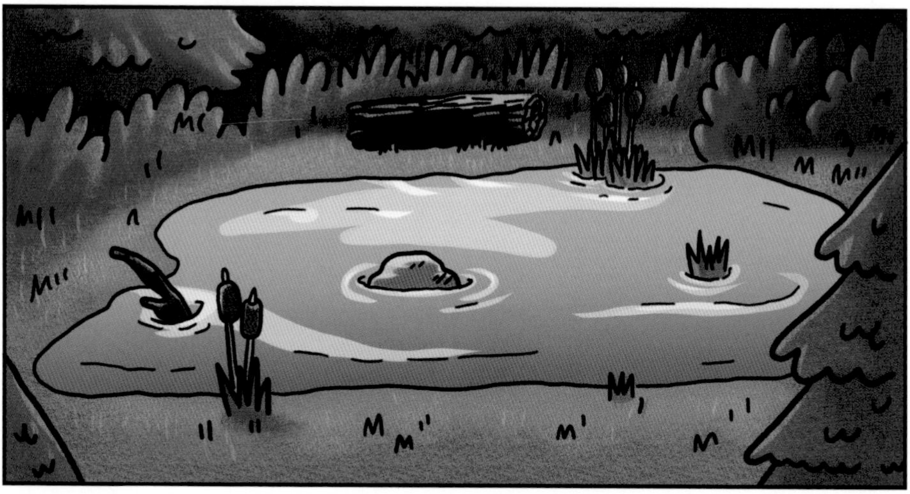

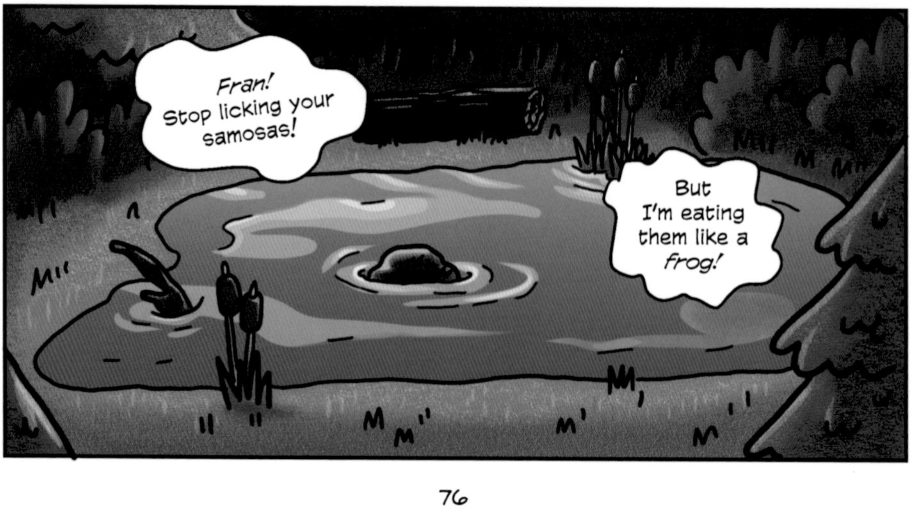
Fran! Stop licking your samosas!
But I'm eating them like a *frog!*

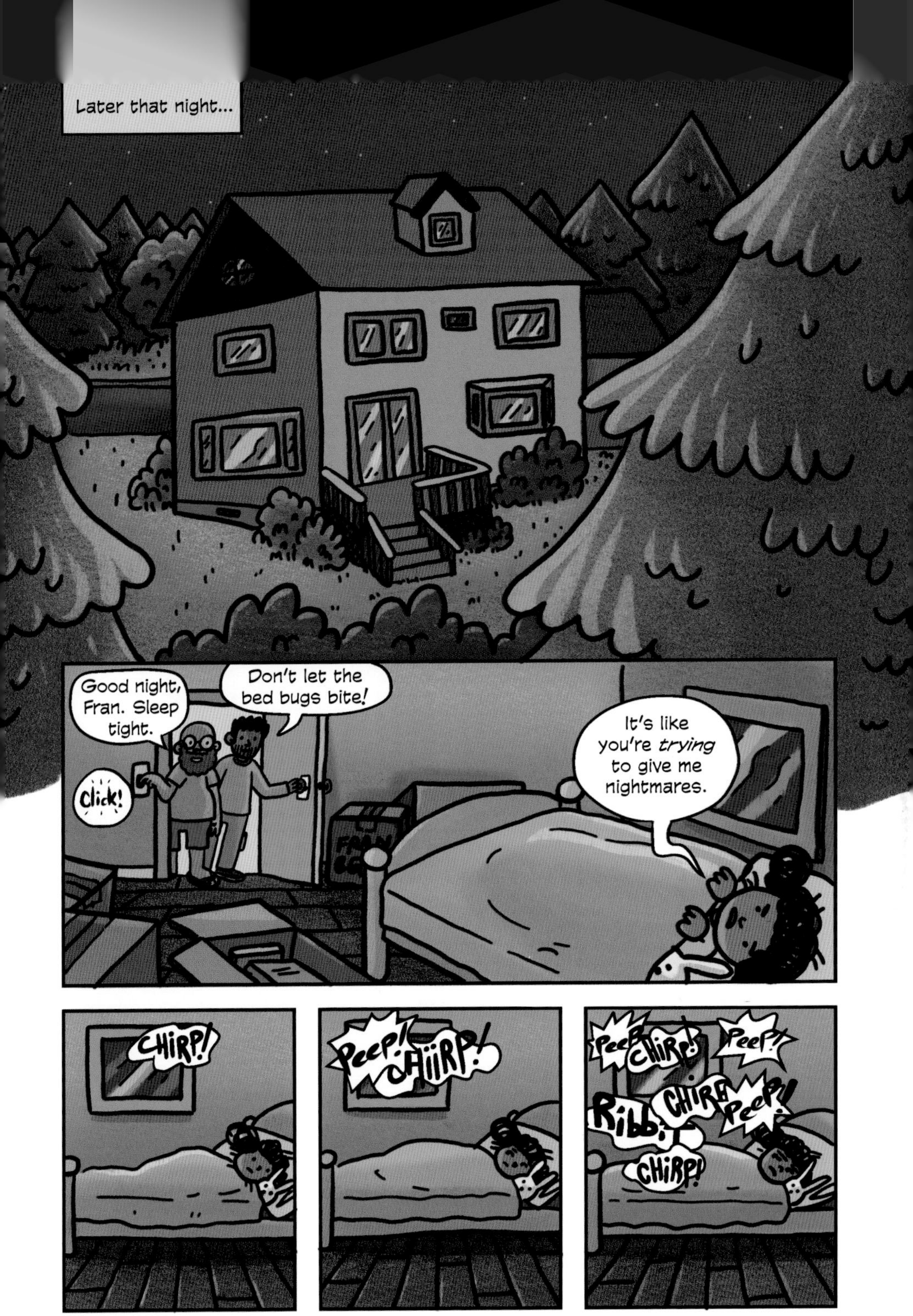
Later that night...
Good night, Fran. Sleep tight.
Don't let the bed bugs bite!
Click!
It's like you're *trying* to give me nightmares.
CHIRP!
Peep!
CHIIRP!
CHIRP!
Peep!
Ribb
Peep!
CHIRP!

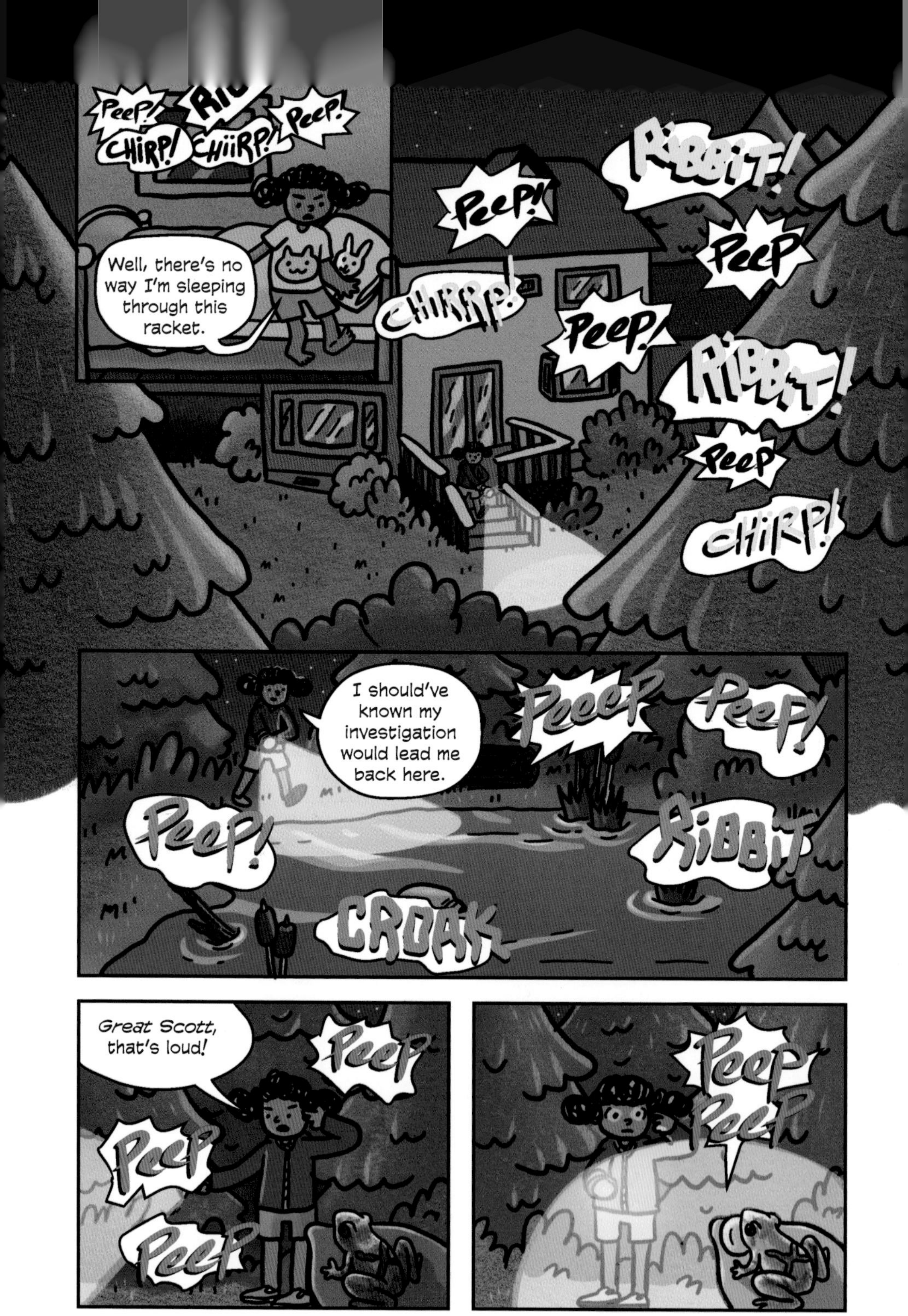
Peep!
CHIRP!
CHIIRP!
Peep!
Well, there's no way I'm sleeping through this racket.
PEEP!
RIBBIT!
CHIRRP!
PEEP
PEEP!
RIBBIT!
PEEP
CHIRP!
I should've known my investigation would lead me back here.
PEEEP
PEEP!
PEEP!
RIBBIT
CROAK
Great Scott, that's loud!
PEEP
PEEP
PEEP
PEEP
PEEP

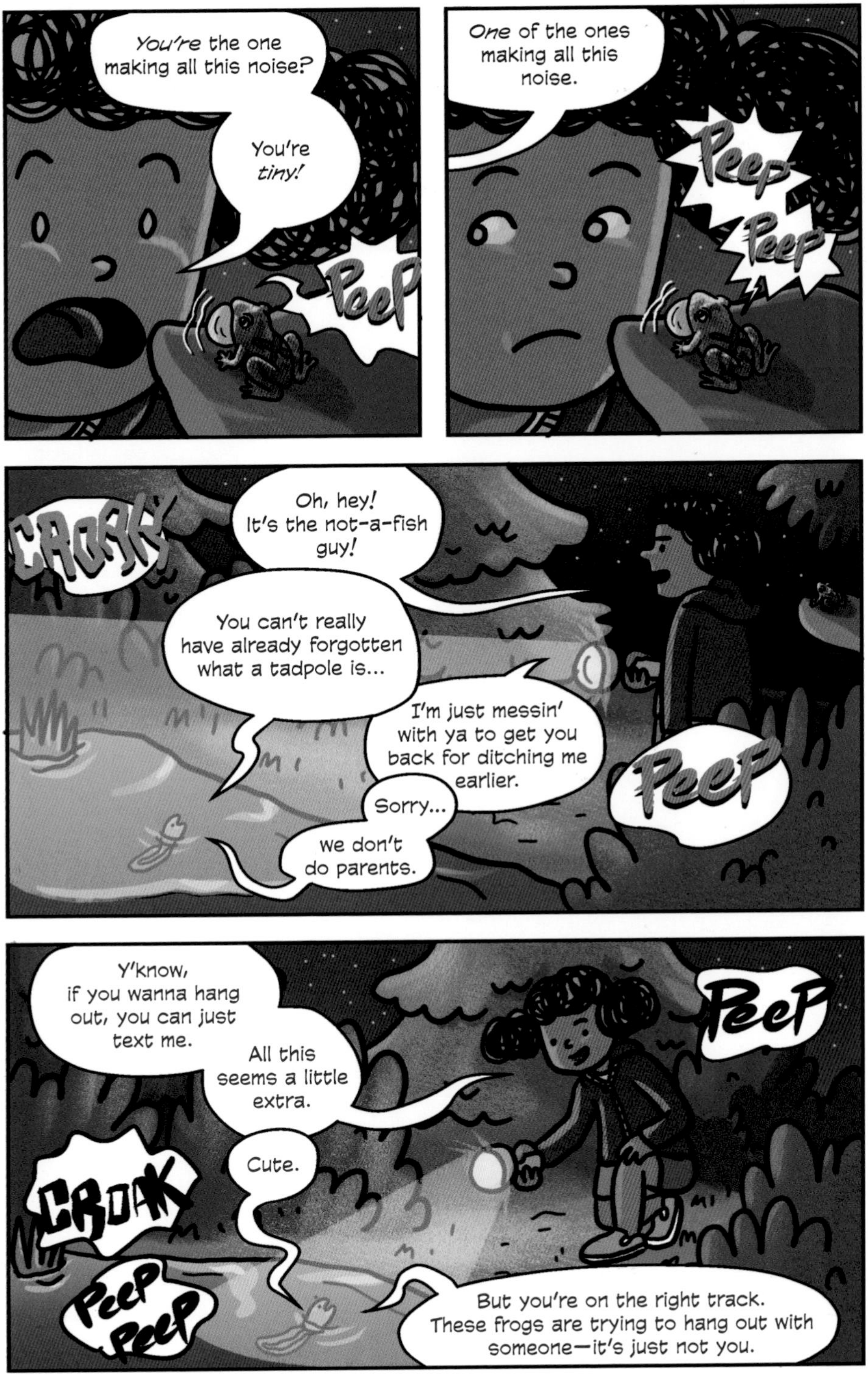
You're the one making all this noise?
You're tiny!
PEEP
One of the ones making all this noise.
PEEP
PEEP
CROAK
Oh, hey! It's the not-a-fish guy!
You can't really have already forgotten what a tadpole is...
I'm just messin' with ya to get you back for ditching me earlier.
PEEP
Sorry...
we don't do parents.
Y'know, if you wanna hang out, you can just text me.
All this seems a little extra.
PEEP
Cute.
CROAK
PEEP PEEP
But you're on the right track. These frogs are trying to hang out with someone—it's just not you.

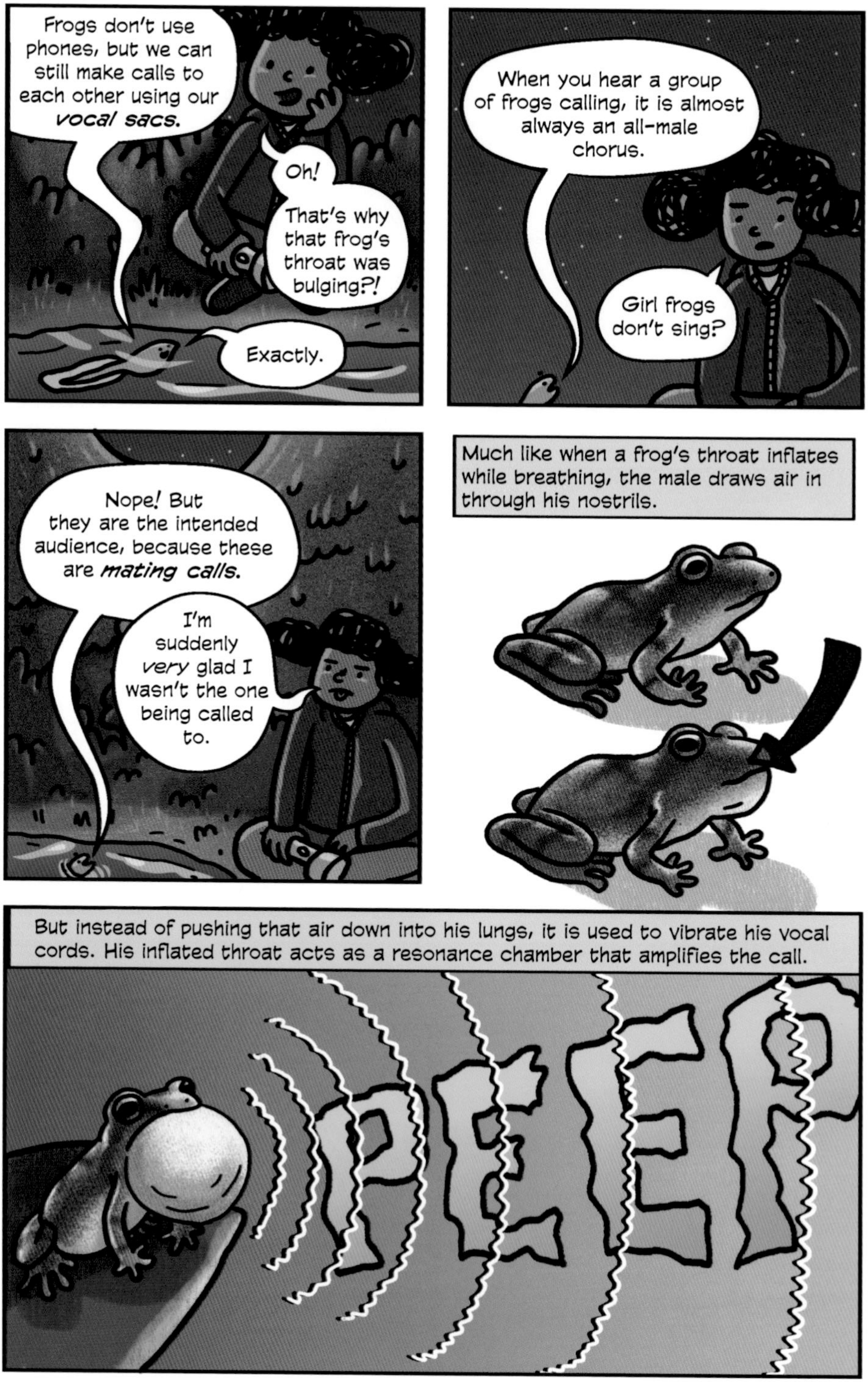
Frogs don't use phones, but we can still make calls to each other using our *vocal sacs.*
Oh!
That's why that frog's throat was bulging?!
Exactly.
When you hear a group of frogs calling, it is almost always an all-male chorus.
Girl frogs don't sing?
Nope! But they are the intended audience, because these are *mating calls.*
I'm suddenly *very* glad I wasn't the one being called to.
Much like when a frog's throat inflates while breathing, the male draws air in through his nostrils.
But instead of pushing that air down into his lungs, it is used to vibrate his vocal cords. His inflated throat acts as a resonance chamber that amplifies the call.
PEEP

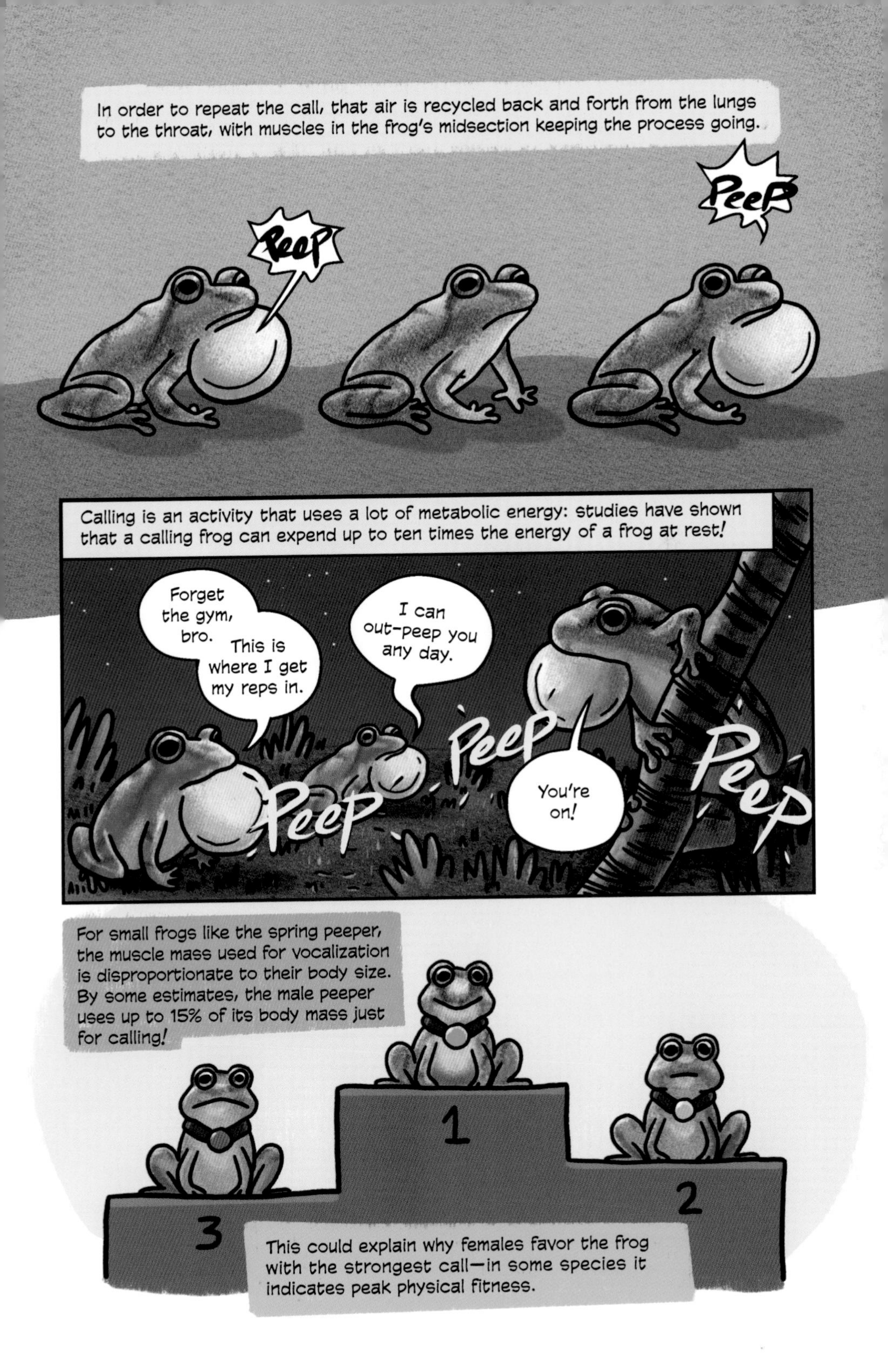
In order to repeat the call, that air is recycled back and forth from the lungs to the throat, with muscles in the frog's midsection keeping the process going.
PEEP
PEEP
Calling is an activity that uses a lot of metabolic energy: studies have shown that a calling frog can expend up to ten times the energy of a frog at rest!
Forget the gym, bro. This is where I get my reps in.
I can out-peep you any day.
Peep
Peep
You're on!
Peep
For small frogs like the spring peeper, the muscle mass used for vocalization is disproportionate to their body size. By some estimates, the male peeper uses up to 15% of its body mass just for calling!
1
2
3
This could explain why females favor the frog with the strongest call—in some species it indicates peak physical fitness.

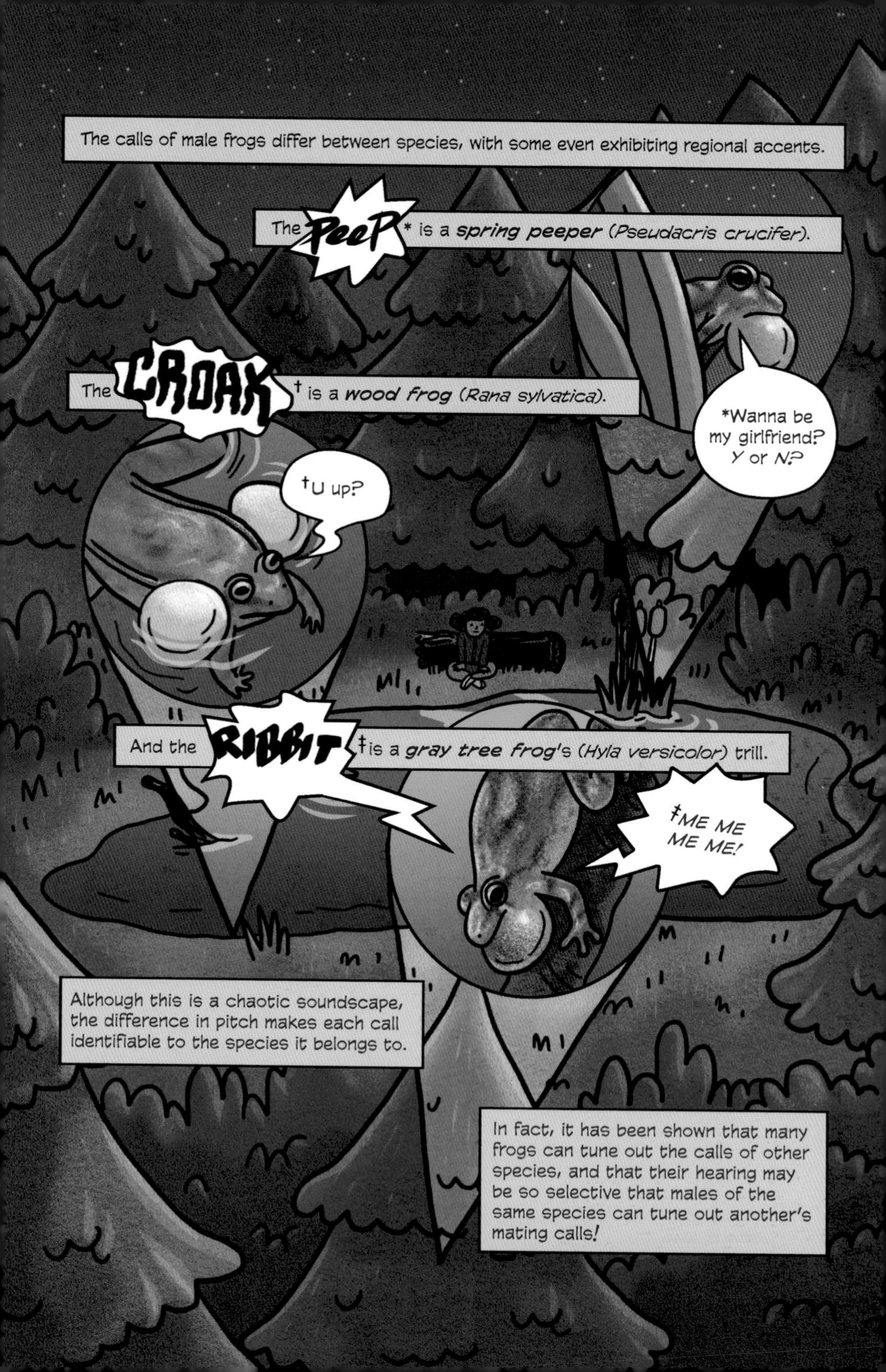

The calls of male frogs differ between species, with some even exhibiting regional accents.
The PEEP* is a spring peeper (Pseudacris crucifer).
*Wanna be my girlfriend? Y or N?
The CROAK† is a wood frog (Rana sylvatica).
†U up?
And the RIBBIT‡ is a gray tree frog's (Hyla versicolor) trill.
‡ME ME ME ME!
Although this is a chaotic soundscape, the difference in pitch makes each call identifiable to the species it belongs to.
In fact, it has been shown that many frogs can tune out the calls of other species, and that their hearing may be so selective that males of the same species can tune out another's mating calls!

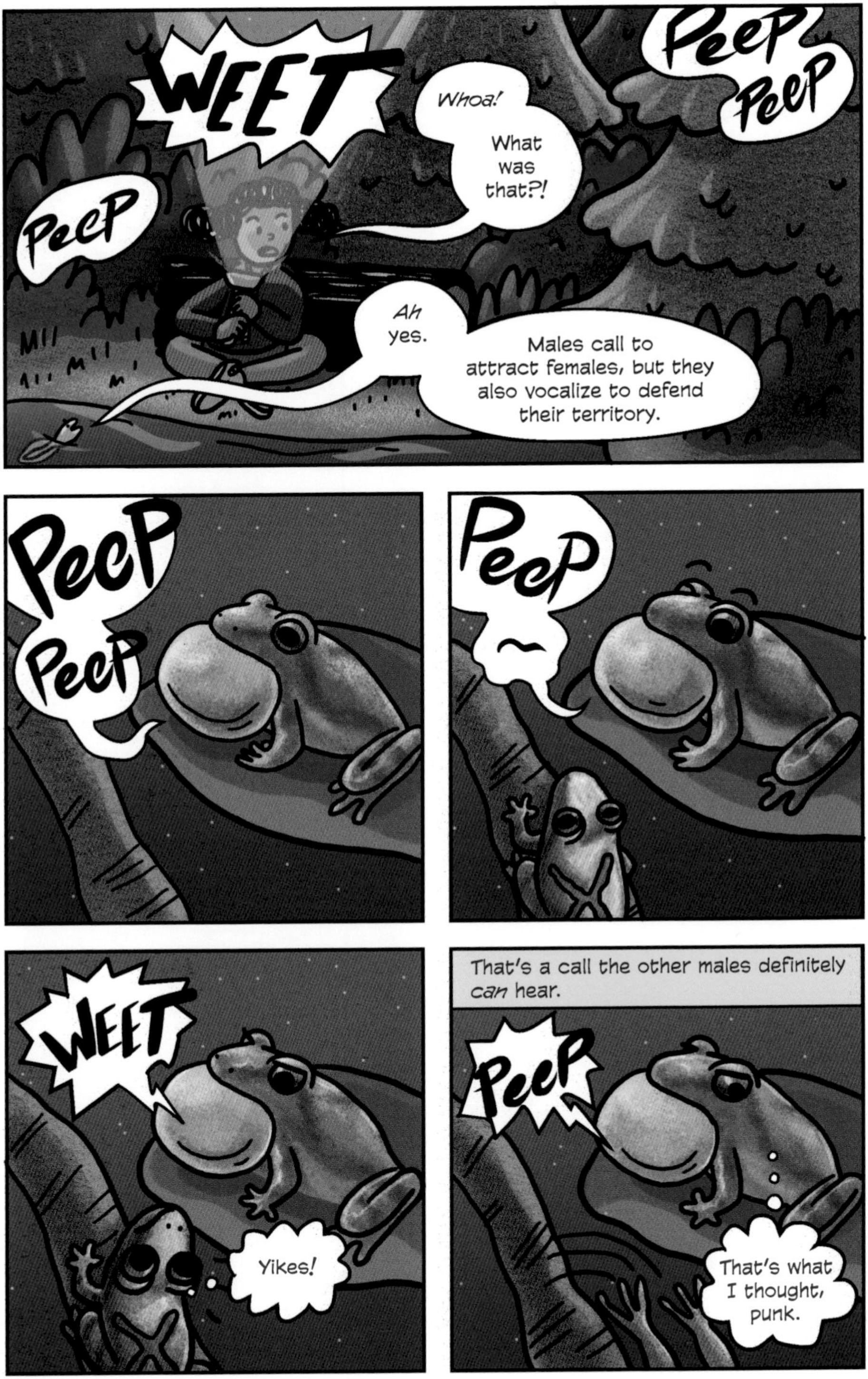
WEET
Peep
Whoa!
What was that?!
Peep Peep
Ah yes.
Males call to attract females, but they also vocalize to defend their territory.
Peep
Peep
Peep
~
WEET
Yikes!
That's a call the other males definitely *can* hear.
Peep
That's what I thought, punk.

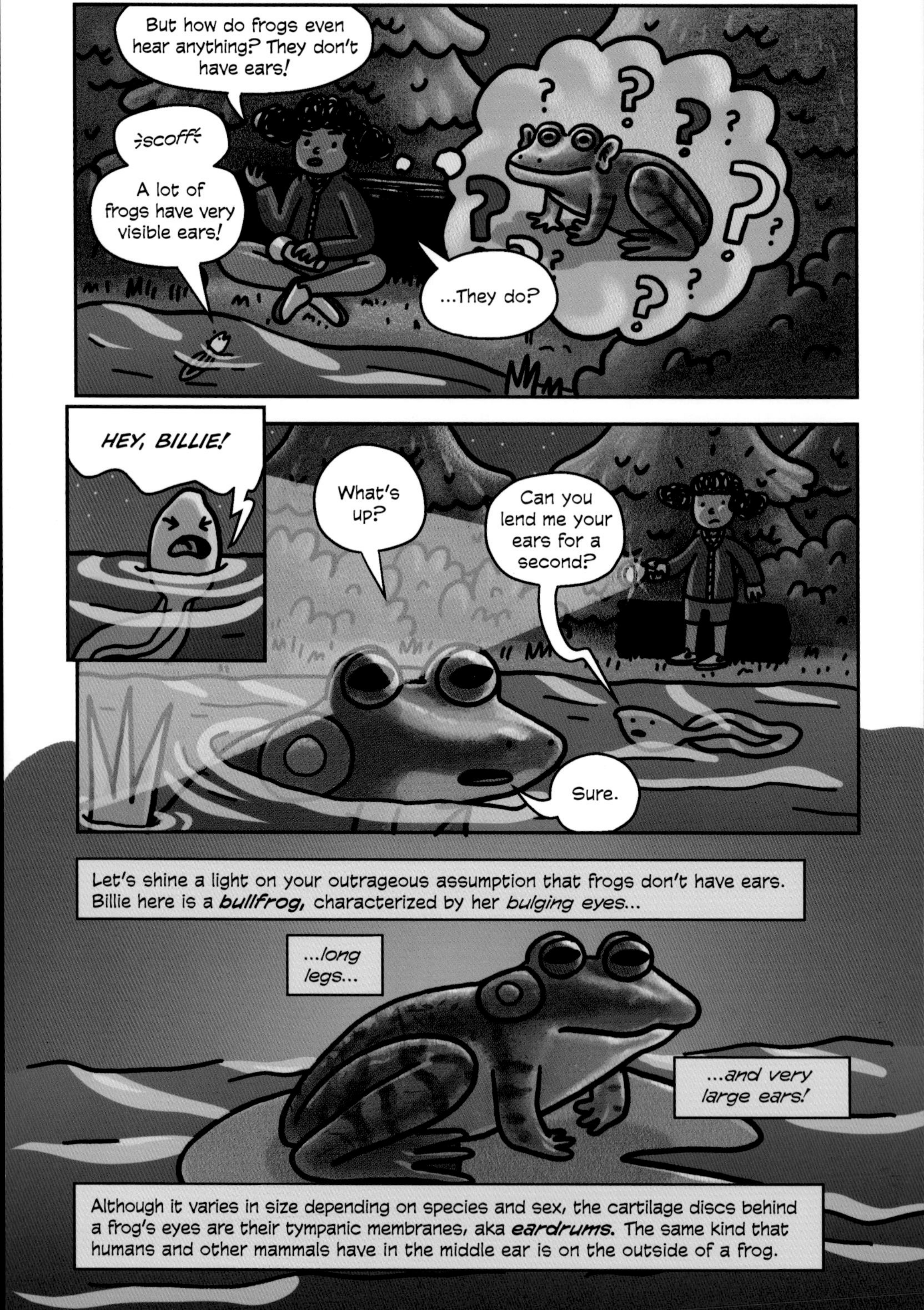
But how do frogs even hear anything? They don't have ears!
⪢scoff⪡
A lot of frogs have very visible ears!
...They do?
HEY, BILLIE!
What's up?
Can you lend me your ears for a second?
Sure.
Let's shine a light on your outrageous assumption that frogs don't have ears. Billie here is a ***bullfrog,*** characterized by her *bulging eyes*...
...long legs...
...and very large ears!
Although it varies in size depending on species and sex, the cartilage discs behind a frog's eyes are their tympanic membranes, aka ***eardrums.*** The same kind that humans and other mammals have in the middle ear is on the outside of a frog.

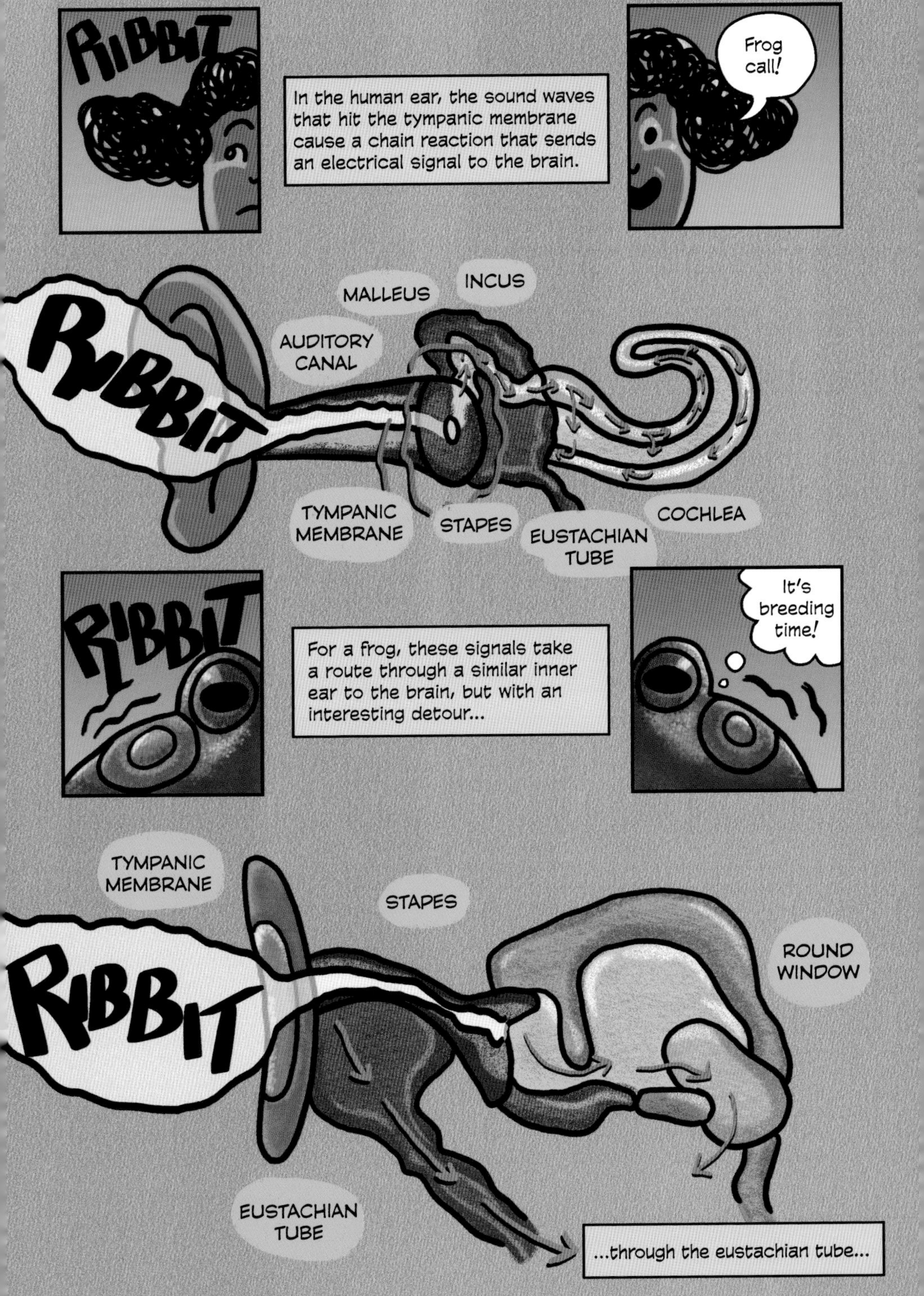
RIBBIT
In the human ear, the sound waves that hit the tympanic membrane cause a chain reaction that sends an electrical signal to the brain.
Frog call!
RIBBIT
MALLEUS
INCUS
AUDITORY CANAL
TYMPANIC MEMBRANE
STAPES
EUSTACHIAN TUBE
COCHLEA
RIBBIT
For a frog, these signals take a route through a similar inner ear to the brain, but with an interesting detour...
It's breeding time!
TYMPANIC MEMBRANE
STAPES
RIBBIT
ROUND WINDOW
EUSTACHIAN TUBE
...through the eustachian tube...

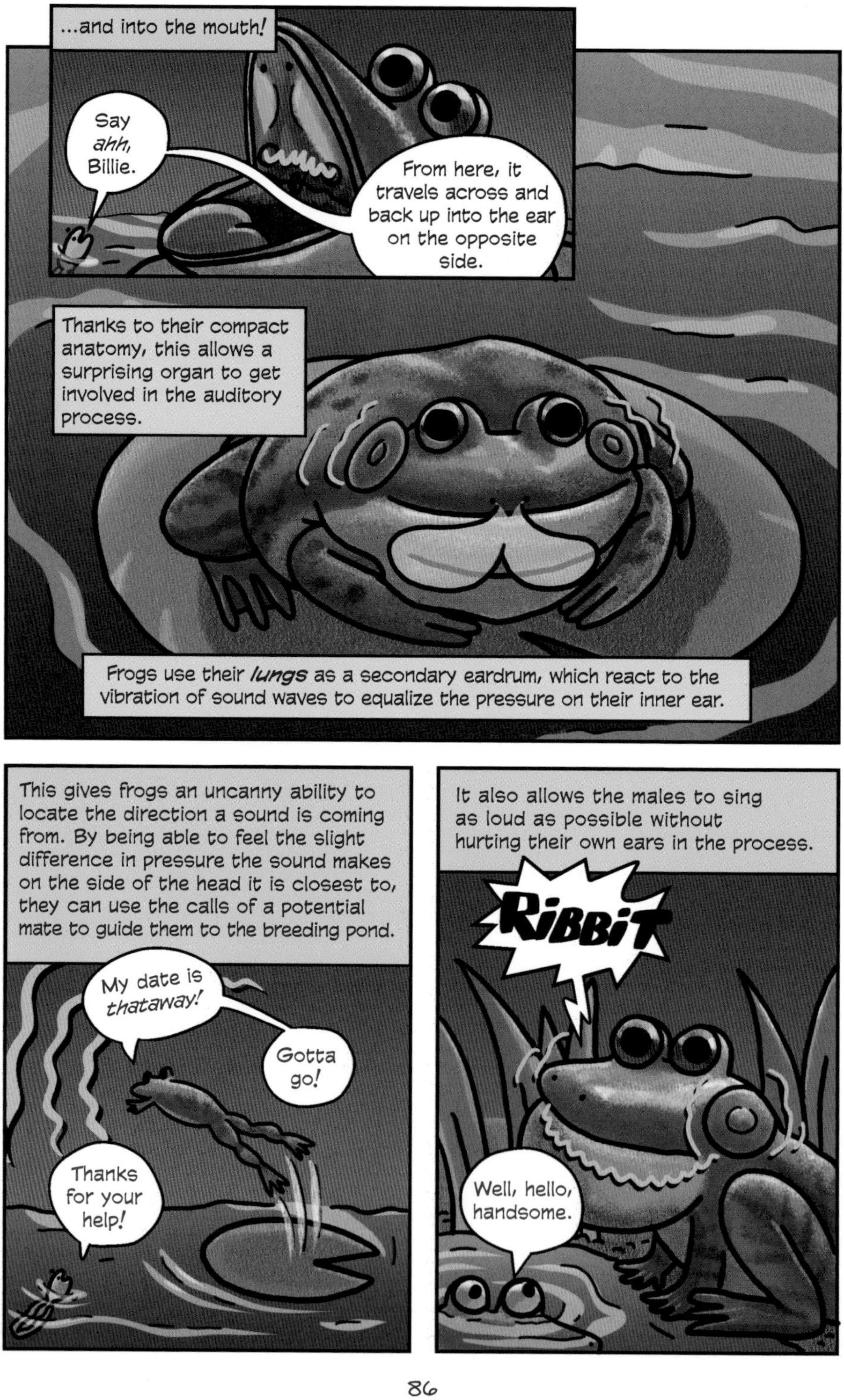
...and into the mouth!
Say *ahh*, Billie.
From here, it travels across and back up into the ear on the opposite side.
Thanks to their compact anatomy, this allows a surprising organ to get involved in the auditory process.
Frogs use their *lungs* as a secondary eardrum, which react to the vibration of sound waves to equalize the pressure on their inner ear.
This gives frogs an uncanny ability to locate the direction a sound is coming from. By being able to feel the slight difference in pressure the sound makes on the side of the head it is closest to, they can use the calls of a potential mate to guide them to the breeding pond.
My date is *thataway!*
Gotta go!
Thanks for your help!
It also allows the males to sing as loud as possible without hurting their own ears in the process.
RIBBIT
Well, hello, handsome.

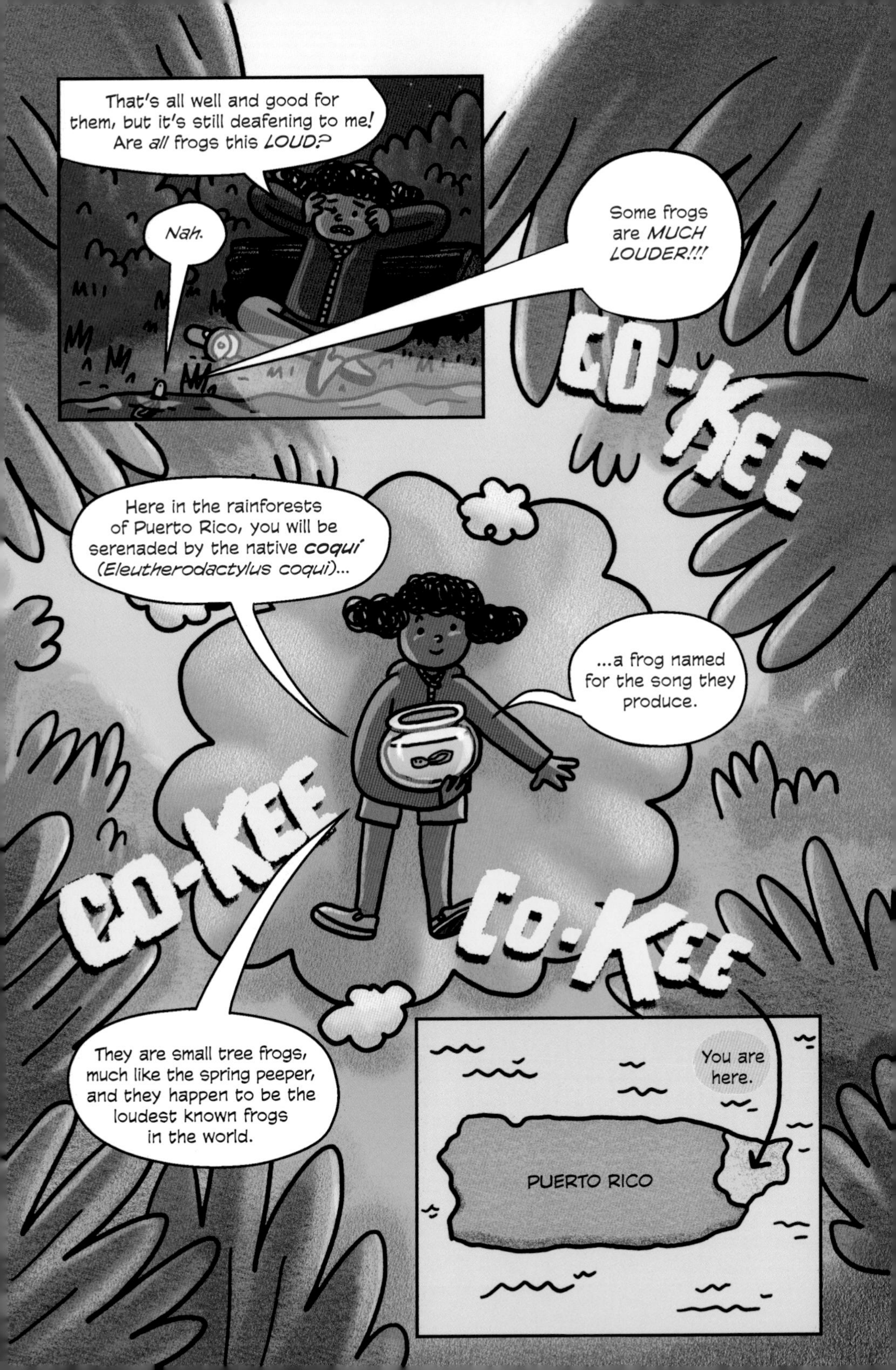
That's all well and good for them, but it's still deafening to me! Are *all* frogs this *LOUD?*
Nah.
Some frogs are *MUCH LOUDER!!!*
CO-KEE
Here in the rainforests of Puerto Rico, you will be serenaded by the native ***coquí*** (*Eleutherodactylus coqui*)...
...a frog named for the song they produce.
CO-KEE
CO-KEE
They are small tree frogs, much like the spring peeper, and they happen to be the loudest known frogs in the world.
You are here.
PUERTO RICO

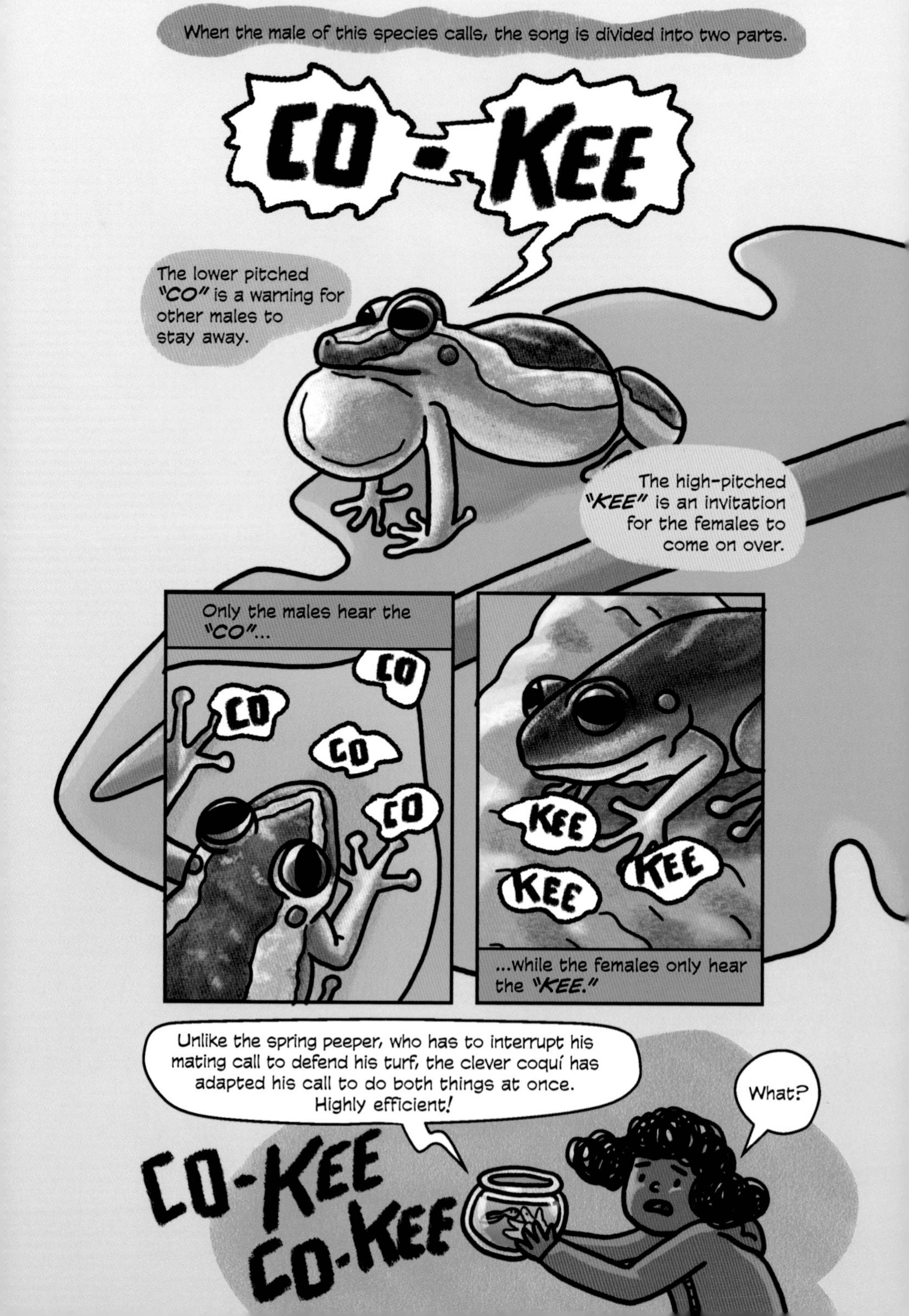
When the male of this species calls, the song is divided into two parts.
CO-KEE
The lower pitched "CO" is a warning for other males to stay away.
The high-pitched "KEE" is an invitation for the females to come on over.
Only the males hear the "CO"...
CO
CO
CO
CO
KEE
KEE
KEE
...while the females only hear the "KEE."
Unlike the spring peeper, who has to interrupt his mating call to defend his turf, the clever coquí has adapted his call to do both things at once. Highly efficient!
What?
CO-KEE CO-KEE

Okay, I can take a hint. If we make a trip to the island of Borneo in Southeast Asia, we can meet a frog who is a little quieter.

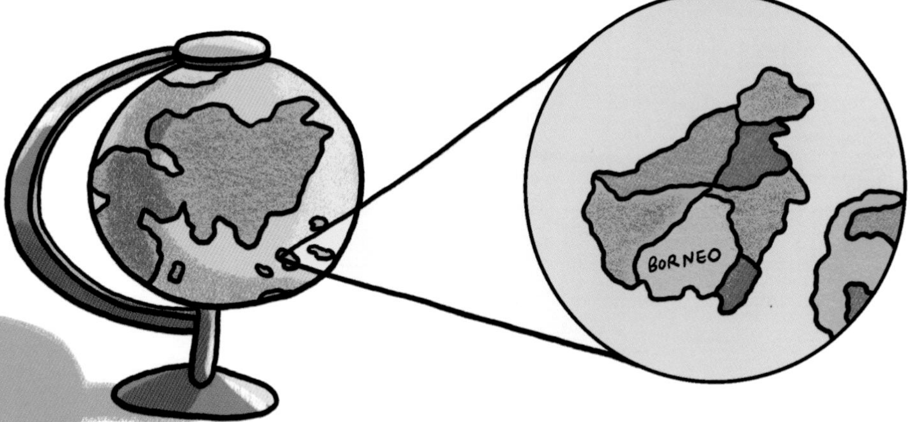
BORNEO

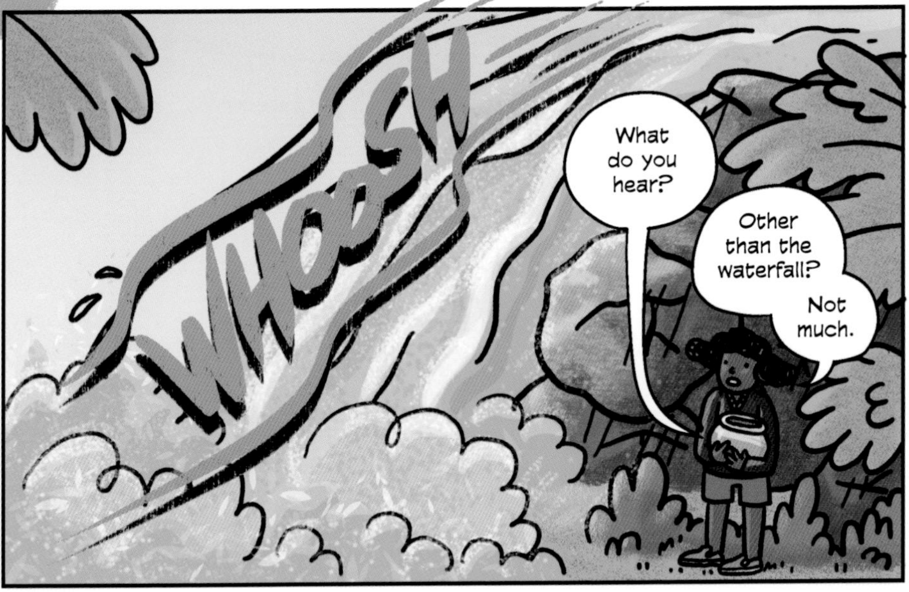
WHOOSH
What do you hear?
Other than the waterfall?
Not much.

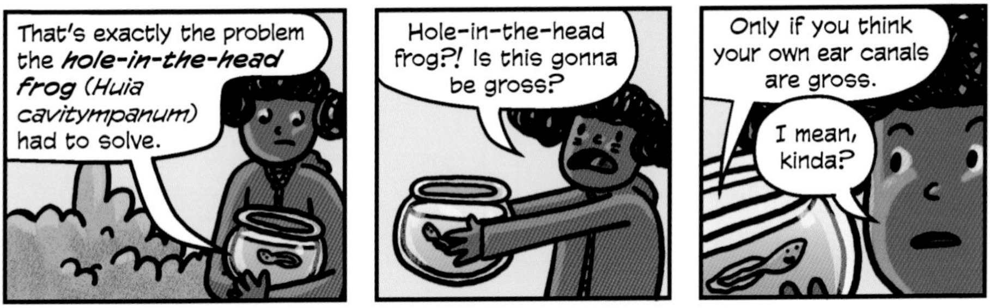
That's exactly the problem the ***hole-in-the-head frog*** (*Huia cavitympanum*) had to solve.
Hole-in-the-head frog?! Is this gonna be gross?
Only if you think your own ear canals are gross.
I mean, kinda?

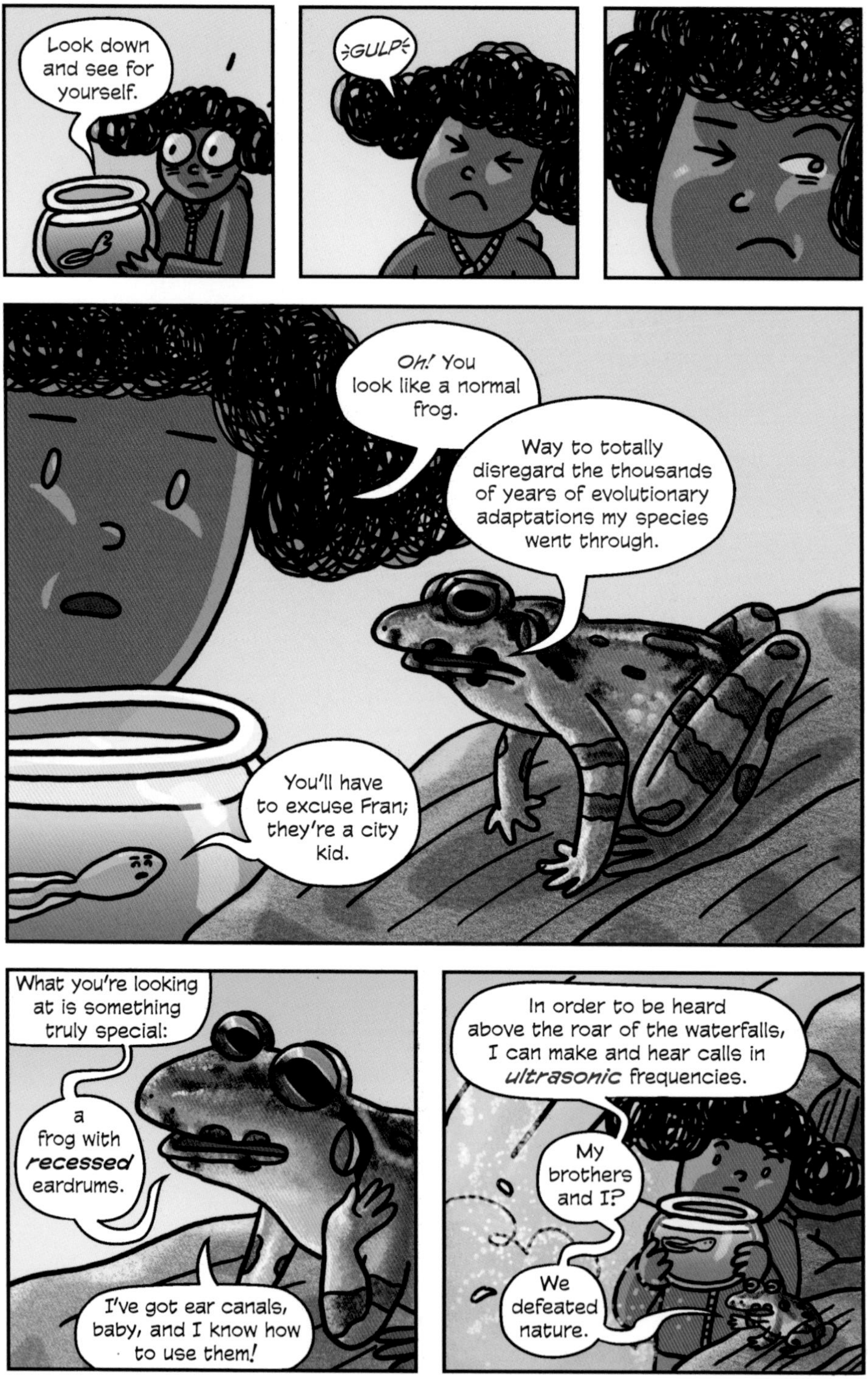

Look down and see for yourself.
GULP
Oh! You look like a normal frog.
Way to totally disregard the thousands of years of evolutionary adaptations my species went through.
You'll have to excuse Fran; they're a city kid.
What you're looking at is something truly special:
a frog with *recessed* eardrums.
I've got ear canals, baby, and I know how to use them!
In order to be heard above the roar of the waterfalls, I can make and hear calls in *ultrasonic* frequencies.
My brothers and I?
We defeated nature.

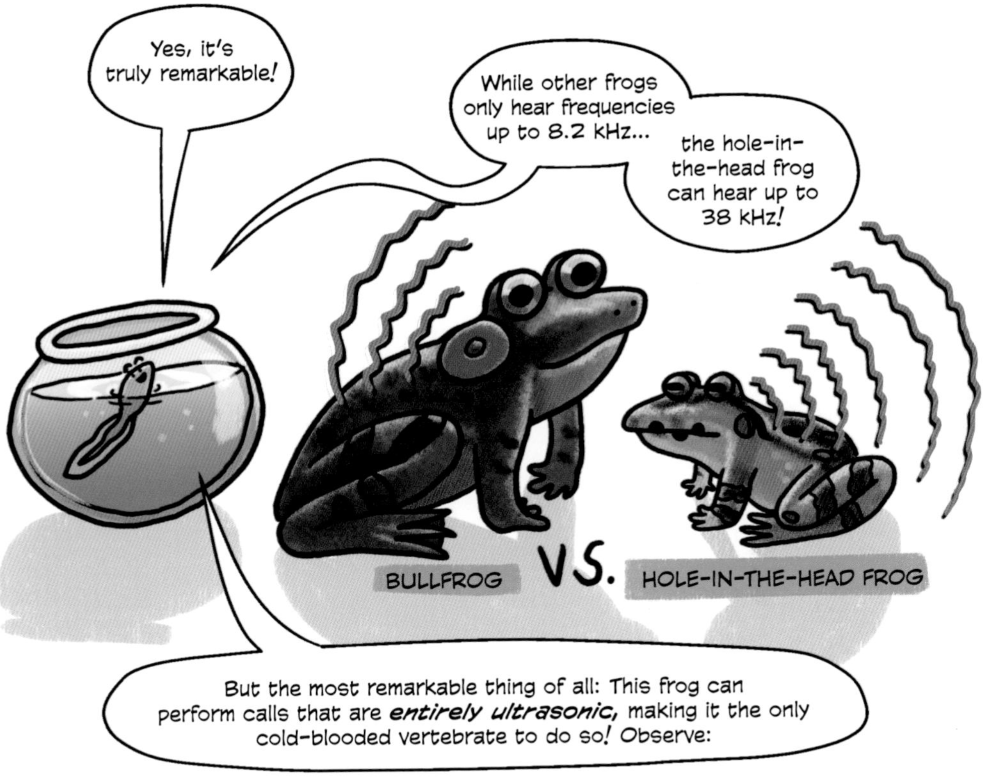
Yes, it's truly remarkable!
While other frogs only hear frequencies up to 8.2 kHz...
the hole-in-the-head frog can hear up to 38 kHz!
BULLFROG
VS.
HOLE-IN-THE-HEAD FROG
But the most remarkable thing of all: This frog can perform calls that are *entirely ultrasonic,* making it the only cold-blooded vertebrate to do so! Observe:

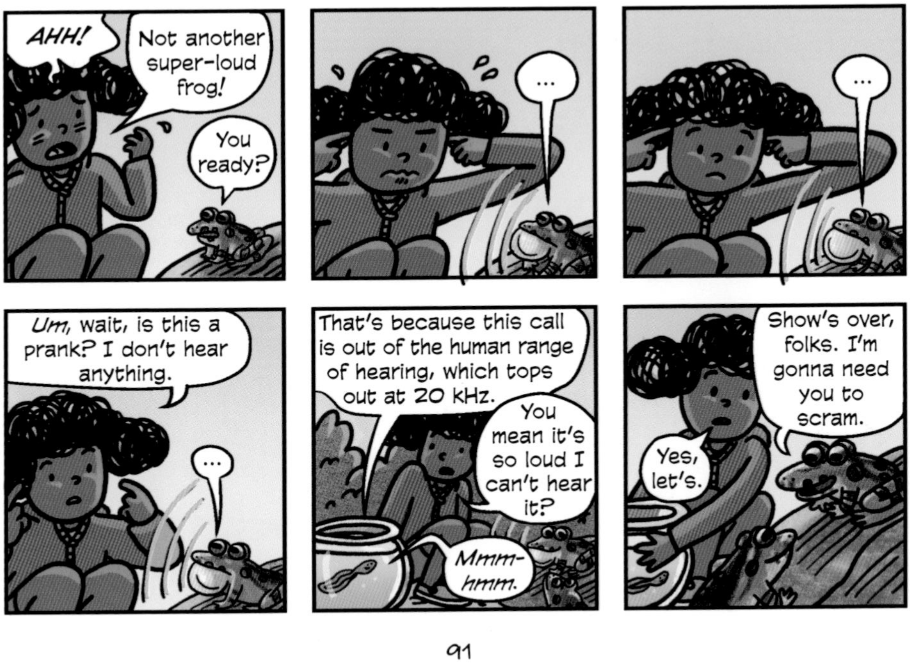
AHH!
Not another super-loud frog!
You ready?
...
...
Um, wait, is this a prank? I don't hear anything.
...
That's because this call is out of the human range of hearing, which tops out at 20 kHz.
You mean it's so loud I can't hear it?
Mmm-hmm.
Show's over, folks. I'm gonna need you to scram.
Yes, let's.

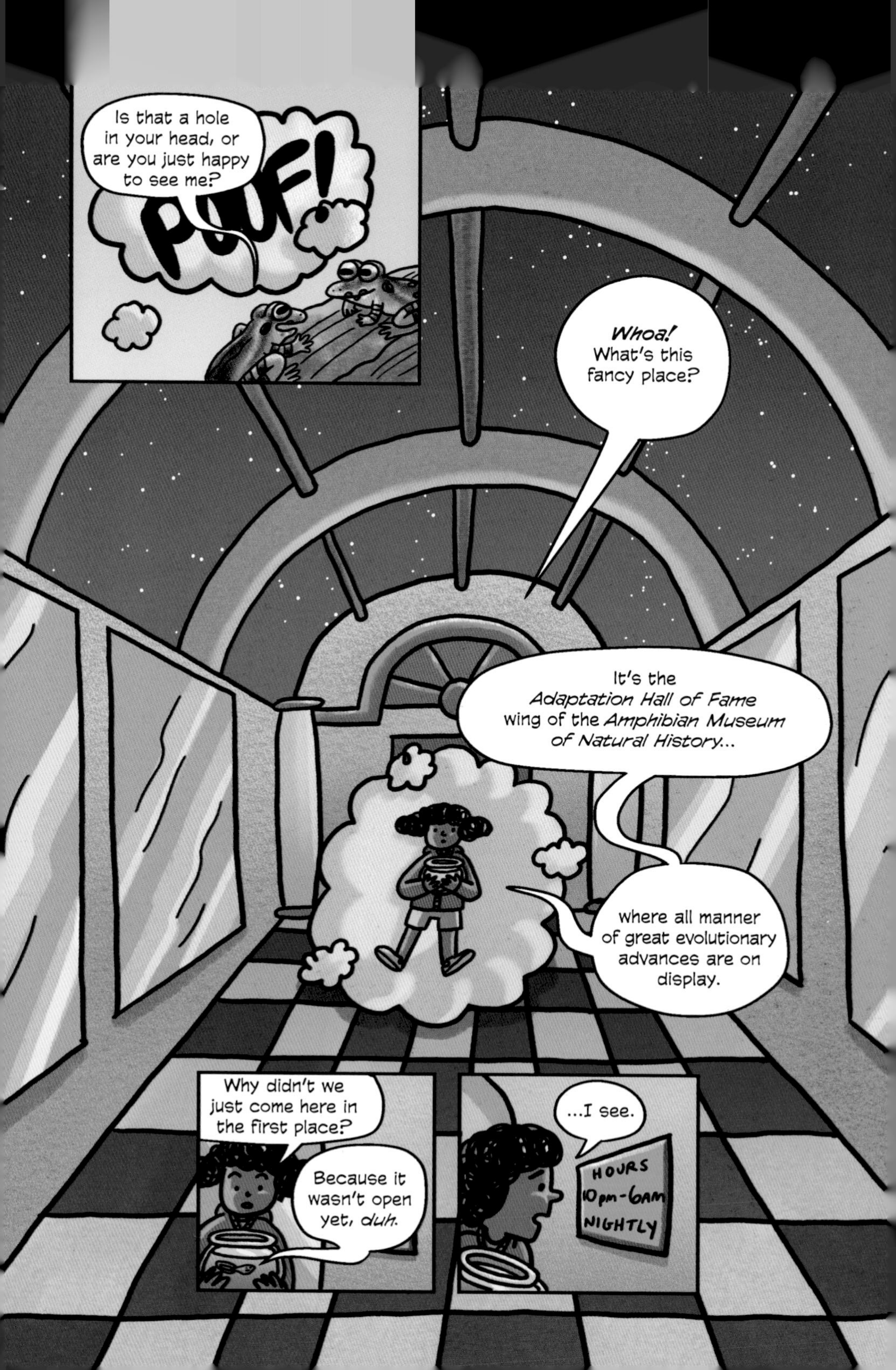
Is that a hole in your head, or are you just happy to see me?
POOF!
Whoa! What's this fancy place?
It's the Adaptation Hall of Fame wing of the Amphibian Museum of Natural History...
where all manner of great evolutionary advances are on display.
Why didn't we just come here in the first place?
Because it wasn't open yet, duh.
...I see.
HOURS
10pm-6AM
NIGHTLY

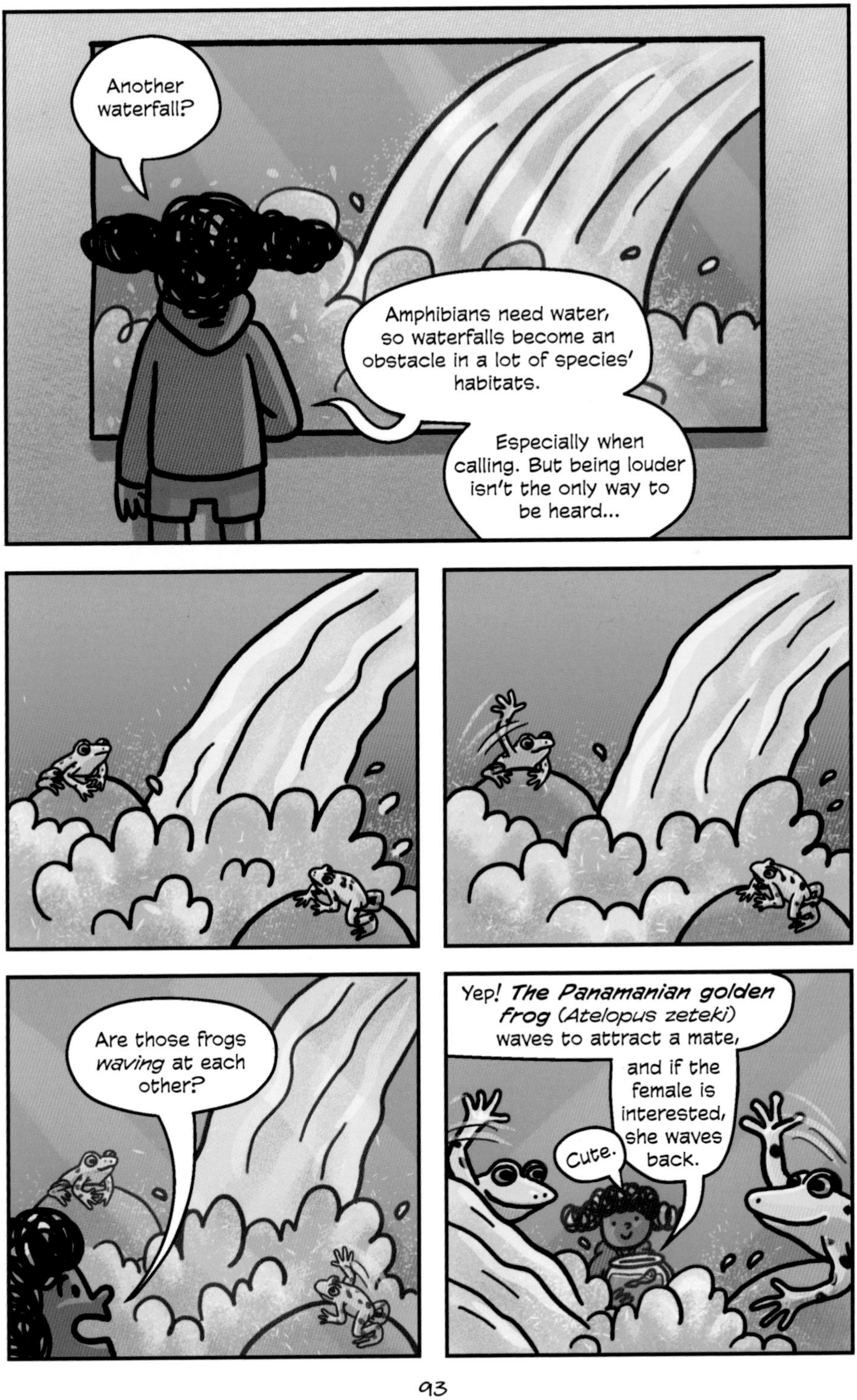
Another waterfall?
Amphibians need water, so waterfalls become an obstacle in a lot of species' habitats.
Especially when calling. But being louder isn't the only way to be heard...
Are those frogs *waving* at each other?
Yep! ***The Panamanian golden frog*** *(Atelopus zeteki)* waves to attract a mate,
and if the female is interested, she waves back.
Cute.

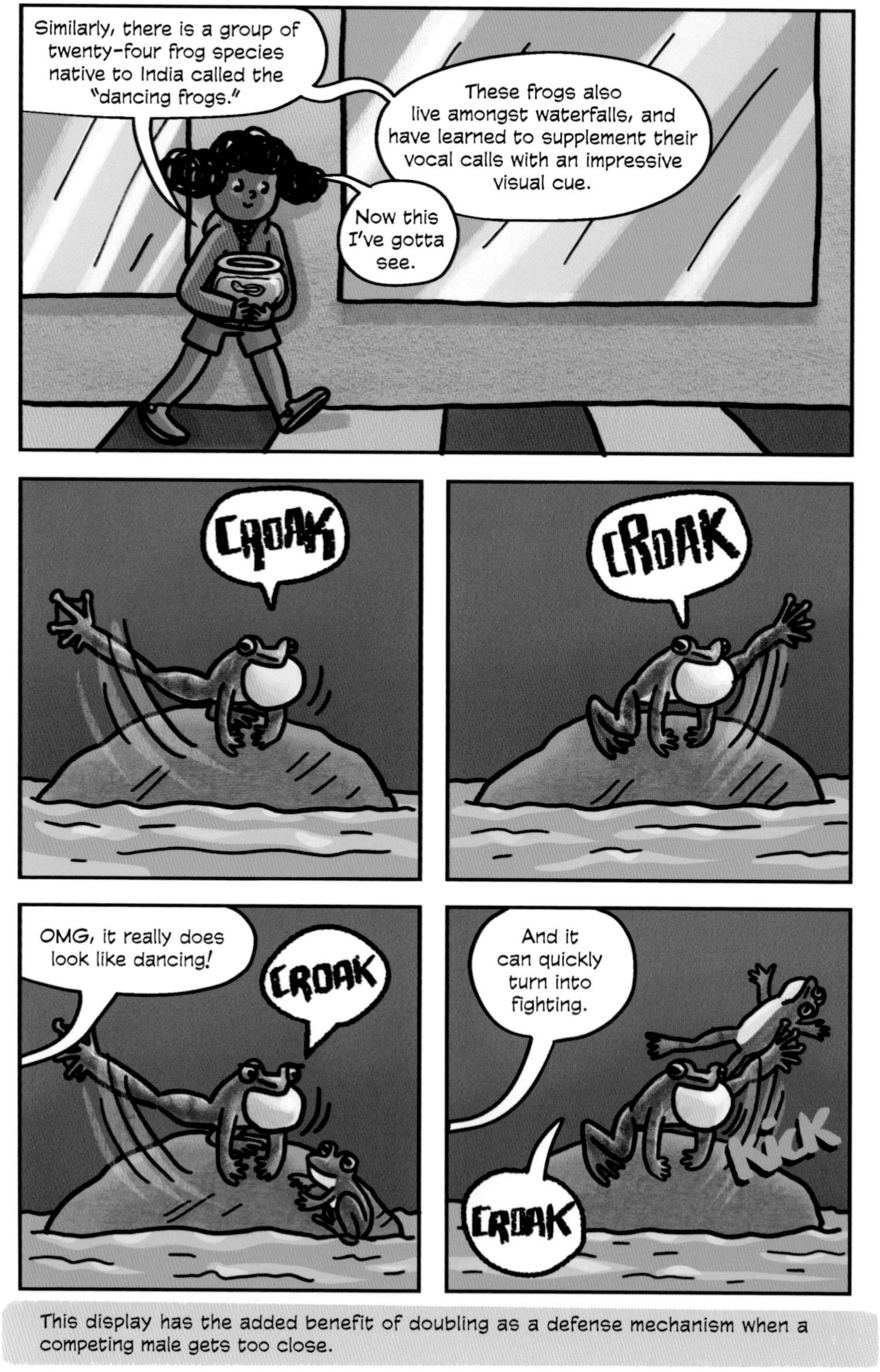
Similarly, there is a group of twenty-four frog species native to India called the "dancing frogs."
These frogs also live amongst waterfalls, and have learned to supplement their vocal calls with an impressive visual cue.
Now this I've gotta see.
CROAK
CROAK
OMG, it really does look like dancing!
CROAK
And it can quickly turn into fighting.
KICK
CROAK
This display has the added benefit of doubling as a defense mechanism when a competing male gets too close.

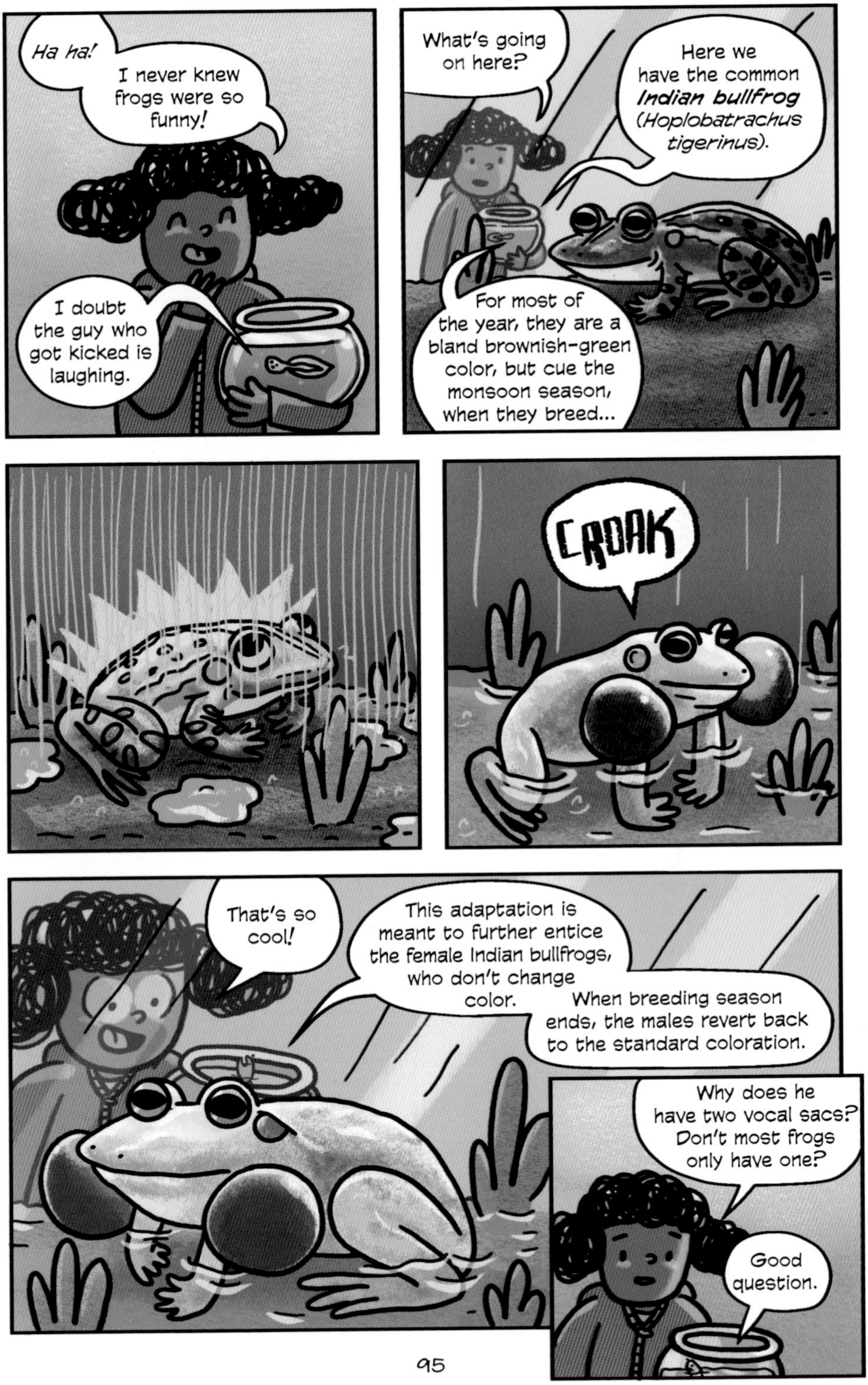
Ha ha!
I never knew frogs were so funny!
I doubt the guy who got kicked is laughing.
What's going on here?
Here we have the common ***Indian bullfrog*** *(Hoplobatrachus tigerinus)*.
For most of the year, they are a bland brownish-green color, but cue the monsoon season, when they breed...
CROAK
That's so cool!
This adaptation is meant to further entice the female Indian bullfrogs, who don't change color.
When breeding season ends, the males revert back to the standard coloration.
Why does he have two vocal sacs? Don't most frogs only have one?
Good question.

There are three types of vocal sacs:

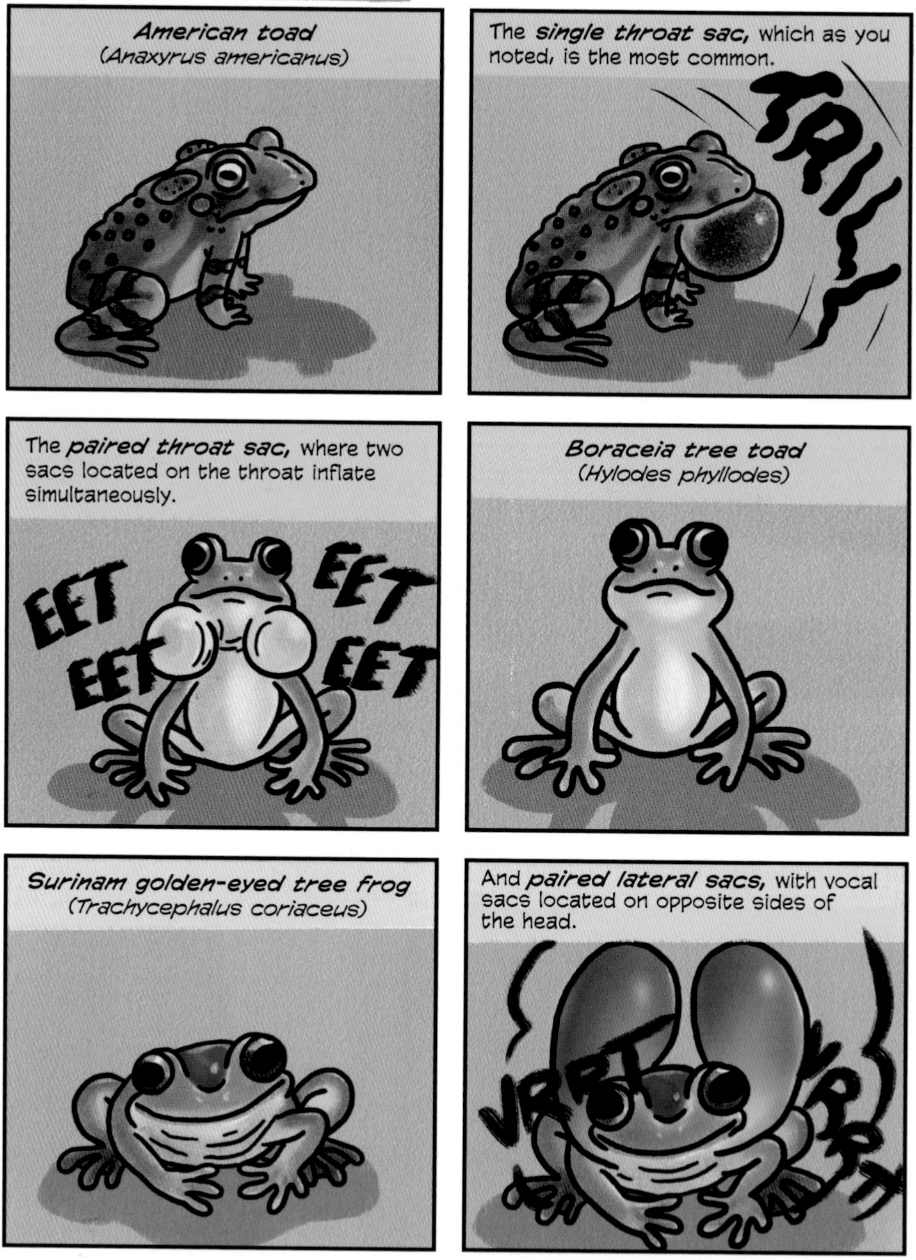
American toad
(Anaxyrus americanus)
The single throat sac, which as you noted, is the most common.
TRILL
The paired throat sac, where two sacs located on the throat inflate simultaneously.
EET
EET
EET
EET
Boraceia tree toad
(Hylodes phyllodes)
Surinam golden-eyed tree frog
(Trachycephalus coriaceus)
And paired lateral sacs, with vocal sacs located on opposite sides of the head.
VRRT
VRRT

Each vocal sac type distributes the call differently, which may help in situations where frogs might be calling through water, or when there is a vibrational or visual element to their calls.

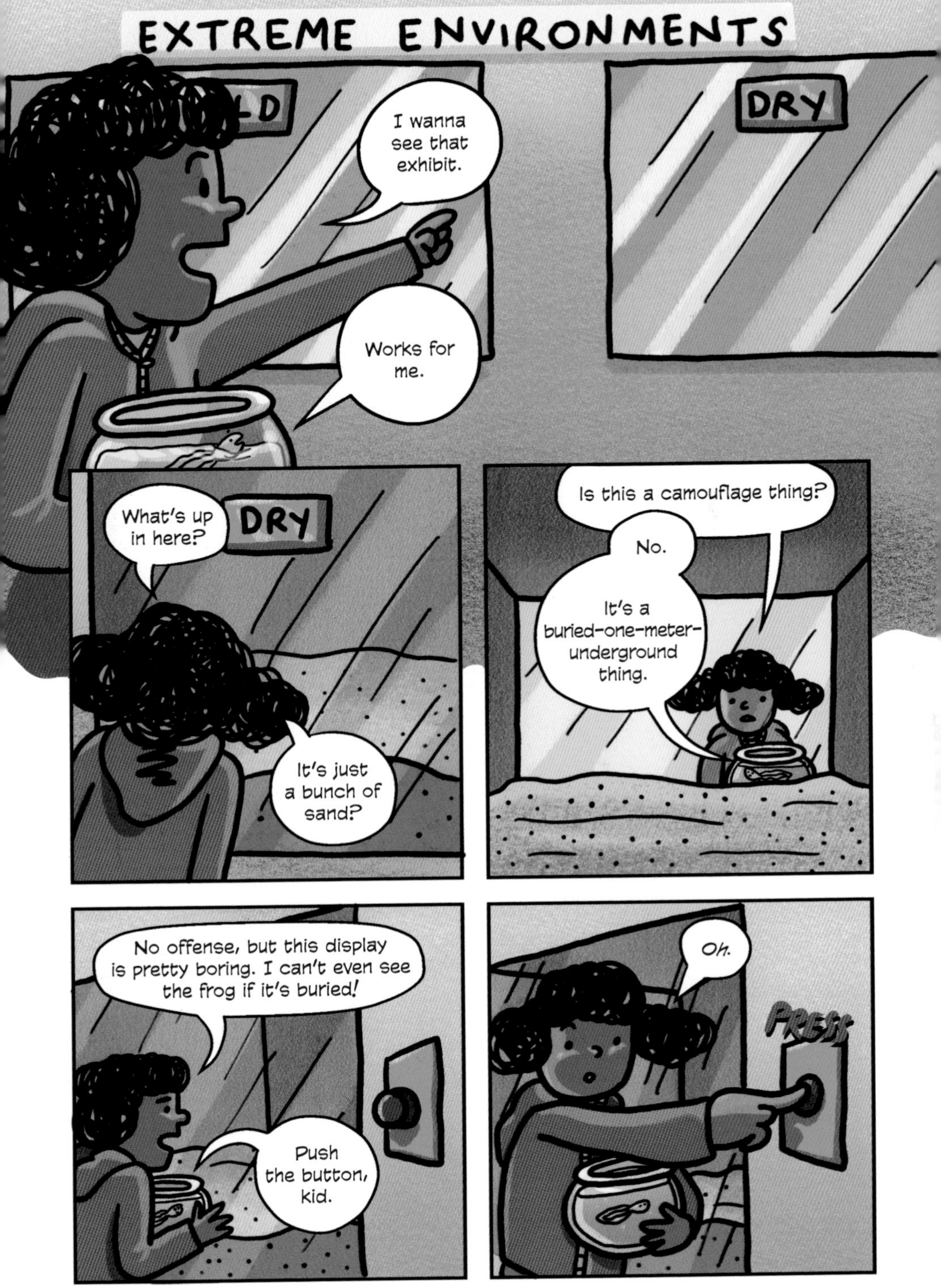
EXTREME ENVIRONMENTS
DRY
I wanna see that exhibit.
Works for me.
DRY
What's up in here?
It's just a bunch of sand?
Is this a camouflage thing?
No.
It's a buried-one-meter-underground thing.
No offense, but this display is pretty boring. I can't even see the frog if it's buried!
Push the button, kid.
Oh.
PRESS

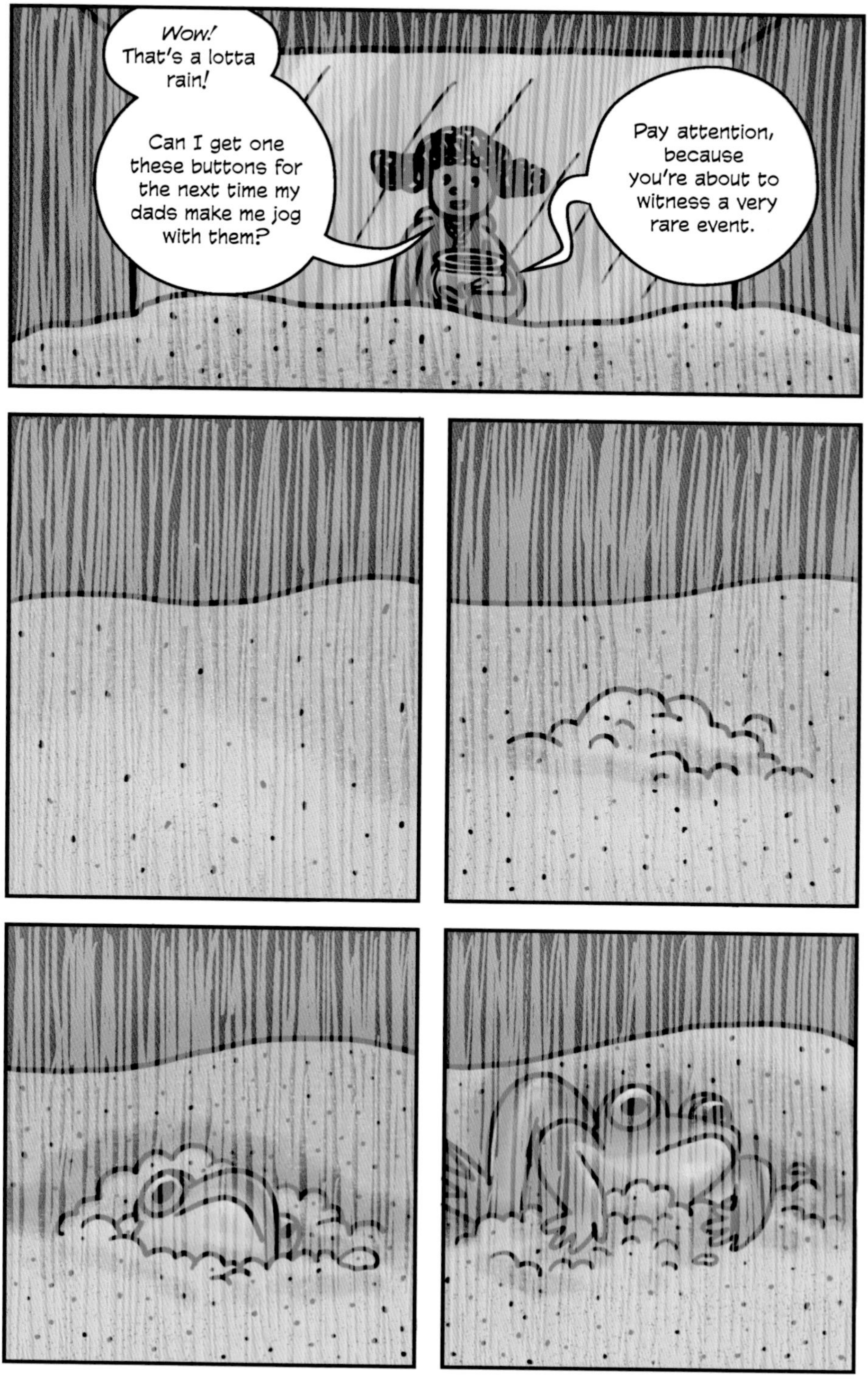
Wow! That's a lotta rain!
Can I get one these buttons for the next time my dads make me jog with them?
Pay attention, because you're about to witness a very rare event.

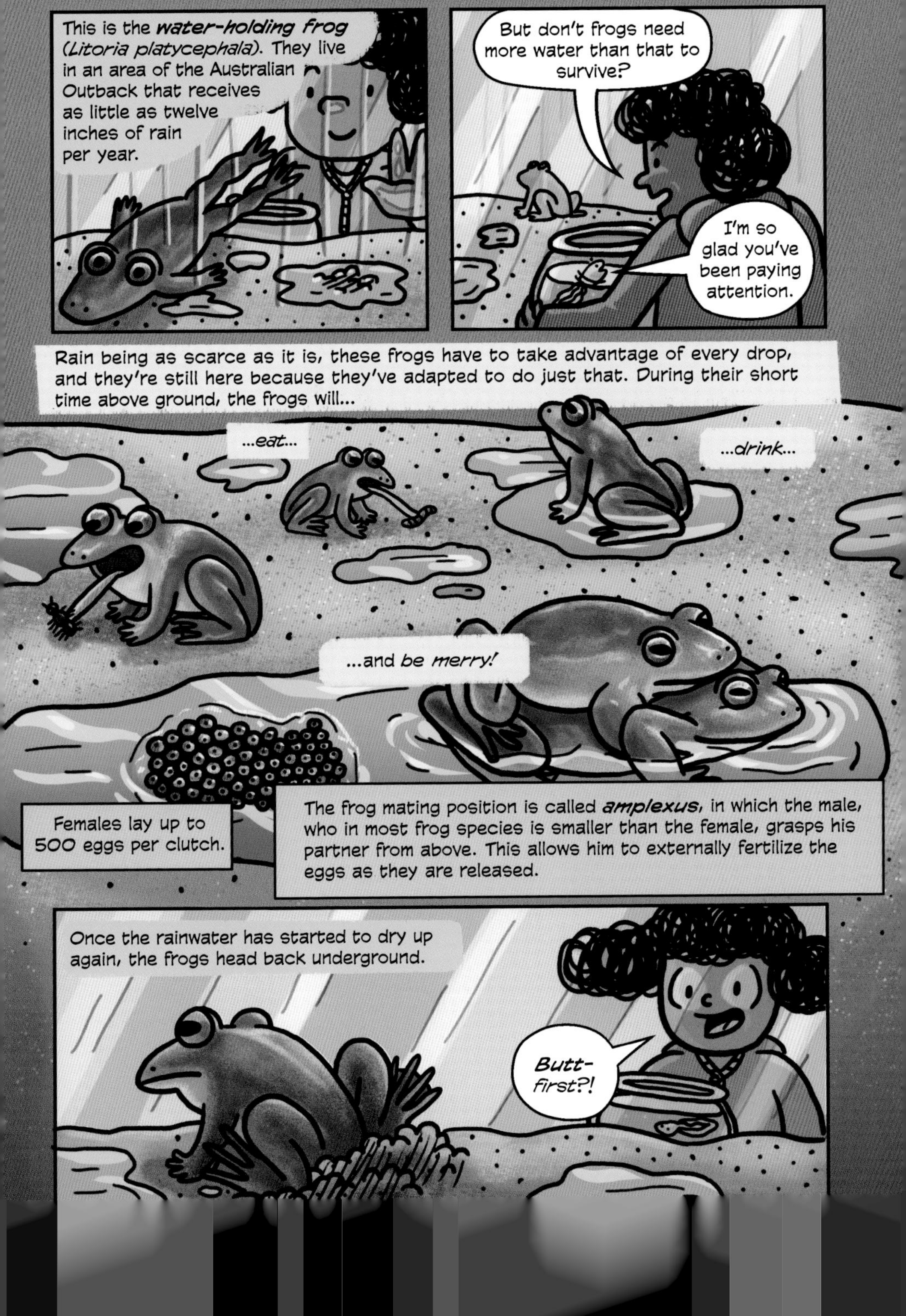

This is the *water-holding frog* (*Litoria platycephala*). They live in an area of the Australian Outback that receives as little as twelve inches of rain per year.
But don't frogs need more water than that to survive?
I'm so glad you've been paying attention.
Rain being as scarce as it is, these frogs have to take advantage of every drop, and they're still here because they've adapted to do just that. During their short time above ground, the frogs will...
...*eat*...
...*drink*...
...and *be merry!*
Females lay up to 500 eggs per clutch.
The frog mating position is called ***amplexus***, in which the male, who in most frog species is smaller than the female, grasps his partner from above. This allows him to externally fertilize the eggs as they are released.
Once the rainwater has started to dry up again, the frogs head back underground.
Butt-first?!

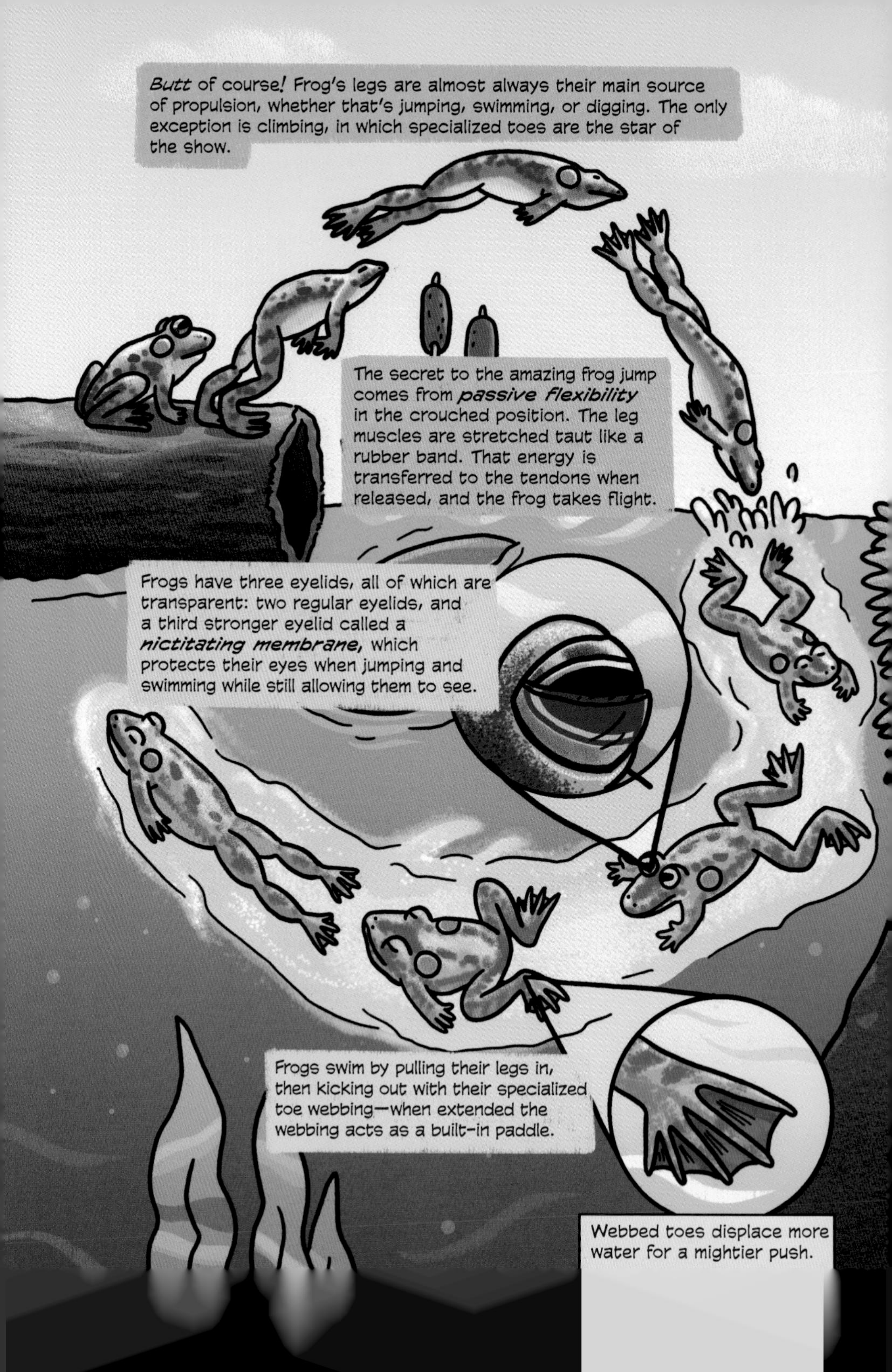
Butt of course! Frog's legs are almost always their main source of propulsion, whether that's jumping, swimming, or digging. The only exception is climbing, in which specialized toes are the star of the show.
The secret to the amazing frog jump comes from ***passive flexibility*** in the crouched position. The leg muscles are stretched taut like a rubber band. That energy is transferred to the tendons when released, and the frog takes flight.
Frogs have three eyelids, all of which are transparent: two regular eyelids, and a third stronger eyelid called a ***nictitating membrane,*** which protects their eyes when jumping and swimming while still allowing them to see.
Frogs swim by pulling their legs in, then kicking out with their specialized toe webbing—when extended the webbing acts as a built-in paddle.
Webbed toes displace more water for a mightier push.

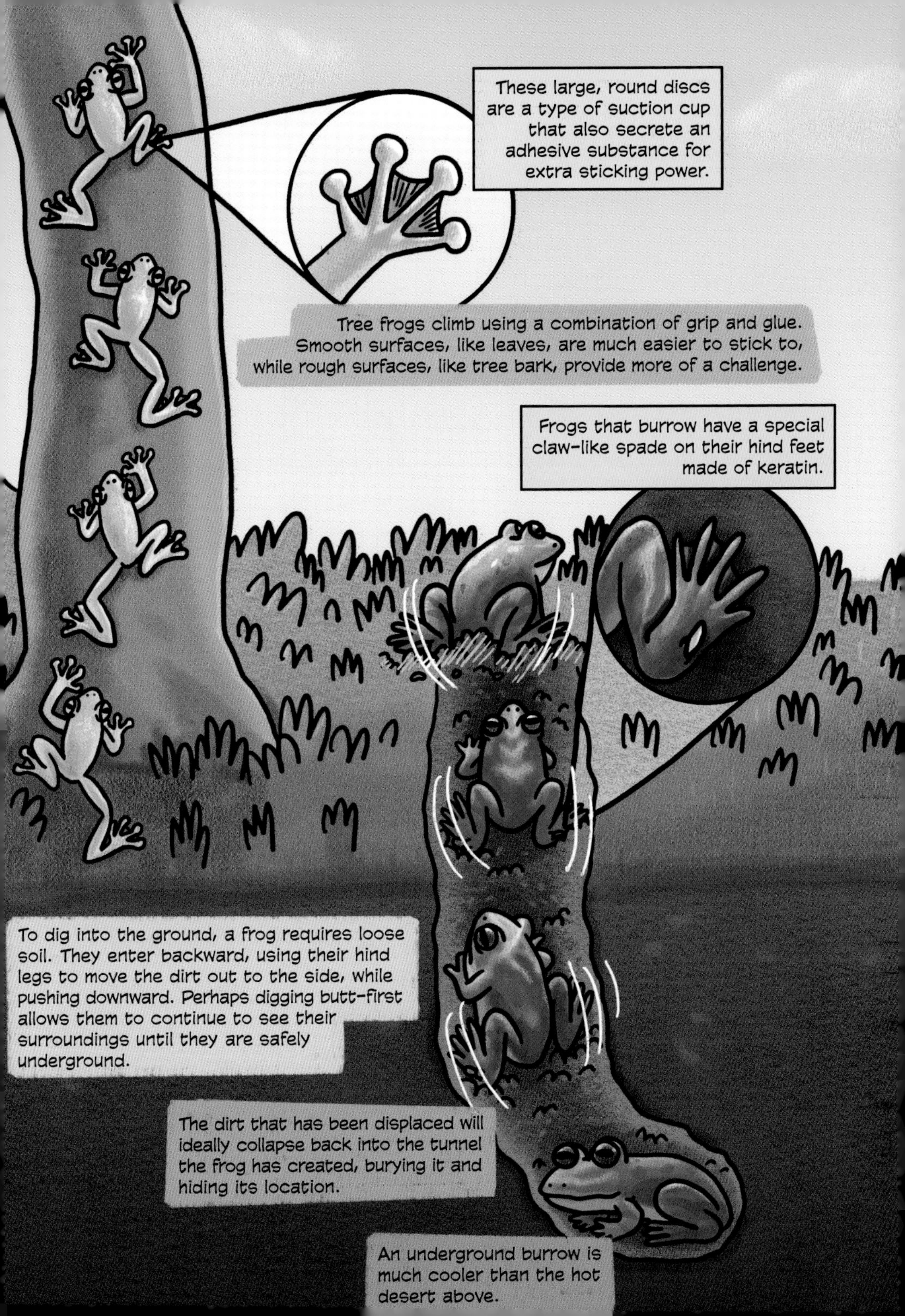
These large, round discs are a type of suction cup that also secrete an adhesive substance for extra sticking power.
Tree frogs climb using a combination of grip and glue. Smooth surfaces, like leaves, are much easier to stick to, while rough surfaces, like tree bark, provide more of a challenge.
Frogs that burrow have a special claw-like spade on their hind feet made of keratin.
To dig into the ground, a frog requires loose soil. They enter backward, using their hind legs to move the dirt out to the side, while pushing downward. Perhaps digging butt-first allows them to continue to see their surroundings until they are safely underground.
The dirt that has been displaced will ideally collapse back into the tunnel the frog has created, burying it and hiding its location.
An underground burrow is much cooler than the hot desert above.

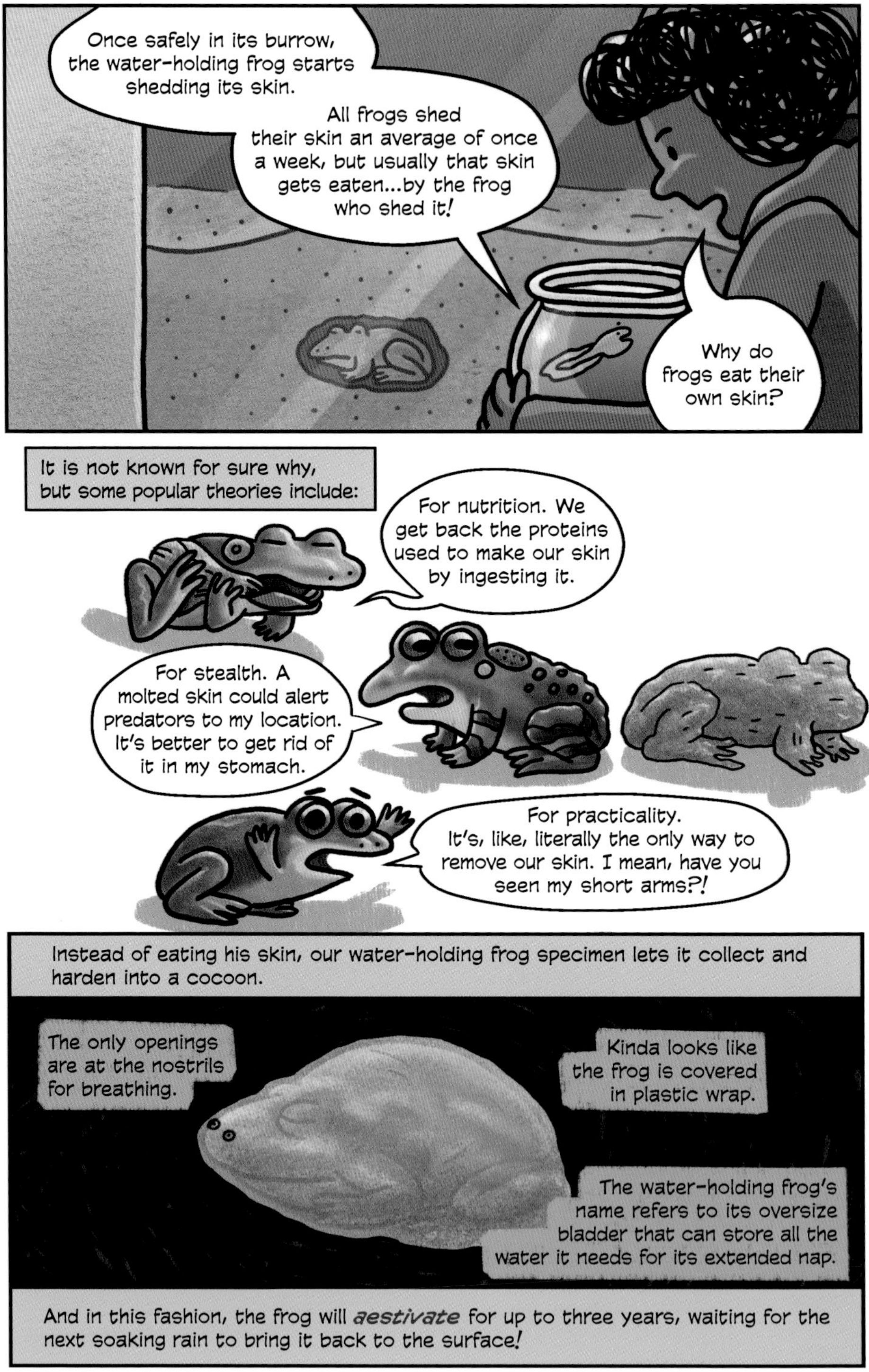
Once safely in its burrow, the water-holding frog starts shedding its skin.
All frogs shed their skin an average of once a week, but usually that skin gets eaten...by the frog who shed it!
Why do frogs eat their own skin?
It is not known for sure why, but some popular theories include:
For nutrition. We get back the proteins used to make our skin by ingesting it.
For stealth. A molted skin could alert predators to my location. It's better to get rid of it in my stomach.
For practicality. It's, like, literally the only way to remove our skin. I mean, have you seen my short arms?!
Instead of eating his skin, our water-holding frog specimen lets it collect and harden into a cocoon.
The only openings are at the nostrils for breathing.
Kinda looks like the frog is covered in plastic wrap.
The water-holding frog's name refers to its oversize bladder that can store all the water it needs for its extended nap.
And in this fashion, the frog will *aestivate* for up to three years, waiting for the next soaking rain to bring it back to the surface!

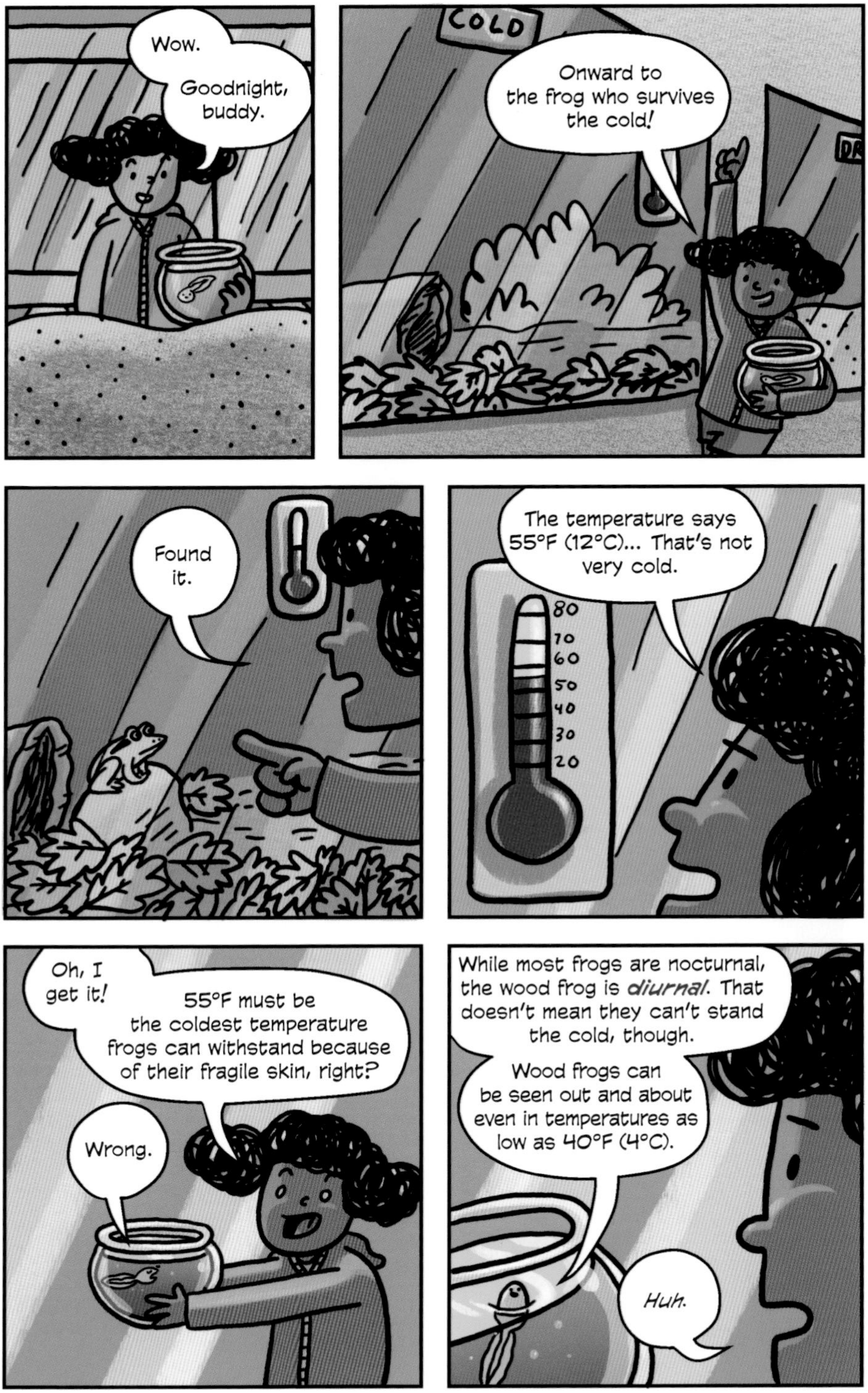
Wow.
Goodnight, buddy.
COLD
Onward to the frog who survives the cold!
Found it.
The temperature says 55°F (12°C)... That's not very cold.
80
70
60
50
40
30
20
Oh, I get it!
55°F must be the coldest temperature frogs can withstand because of their fragile skin, right?
Wrong.
While most frogs are nocturnal, the wood frog is *diurnal*. That doesn't mean they can't stand the cold, though.
Wood frogs can be seen out and about even in temperatures as low as 40°F (4°C).
Huh.

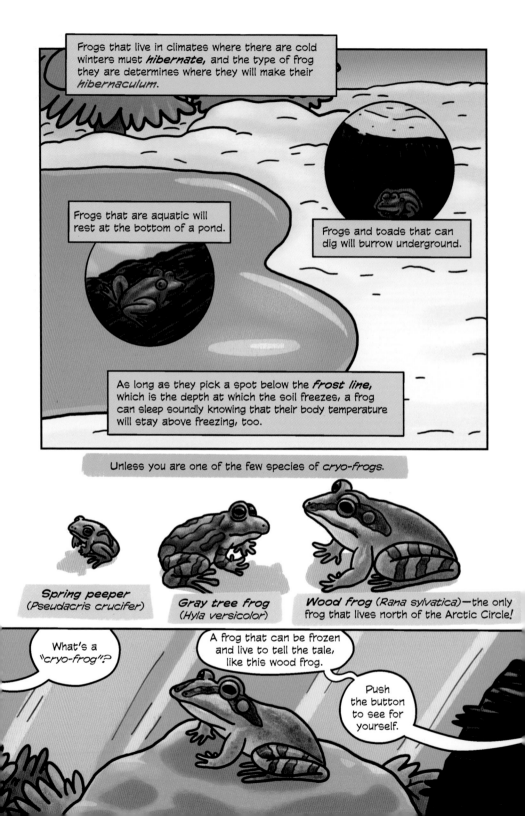

Frogs that live in climates where there are cold winters must *hibernate,* and the type of frog they are determines where they will make their *hibernaculum.*

Frogs that are aquatic will rest at the bottom of a pond.

Frogs and toads that can dig will burrow underground.

As long as they pick a spot below the *frost line,* which is the depth at which the soil freezes, a frog can sleep soundly knowing that their body temperature will stay above freezing, too.

Unless you are one of the few species of *cryo-frogs.*

Spring peeper
(Pseudacris crucifer)

Gray tree frog
(Hyla versicolor)

Wood frog *(Rana sylvatica)*—the only frog that lives north of the Arctic Circle!

What's a "cryo-frog"?

A frog that can be frozen and live to tell the tale, like this wood frog.

Push the button to see for yourself.

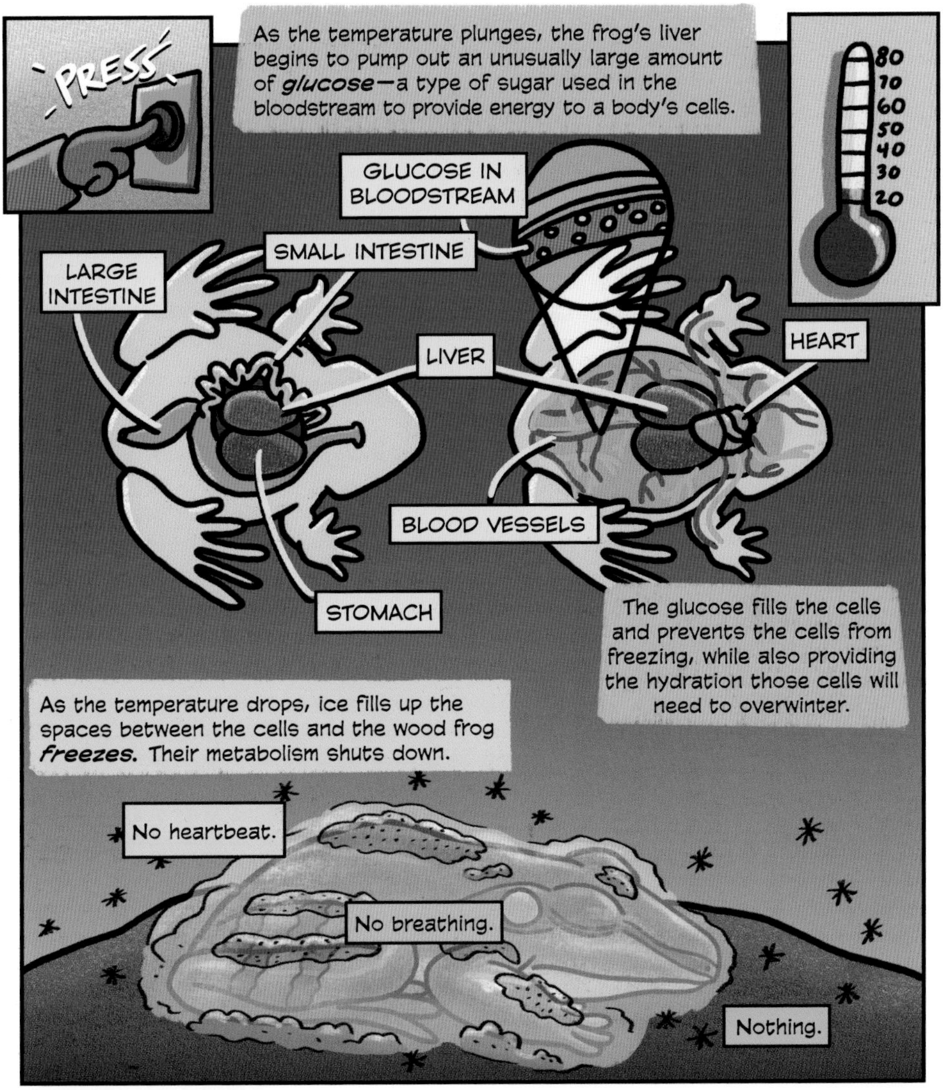
PRESS
As the temperature plunges, the frog's liver begins to pump out an unusually large amount of *glucose*—a type of sugar used in the bloodstream to provide energy to a body's cells.
80
70
60
50
40
30
20
GLUCOSE IN BLOODSTREAM
SMALL INTESTINE
LARGE INTESTINE
LIVER
HEART
BLOOD VESSELS
STOMACH
The glucose fills the cells and prevents the cells from freezing, while also providing the hydration those cells will need to overwinter.
As the temperature drops, ice fills up the spaces between the cells and the wood frog *freezes*. Their metabolism shuts down.
No heartbeat.
No breathing.
Nothing.

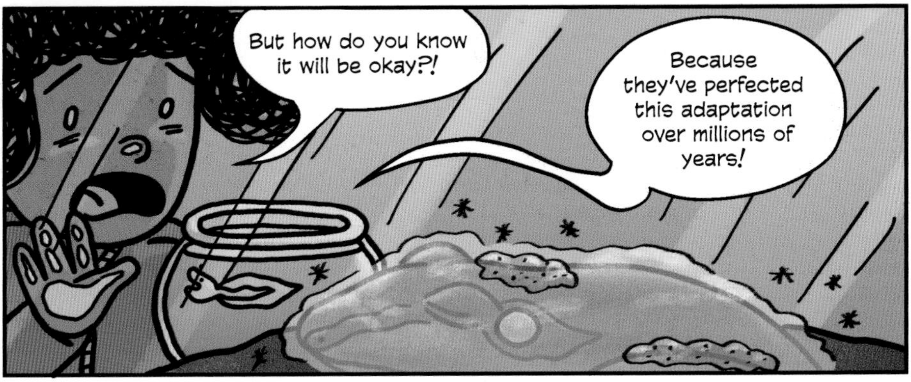
But how do you know it will be okay?!
Because they've perfected this adaptation over millions of years!

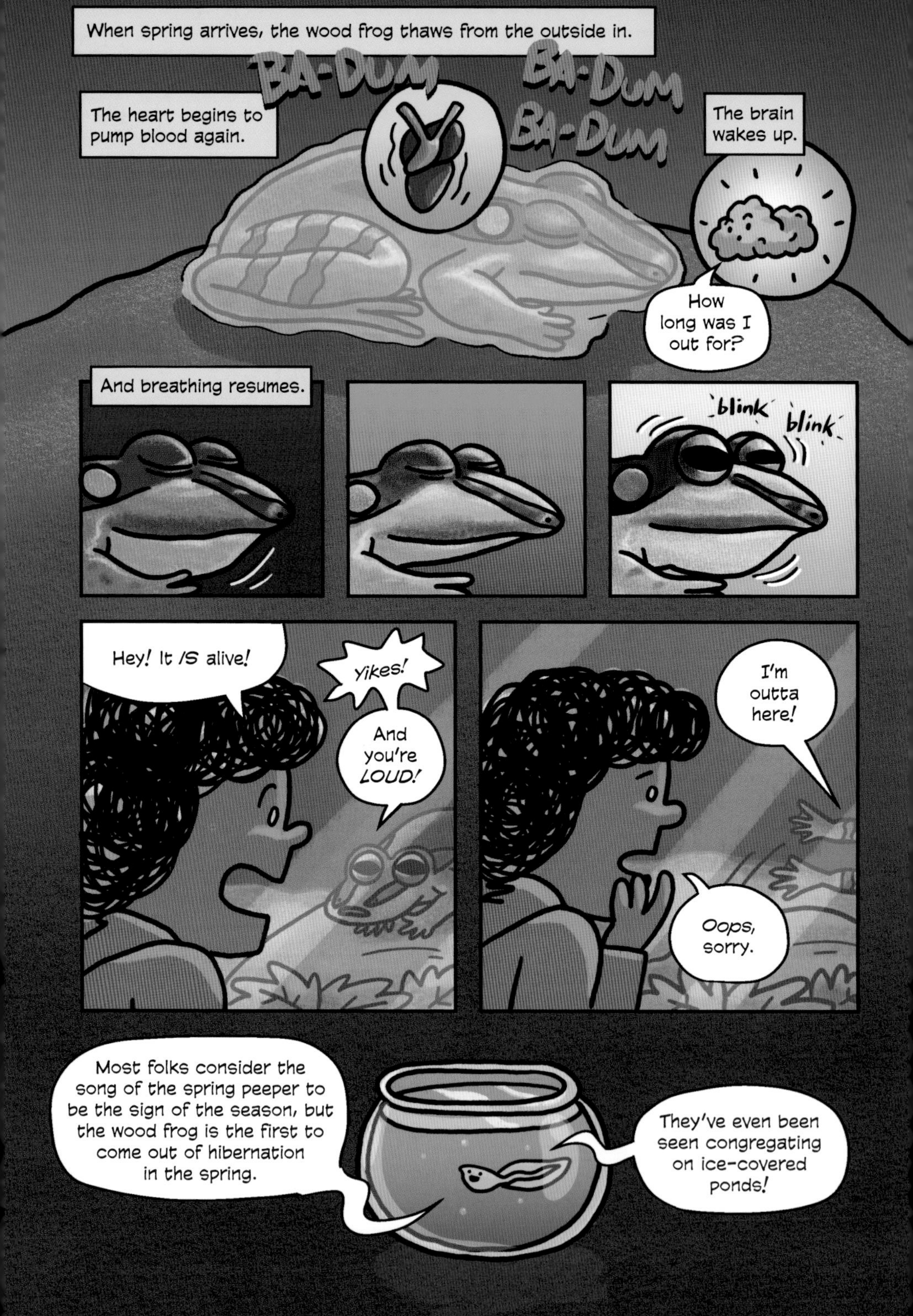
When spring arrives, the wood frog thaws from the outside in.
BA-DUM
BA-DUM
BA-DUM
The heart begins to pump blood again.
The brain wakes up.
How long was I out for?
And breathing resumes.
blink
blink
Hey! It IS alive!
Yikes!
And you're LOUD!
I'm outta here!
Oops, sorry.
Most folks consider the song of the spring peeper to be the sign of the season, but the wood frog is the first to come out of hibernation in the spring.
They've even been seen congregating on ice-covered ponds!

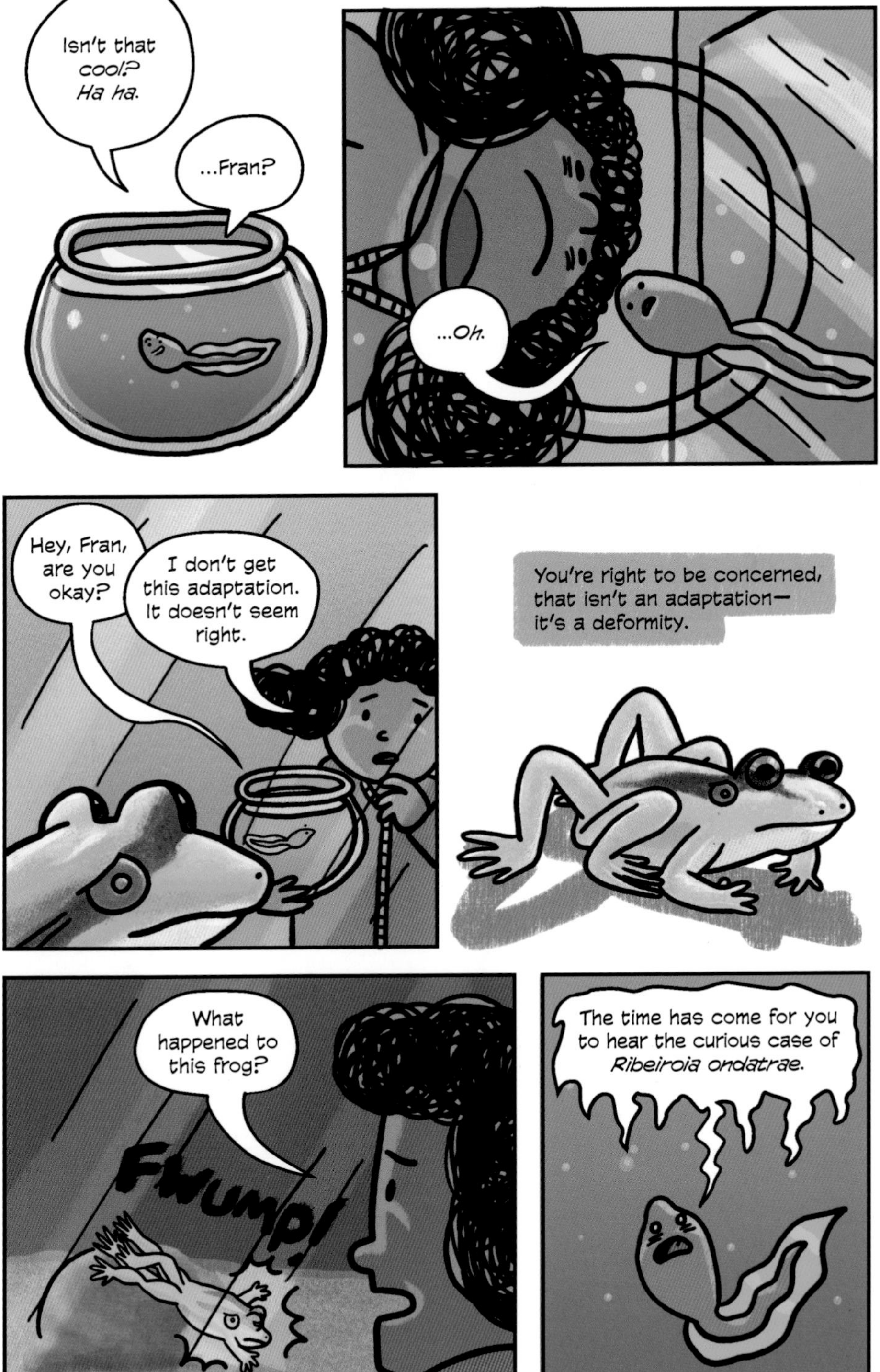

Isn't that *cool?* *Ha ha.*
...Fran?
...*Oh.*
Hey, Fran, are you okay?
I don't get this adaptation. It doesn't seem right.
You're right to be concerned, that isn't an adaptation—it's a deformity.
What happened to this frog?
FWUMP!
The time has come for you to hear the curious case of *Ribeiroia ondatrae*.

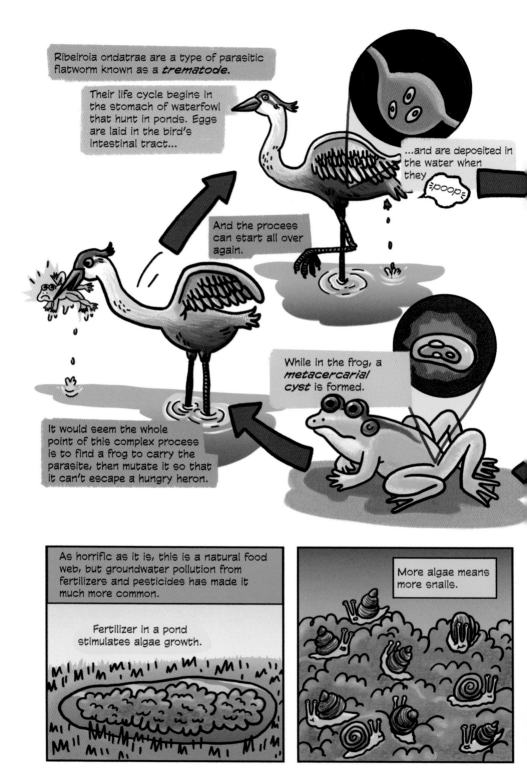

Ribeiroia ondatrae are a type of parasitic flatworm known as a *trematode*.

Their life cycle begins in the stomach of waterfowl that hunt in ponds. Eggs are laid in the bird's intestinal tract...

...and are deposited in the water when they

poop

And the process can start all over again.

While in the frog, a *metacercarial cyst* is formed.

It would seem the whole point of this complex process is to find a frog to carry the parasite, then mutate it so that it can't escape a hungry heron.

As horrific as it is, this is a natural food web, but groundwater pollution from fertilizers and pesticides has made it much more common.

Fertilizer in a pond stimulates algae growth.

More algae means more snails.

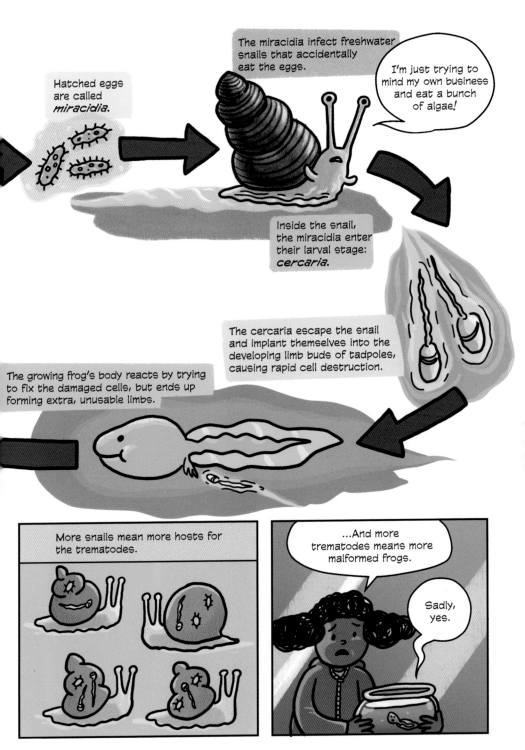

Hatched eggs are called *miracidia*.

The miracidia infect freshwater snails that accidentally eat the eggs.

I'm just trying to mind my own business and eat a bunch of algae!

Inside the snail, the miracidia enter their larval stage: *cercaria*.

The cercaria escape the snail and implant themselves into the developing limb buds of tadpoles, causing rapid cell destruction.

The growing frog's body reacts by trying to fix the damaged cells, but ends up forming extra, unusable limbs.

More snails mean more hosts for the trematodes.

...And more trematodes means more malformed frogs.

Sadly, yes.

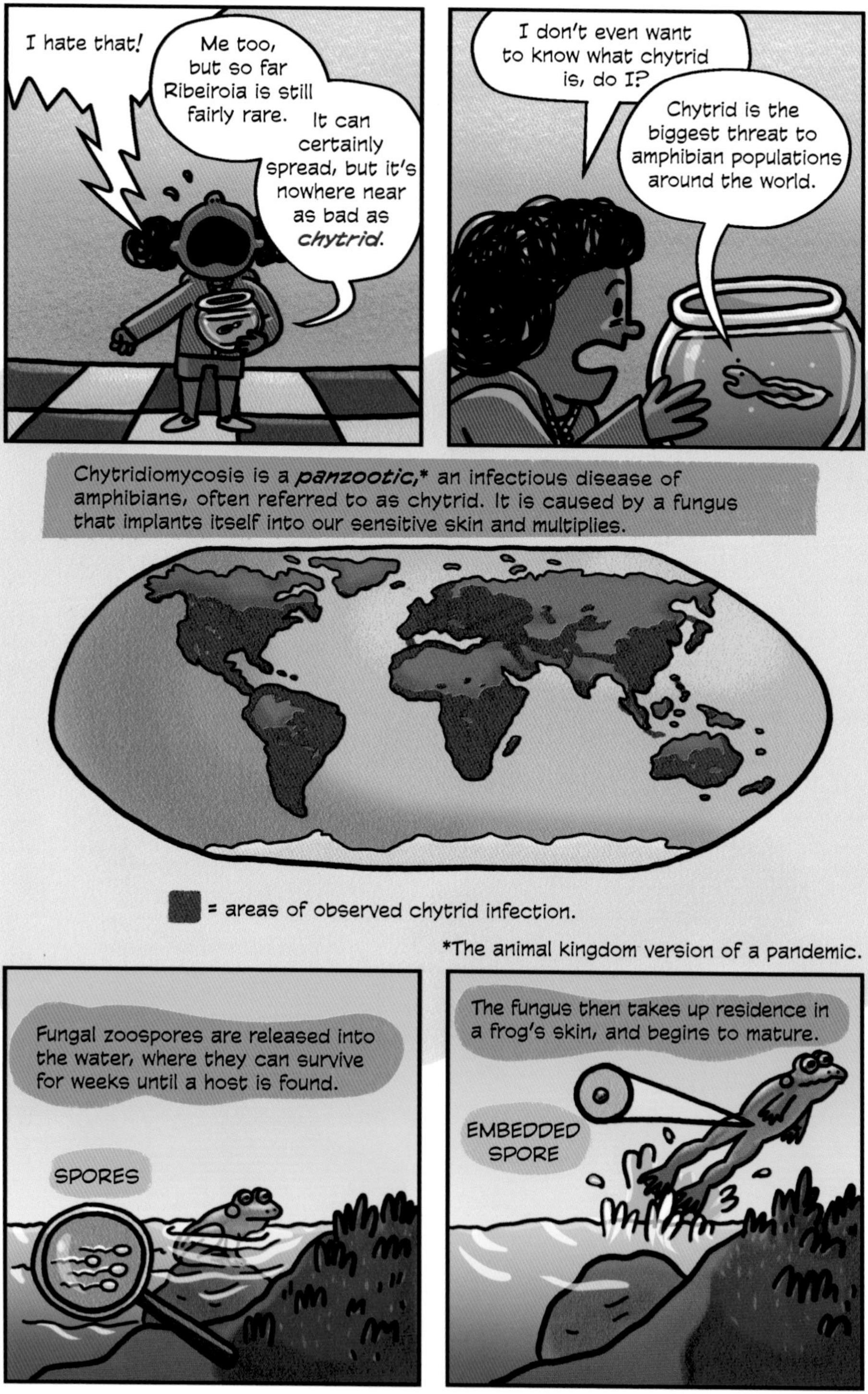
I hate that!
Me too, but so far Ribeiroia is still fairly rare.
It can certainly spread, but it's nowhere near as bad as *chytrid*.
I don't even want to know what chytrid is, do I?
Chytrid is the biggest threat to amphibian populations around the world.
Chytridiomycosis is a *panzootic,** an infectious disease of amphibians, often referred to as chytrid. It is caused by a fungus that implants itself into our sensitive skin and multiplies.
= areas of observed chytrid infection.
*The animal kingdom version of a pandemic.
Fungal zoospores are released into the water, where they can survive for weeks until a host is found.
SPORES
The fungus then takes up residence in a frog's skin, and begins to mature.
EMBEDDED SPORE

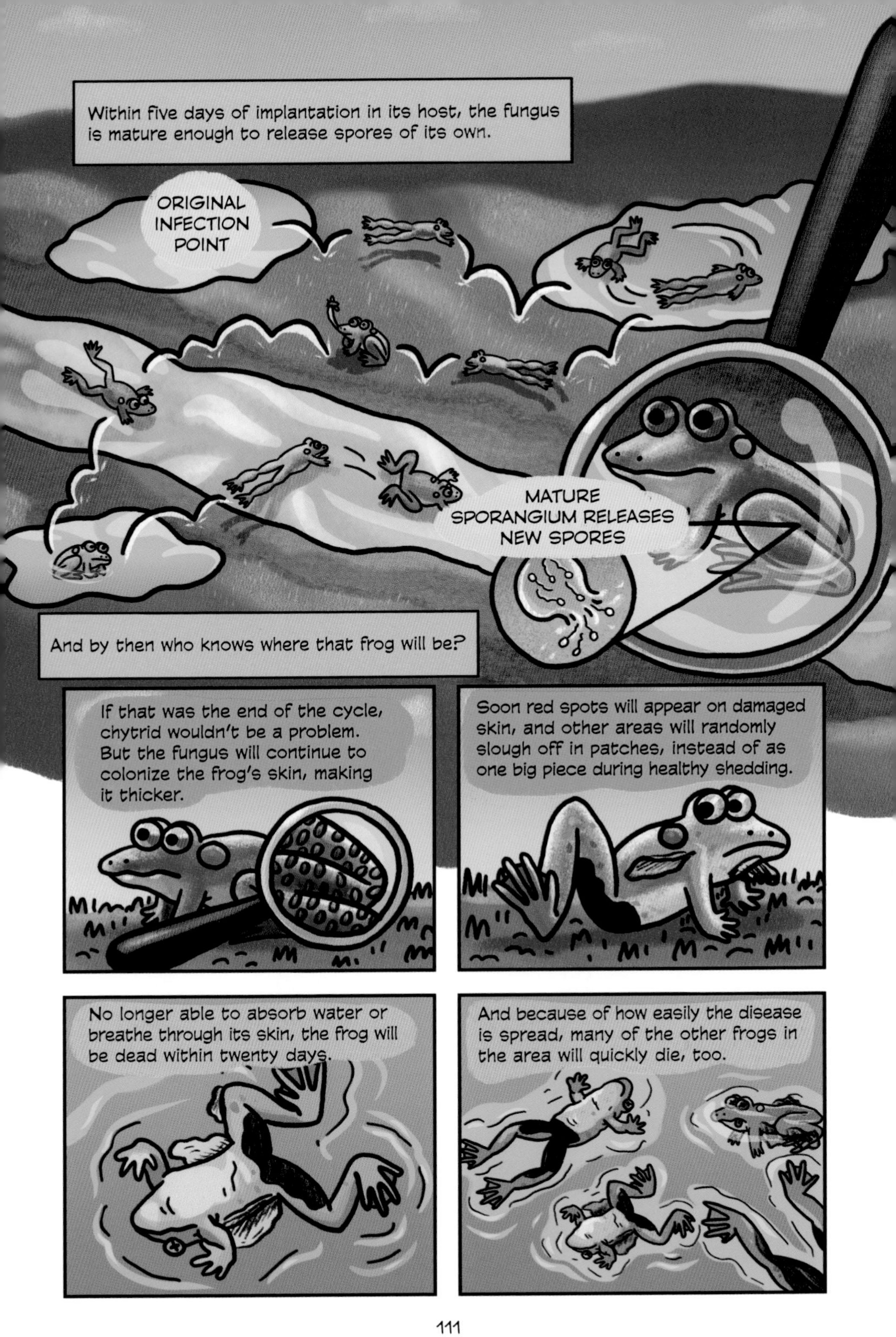

Within five days of implantation in its host, the fungus is mature enough to release spores of its own.
ORIGINAL INFECTION POINT
MATURE SPORANGIUM RELEASES NEW SPORES
And by then who knows where that frog will be?
If that was the end of the cycle, chytrid wouldn't be a problem. But the fungus will continue to colonize the frog's skin, making it thicker.
Soon red spots will appear on damaged skin, and other areas will randomly slough off in patches, instead of as one big piece during healthy shedding.
No longer able to absorb water or breathe through its skin, the frog will be dead within twenty days.
And because of how easily the disease is spread, many of the other frogs in the area will quickly die, too.

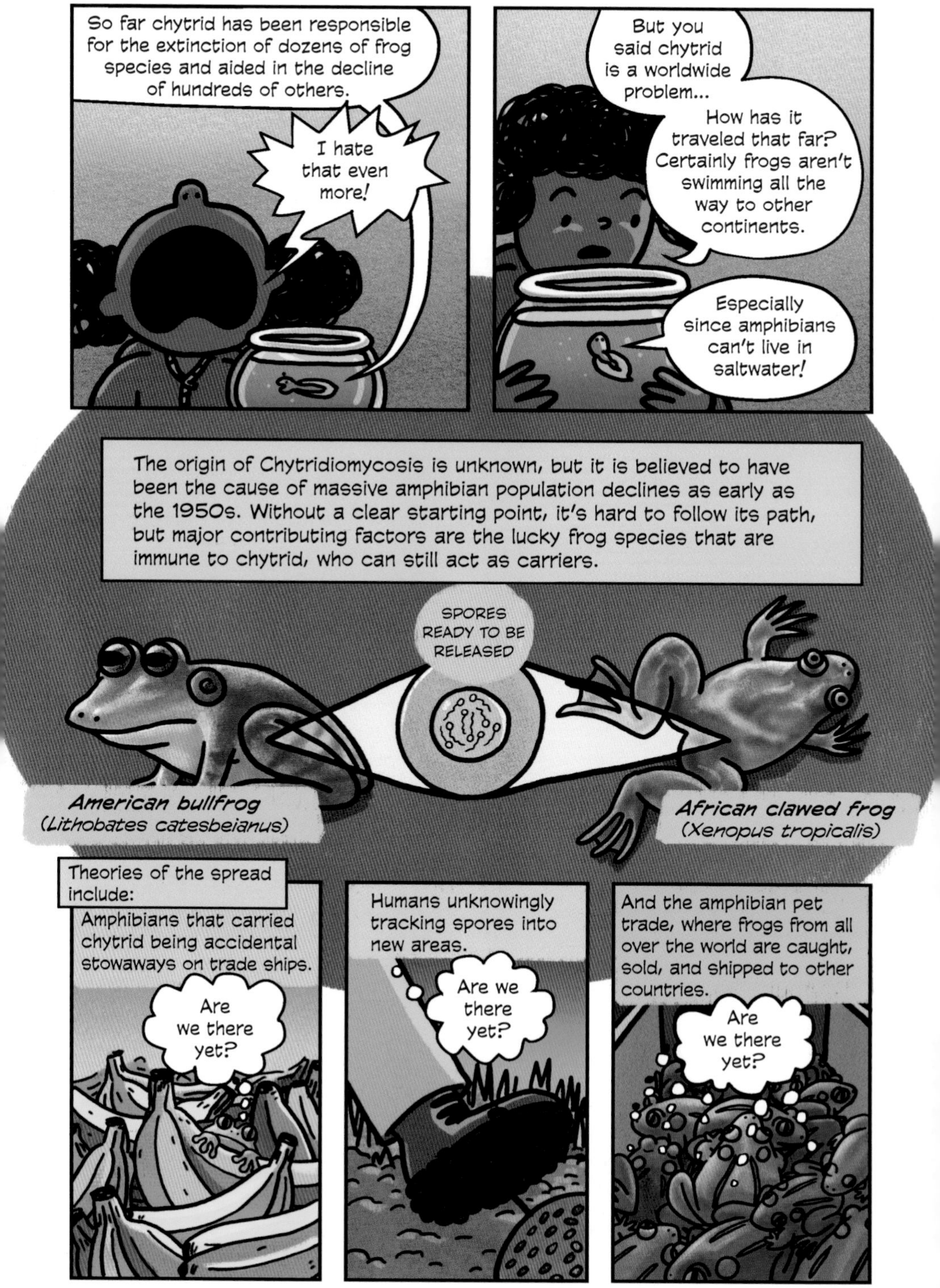
So far chytrid has been responsible for the extinction of dozens of frog species and aided in the decline of hundreds of others.
I hate that even more!
But you said chytrid is a worldwide problem...
How has it traveled that far? Certainly frogs aren't swimming all the way to other continents.
Especially since amphibians can't live in saltwater!
The origin of Chytridiomycosis is unknown, but it is believed to have been the cause of massive amphibian population declines as early as the 1950s. Without a clear starting point, it's hard to follow its path, but major contributing factors are the lucky frog species that are immune to chytrid, who can still act as carriers.
SPORES READY TO BE RELEASED
American bullfrog (Lithobates catesbeianus)
African clawed frog (Xenopus tropicalis)
Theories of the spread include:
Amphibians that carried chytrid being accidental stowaways on trade ships.
Are we there yet?
Humans unknowingly tracking spores into new areas.
Are we there yet?
And the amphibian pet trade, where frogs from all over the world are caught, sold, and shipped to other countries.
Are we there yet?

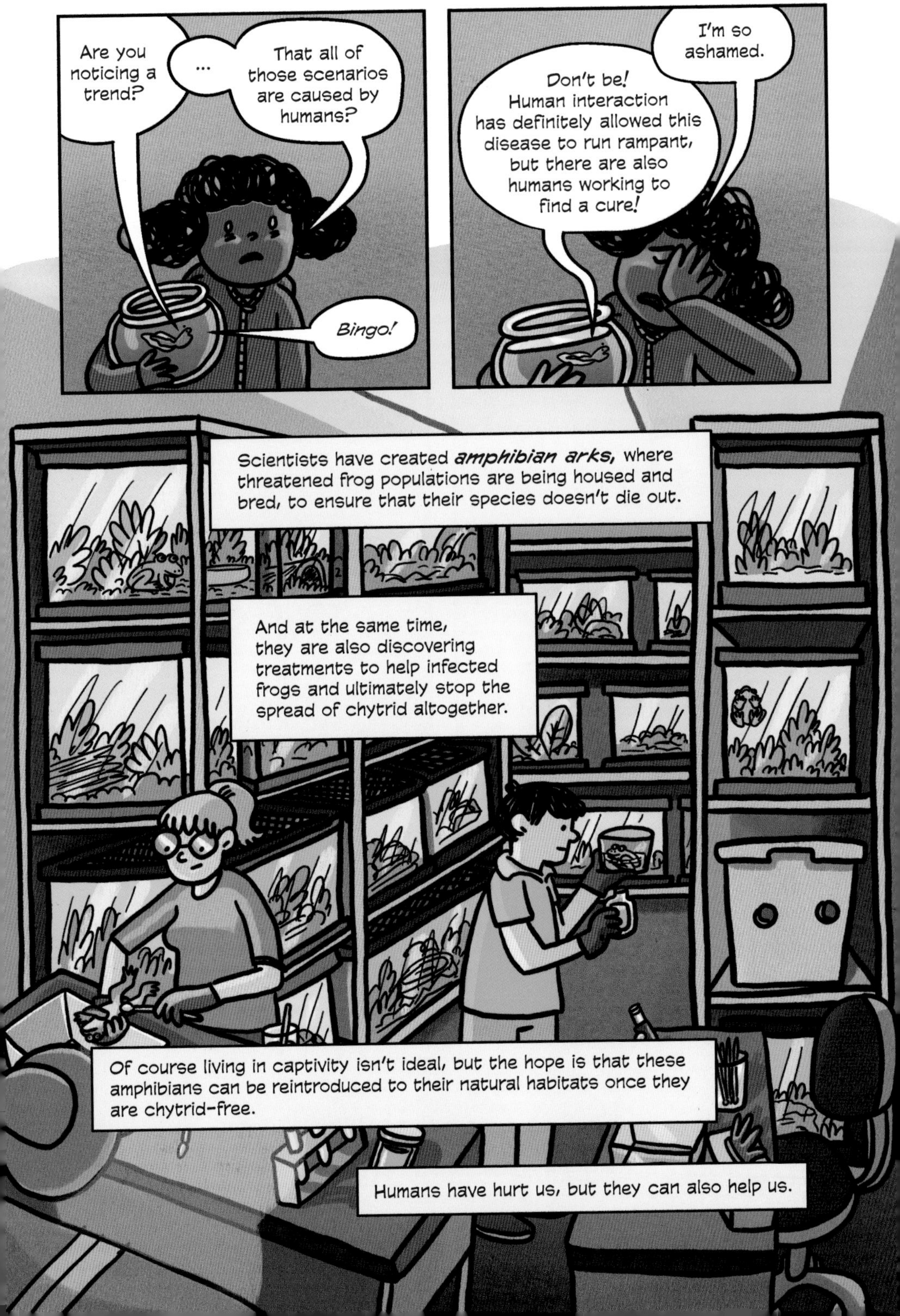
Are you noticing a trend?
...
That all of those scenarios are caused by humans?
Bingo!
I'm so ashamed.
Don't be! Human interaction has definitely allowed this disease to run rampant, but there are also humans working to find a cure!
Scientists have created amphibian arks, where threatened frog populations are being housed and bred, to ensure that their species doesn't die out.
And at the same time, they are also discovering treatments to help infected frogs and ultimately stop the spread of chytrid altogether.
Of course living in captivity isn't ideal, but the hope is that these amphibians can be reintroduced to their natural habitats once they are chytrid-free.
Humans have hurt us, but they can also help us.

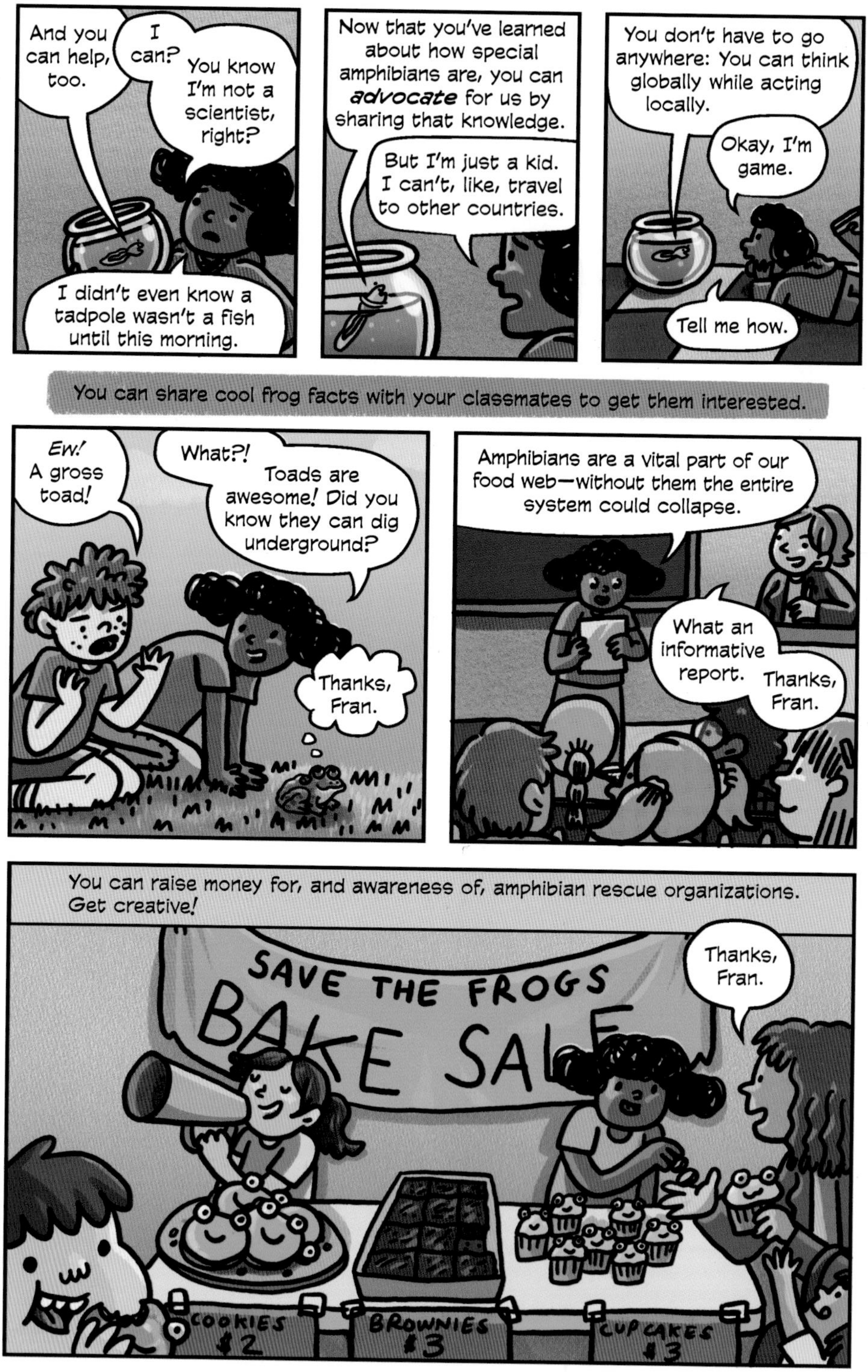
And you can help, too.
I can?
You know I'm not a scientist, right?
I didn't even know a tadpole wasn't a fish until this morning.
Now that you've learned about how special amphibians are, you can *advocate* for us by sharing that knowledge.
But I'm just a kid. I can't, like, travel to other countries.
You don't have to go anywhere: You can think globally while acting locally.
Okay, I'm game.
Tell me how.
You can share cool frog facts with your classmates to get them interested.
Ew! A gross toad!
What?!
Toads are awesome! Did you know they can dig underground?
Thanks, Fran.
Amphibians are a vital part of our food web—without them the entire system could collapse.
What an informative report.
Thanks, Fran.
You can raise money for, and awareness of, amphibian rescue organizations. Get creative!
SAVE THE FROGS
BAKE SALE
Thanks, Fran.
COOKIES $2
BROWNIES $3
CUPCAKES $3

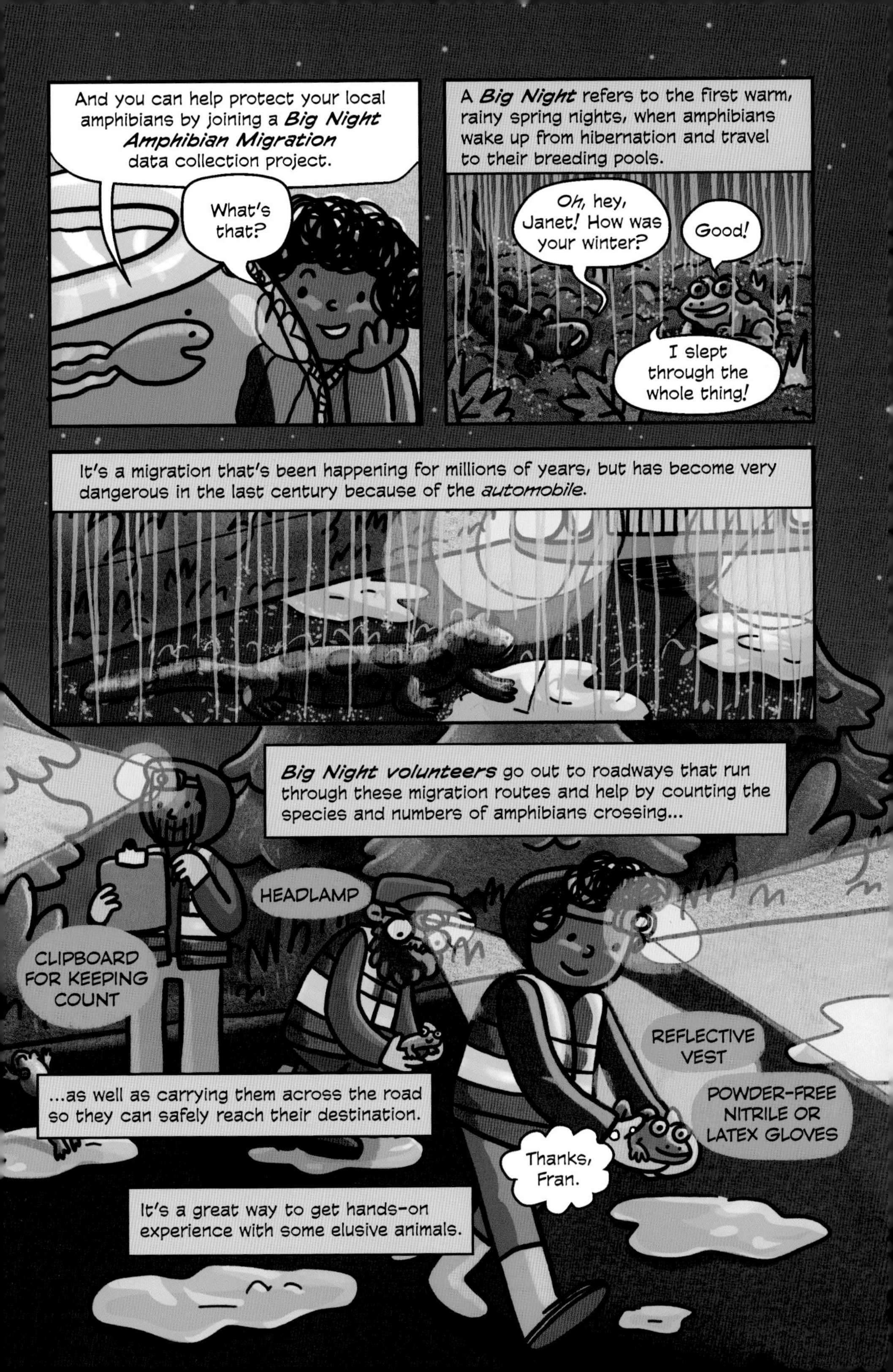
And you can help protect your local amphibians by joining a ***Big Night Amphibian Migration*** data collection project.
What's that?
A ***Big Night*** refers to the first warm, rainy spring nights, when amphibians wake up from hibernation and travel to their breeding pools.
Oh, hey, Janet! How was your winter?
Good!
I slept through the whole thing!
It's a migration that's been happening for millions of years, but has become very dangerous in the last century because of the *automobile*.
Big Night volunteers go out to roadways that run through these migration routes and help by counting the species and numbers of amphibians crossing...
HEADLAMP
CLIPBOARD FOR KEEPING COUNT
REFLECTIVE VEST
POWDER-FREE NITRILE OR LATEX GLOVES
...as well as carrying them across the road so they can safely reach their destination.
Thanks, Fran.
It's a great way to get hands-on experience with some elusive animals.

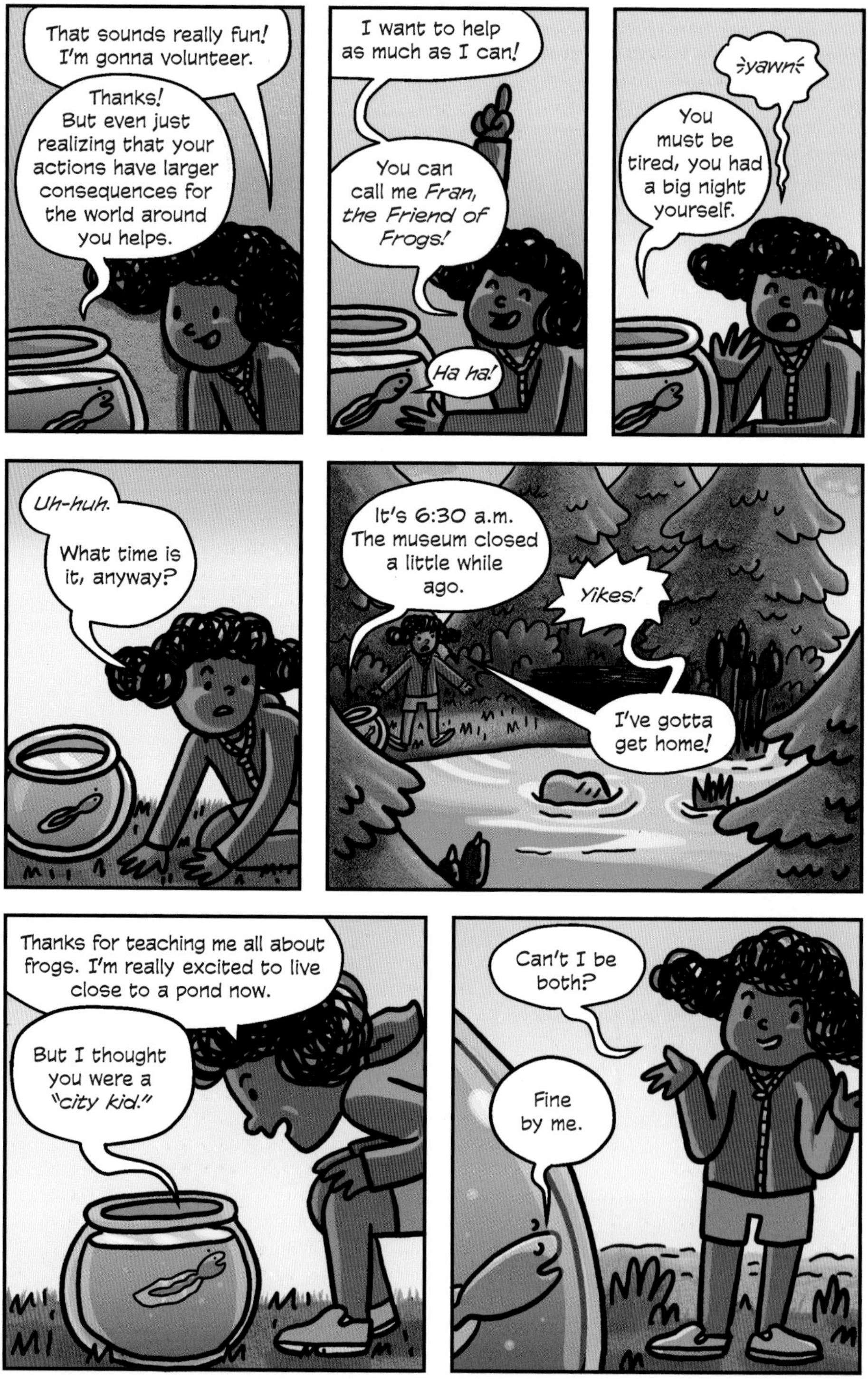
That sounds really fun! I'm gonna volunteer.
Thanks! But even just realizing that your actions have larger consequences for the world around you helps.
I want to help as much as I can!
You can call me *Fran, the Friend of Frogs!*
Ha ha!
yawn
You must be tired, you had a big night yourself.
Uh-huh.
What time is it, anyway?
It's 6:30 a.m. The museum closed a little while ago.
Yikes!
I've gotta get home!
Thanks for teaching me all about frogs. I'm really excited to live close to a pond now.
But I thought you were a "*city kid.*"
Can't I be both?
Fine by me.

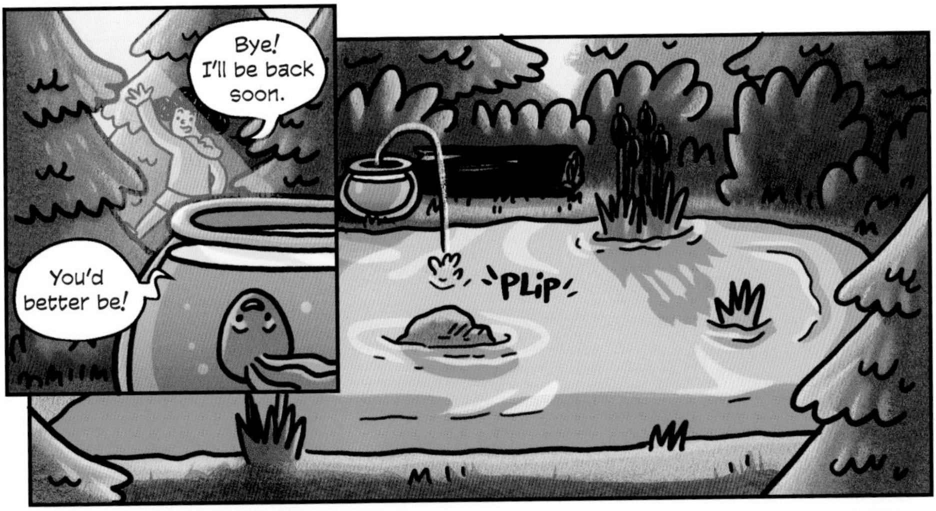
Bye! I'll be back soon.
You'd better be!
PLIP

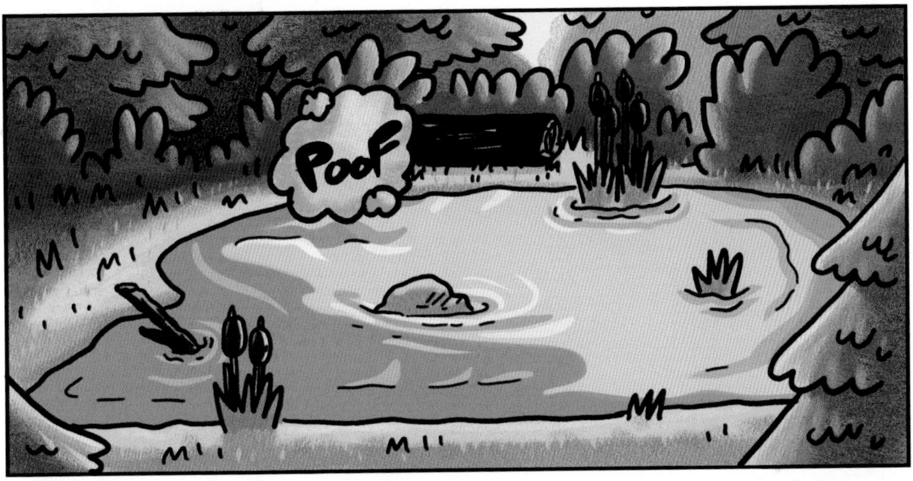
POOF

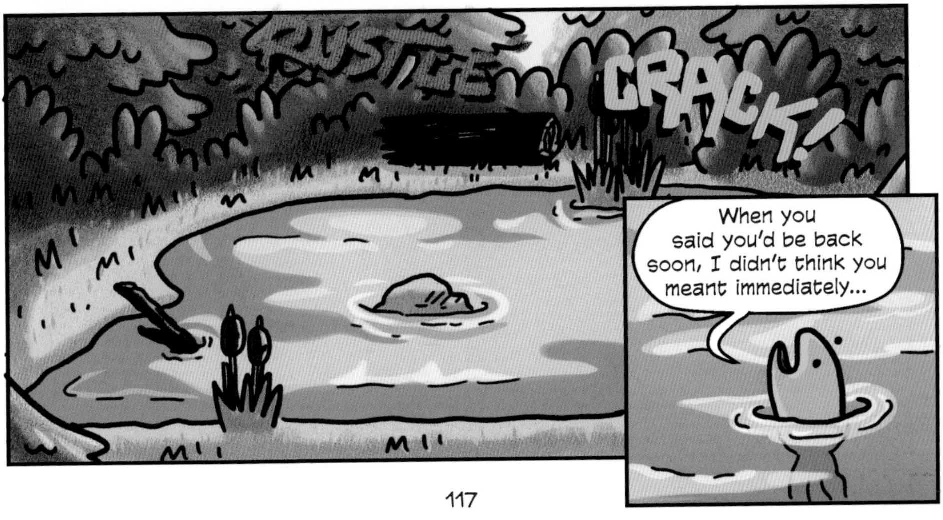
RUSTLE
CRACK!
When you said you'd be back soon, I didn't think you meant immediately...

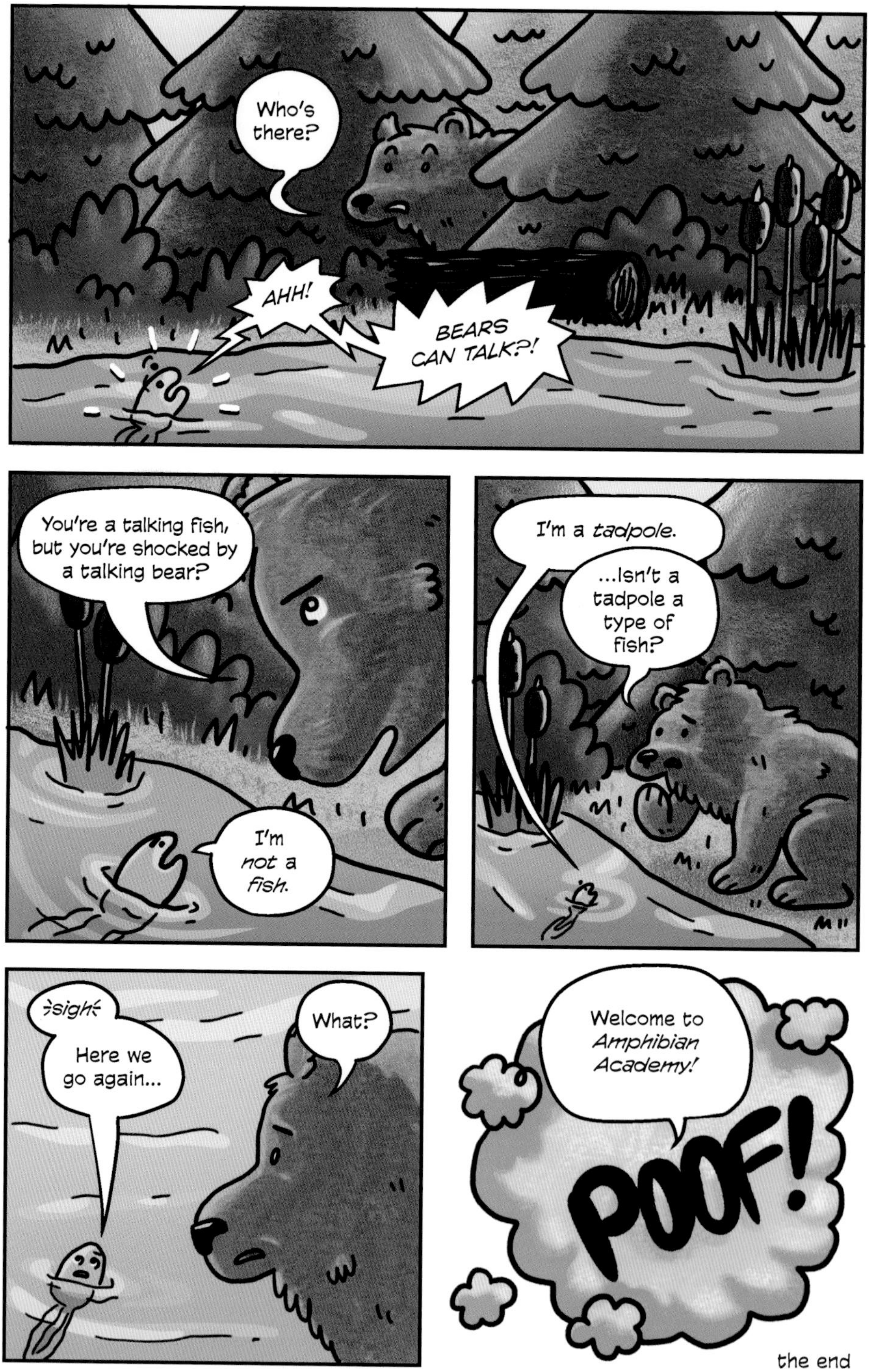
Who's there?
AHH!
BEARS CAN TALK?!
You're a talking fish, but you're shocked by a talking bear?
I'm *not* a *fish*.
I'm a *tadpole*.
...Isn't a tadpole a type of fish?
sigh
Here we go again...
What?
Welcome to *Amphibian Academy!*
POOF!

the end

—GLOSSARY—

Adaptation
The evolutionary process of an organism becoming specialized for life in its specific environment.

Aestivate
To go into an extended state of dormancy during a prolonged hot and dry period.

Alkaloids
Basic, naturally occurring organic compounds that contain at least one nitrogen atom and have a physiological effect on other organisms.

Apoptosis
When cells are biologically programmed to die in the process of an organism's growth; during apoptosis, the dead cells are usually reused as building blocks for the next stage of development.

Aposematism
A visual way for an organism to communicate that it is poisonous and/or toxic, and should be avoided.

Camouflage
Coloration that is used to conceal oneself in one's environment.

Chytrid
Shorthand for *Batrachochytrium dendrobatidis*, sometimes also called *Bd* or the amphibian chytrid fungus, is a fungus that causes the highly infectious disease chytridiomycosis in amphibians.

Colonize
To settle in a specific area.

Dermal papillae
A superficial extension of the skin and its layers underneath.

Diaphragm
A muscular partition that plays a major role in breathing, as its contraction increases the volume of the thorax and so inflates the lungs.

Diurnal
Active during the day.

Hibernaculum

    A shelter occupied by an organism during hibernation.

Metamorph

    An organism that has undergone metamorphosis. In frogs, it refers to the stage between starting life on land and fully maturing into an adult.

Metamorphosis

    A series of extreme physical changes to an organism after birth.

Nocturnal

    Active at night.

Oophila

    Oophila amblystomatis, single-cell algae that live inside amphibian eggs.

Operculum

    The skin that forms over the gills to protect them during metamorphosis. This is the same skin under which the forelimbs will grow and eventually emerge.

Phytotelmata

    Naturally occurring pools of water that collect in the leaves of terrestrial plants.

Poisonous

    Producing poison as a means of self-defense that acts upon its victim when *ingested.*

Secretion

    A useful substance that is released from a gland or cell.

Symbiosis

    A cooperative relationship between two organisms sharing a habitat.

Taxonomy

    The classification system used for organisms in biology.

Ultrasonic

    Sound waves that consist of frequencies above the auditory limit of the human ear.

Venomous

    Producing poison as a means of self-defense that acts upon its victim when *injected.*

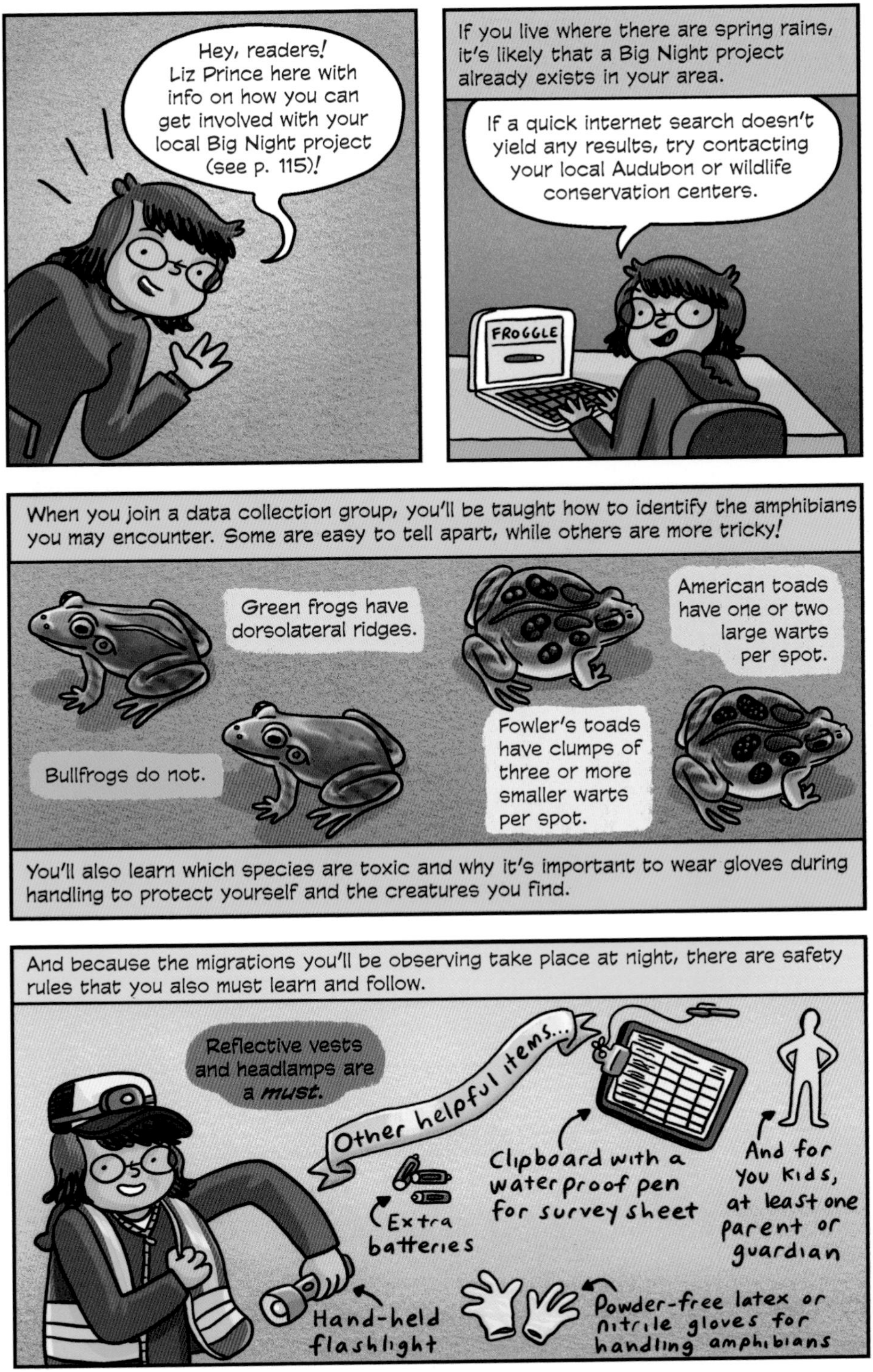
Hey, readers! Liz Prince here with info on how you can get involved with your local Big Night project (see p. 115)!
If you live where there are spring rains, it's likely that a Big Night project already exists in your area.
If a quick internet search doesn't yield any results, try contacting your local Audubon or wildlife conservation centers.
FROGGLE
When you join a data collection group, you'll be taught how to identify the amphibians you may encounter. Some are easy to tell apart, while others are more tricky!
Green frogs have dorsolateral ridges.
Bullfrogs do not.
American toads have one or two large warts per spot.
Fowler's toads have clumps of three or more smaller warts per spot.
You'll also learn which species are toxic and why it's important to wear gloves during handling to protect yourself and the creatures you find.
And because the migrations you'll be observing take place at night, there are safety rules that you also must learn and follow.
Reflective vests and headlamps are a *must.*
Other helpful items...
Extra batteries
Clipboard with a waterproof pen for survey sheet
And for you kids, at least one parent or guardian
Hand-held flashlight
Powder-free latex or nitrile gloves for handling amphibians

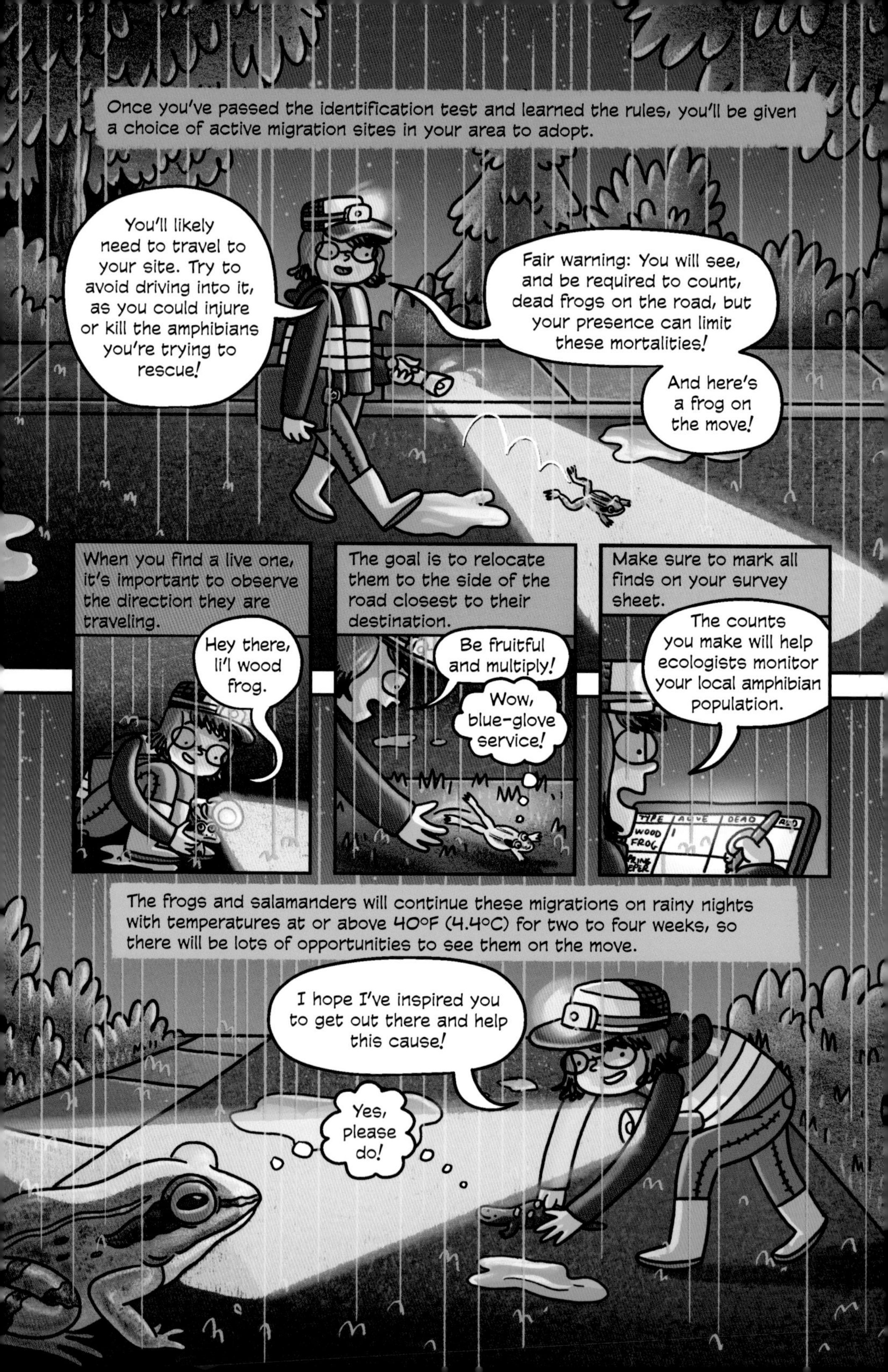

Once you've passed the identification test and learned the rules, you'll be given a choice of active migration sites in your area to adopt.
You'll likely need to travel to your site. Try to avoid driving into it, as you could injure or kill the amphibians you're trying to rescue!
Fair warning: You will see, and be required to count, dead frogs on the road, but your presence can limit these mortalities!
And here's a frog on the move!
When you find a live one, it's important to observe the direction they are traveling.
Hey there, li'l wood frog.
The goal is to relocate them to the side of the road closest to their destination.
Be fruitful and multiply!
Wow, blue-glove service!
Make sure to mark all finds on your survey sheet.
The counts you make will help ecologists monitor your local amphibian population.
TYPE
ALIVE
DEAD
WOOD FROG
The frogs and salamanders will continue these migrations on rainy nights with temperatures at or above 40°F (4.4°C) for two to four weeks, so there will be lots of opportunities to see them on the move.
I hope I've inspired you to get out there and help this cause!
Yes, please do!